Charles Constantine Pise

Saint Ignatius and his first Companions

Charles Constantine Pise

Saint Ignatius and his first Companions

ISBN/EAN: 9783337340858

Printed in Europe, USA, Canada, Australia, Japan

Cover: Foto ©Lupo / pixelio.de

More available books at **www.hansebooks.com**

ST. IGNATIUS

AND

HIS FIRST COMPANIONS

These Portraits are taken from very ancient originals, and are no doubt true likenesses of St Ignatius and the first nine.

NEW YORK
Edward Dunigan & Bro.

THE FOUNDERS OF THE JESUITS.

SAINT IGNATIUS

AND HIS

FIRST COMPANIONS.

BY THE
REV. CHAS. CONSTANTINE PISE, D.D.,
AUTHOR OF "HISTORY OF THE CHURCH," "FATHER ROWLAND,"
"ALETHEIA," ETC.

A NEW EDITION.

NEW YORK:
P. J. KENEDY,
EXCELSIOR CATHOLIC PUBLISHING HOUSE,
5 BARCLAY STREET.

1894.

COPYRIGHT
1886.
P. J. KENEDY.

A. M. D. G.

TO

THE COLLEGE OF GEORGETOWN. D.C.,

MY VENERABLE ALMA MATER, THE NURSE OF LETTERS, SCIENCE, AND VIRTUE,

EVER ANIMATED BY THE SPIRIT OF LOYOLA, AND THE FIRST NINE,

𝔗𝔥𝔦𝔰 𝔙𝔬𝔩𝔲𝔪𝔢,

A TRIFLING, BUT VERY SINCERE, TOKEN OF GRATITUDE, IS MOST RESPECTFULLY AND AFFECTIONATELY INSCRIBED.

PREFACE.

AMONG the nine first companions of St. Ignatius, four preceded him to the tomb; namely, Peter Faber, St. Francis Xavier, Claudius Jaius, and John Cordurius. Of course, in the following pages, their lives are given to their conclusion. Of the others, my purpose was to treat only down to the period when their holy Founder was taken from them. In which space, however, all the important actions of the early Society are comprised. The principal object I had in view, in not carrying out their history after the death of St. Ignatius, was, to exhibit the spirit which he, in person, diffused throughout the body, and thereby confute, by evidence, the vain calumny that he was a fanatic, and his first disciples were intriguers and impostors.

In the performance of my task, ORLANDINUS, the author of a lengthy and elegant History of the Society down to the demise of St. Ignatius, has been my constant and faithful guide. To his great work, references will be found scattered in the notes on almost every page of this volume. The edition in my hands is that of *Coloniæ Agrippinæ, sumptibus Antonii Hierat;* anno Domini MDCXV.: approved by Claudius Aquaviva, General of the Society, in the preceding year (1614). If my present work be worthy the acceptance of the Jesuits in these United States, to them I offer it, as an humble but grateful remuneration for the cares and favors which they bestowed upon my boyhood, while under their salutary and paternal tuition.

CONTENTS.

CHAPTER I.

IGNATIUS.—The proud knight converted to a great saint. Period of his birth. His family, character, sanctity. Book of Exercises. Pilgrimage to Jerusalem. His "Company." Its appellation. Its object. Its polity. He sues the approbation of Paul III. It is approved by Julius III. The General of the order: its various grades. Ecclesiastical honors repudiated. Why. No particular dress. Attack of the Sorbonne. Defence of Father Olauius. It is persecuted. Its efforts for the cause of education. Schools. Colleges. Ignatius' illness and death. His reputation for sanctity. Baronius prays at his tomb............................ 28

CHAPTER II.

PETER FABER.—How gained over by Ignatius. Performs the Exercises. Is ordained Priest. Teaches in the University of Rome. Is sent to Parma; and to Germany. His mission at Ratisbonne. Goes to Spain. Returns to Germany. His labors at Spires; and at Mentz; at Augsburg, and Cologne. Is called to Portugal. Thence to Liege. Returns to Cologne. Defends the Catholic Faith. His manner of treating with heretics. Is sent back to Portugal. Goes to Castile. Distinguishes himself at Salamanca. Goes to Valladolid. His influence at the Court of Philip. Traverses Madrid and Toledo. Is deputed to the Council of Trent. Sickens at Barcelona, and dies at Rome.................... 79

CHAPTER III.

FRANCIS XAVIER.—Converted by Ignatius. Rejects a canonicate. Is sent to the Indies, as Apostolic Legate. His labors at Mozambique, Melinda, and Socotra; on the Fishery-coast; at Goa; at Cape Comorin; at Travancor; in the Island of Manaria; in Ceylon. Visits the tomb of St. Thomas at Meliapor. Goes to Malacca; Amboina; Maluco; to the Isle of Moro; meditates a mission to Japan. Returns to India; to Goa. Departs for Japan. Arrives at Gangoxima. Traverses Japan. First Japanese Christians. Goes to Firando, and to Meaco, and Amangouchi. Disputes with the Bonzees. Conference with the King of Bungo. Returns to the Indies. Departs for China. Arrives at the Island of Sanchin. Dies in the midst of his glory.................................. 103

CHAPTER IV.

JAMES LAYNEZ.—Unites himself to Ignatius. Enters Rome barefoot. Teaches in the Roman Academy. Is sent to Parma. His labors at Venice; at Brescia; at Padua; at Bassano; at Rome. Refuses the purple. Is sent to the Council of Trent. His zeal at Bologna; Florence; Perugio; Monte Pulciano; Sienna; Venice; Naples. Is sent to Sicily. Accompanies Vega to Africa. His labors. Is called to Pisa. Is again sent as theologian of the Pope, to the Council of Trent. Is made Provincial of Italy. Preaches at Genoa. Writes a compendium of theology for the use of the schools of the Society. Is sent back to Germany to the Diet of Augsburg. Returns to Italy. Rejects the Cardinal's hat. His great merits, talents, and actions................................. 153

CHAPTER V.

ALPHONSUS SALMERON.—Called to the Society. Teaches in the *Sapienza*, at Rome. Is sent to Ireland. Seized as a Spy at Lyons. Is called to Modena. Is persecuted. Is sent to the Council of Trent. Draws up a Summary of the Errors of Luther. Goes to Bologna; to Verona; to Germany, at the command of the Pope. Labors at Ingoldstadt. Is recalled to Verona; is sent to Naples; afterwards to Poland; then to Belgium. His labors forever appreciated by that nation—his immortal name.. 191

CHAPTER VI.

Nicholas Bobadilla.—Becomes one of the Nine. Is sent to the island of Ischia. Is destined for the East Indies, but detained by illness. Is deputed to Germany. Labors at Vienna; traverses the different cities of Germany. Refuses the Episcopal dignity. His zeal at Naples. Is made Rector of the Neapolitan College. His lenient government. His trials. His submission. His obedience and other virtues. An example to posterity.. 221

CHAPTER VII.

Simon Rodriguez.—Is numbered among the Nine. Is selected for the Indies. Departs to Portugal. Is there detained. Converts the Ambassador from the Indies. His trials at Lisbon. Is made Tutor to the Son of the King. Is created Provincial. Is called to Rome. Is appointed to preside over the Province of Aragon. Is recalled to Rome. His severe trials. His extreme humility. Another shining example to his brethren for all succeeding times............................... 257

CHAPTER VIII.

Claudius Jaius.—He joins Ignatius. Is sent to Brescia and Favenza. Goes to Germany. Is persecuted. Labors at Ratisbonne, and Ingolstadt. Succeeds Eckius in the Chair of Theology. Attends the Diet of Worms. Founds Seminaries. Is sought after by various Princes. Is sent to the Council of Trent. Refuses the See of Trieste. Goes to Ferrara, at the invitation of the Duke. Goes to Augsburg. Thence to Vienna. Dies. His eulogy. His monument. His immortality..................... 285

CHAPTER IX.

John Cordurius.—One of the Companions. His career brief, but bright. Was destined for Ireland. Was appointed Confessor to Margaret, daughter of Charles V. His death revealed to Ignatius on the Bridge of Sixtus... 329

CHAPTER X.

PASCHASIUS BROËTUS.—The last of the Nine. Is sent to Ireland. Is captured at Lyons as a spy. Is sent to Monte Pulciano, and to Faveza. Is deemed worthy to be made Patriarch of Ethiopia by Ignatius Goes to Bologna. To Ferrara. Is made the first Provincial of Italy. Is sent to France. Labors to establish the Society at Paris. Opposition of the Sorbonne. Triumph of justice. His patience and other virtues. Styled by Ignatius "The Angel of the Society.".......... 887

INTRODUCTION.

INTRODUCTION.

In the different epochs when the Church was afflicted with the dissemination of new errors, God never failed to raise up extraordinary men, and sometimes societies, animated by a holy zeal: and his assistance has always been given, in proportion to her actual necessities. Now, in what age, I will ask, did the Church stand more in need of the special aid of the Divine power, than when she saw herself attacked by a multitude of enemies, whose object and determination were to destroy her very existence? It is not suprising, therefore, if Saint Ignatius and his first companions should be regarded as a strong and peculiar rampart, reared up by the power of Heaven to oppose and withstand the combined assaults of Luther and his fellow-reformists.

That is no unfounded assertion. It is authorized

not only by the experience of past centuries, but by the facts and actions of the new Society. Time only strengthens it; and it has been confirmed by an authority which must have great weight with Catholics, I mean by the decision of the Sovereign Pontiffs. Of these I will cite but one; whose exalted and enlightened character has secured the admiration of Protestants and even of modern philosophers: "It is a constant and common opinion," writes the great pope, Benedict XIV., "and which has been confirmed by the decisions of the Apostolic See, that, as God, by his omnipotence, has raised up at other periods other Saints in his Church, so has he, in like manner, raised up St. Ignatius and his Society, to oppose Luther and the other Heresiarchs of his time."*

I will not here attempt to relate what the Jesuits have done in various parts of the world, since the institution of their order. Some of the deeds of the first disciples of Ignatius the reader will find in the following pages; enough, perhaps, to satisfy him of their wonderful zeal, perseverance, devotion to the cause of truth, and sacrifices for the salvation of souls.

It is incontestable, that the Reformists of the six

---

* Brief given in 1748.

teenth century dreaded the first Jesuits as their most formidable enemies. Hence the origin of the hatred which they evinced towards the Society, and which the lapse of ages has not been able to extinguish in the hearts of their posterity. Wherever the first companions were admitted, the novel doctrines not only made no progress, but entire cities returned to the bosom of the ancient Church. Cologne, Treves, Mentz, and the other towns of Germany that have retained the faith of their ancestors, must attribute that blessing principally to the indefatigable zeal of the Jesuits: to whose cares and labors, likewise, many other cities must acknowledge their gratitude for the perpetuation of the Catholic religion among them.

The legates of the Council of Trent rendered becoming homage to the usefulness and virtues of the infant Society. In that august assembly, there was but one voice in their regard. The ambassadors of princes united their tributes with those of the prelates, and all unanimously agreed, that the most efficacious means of re-establishing religion, and reforming morals, in Germany, would be to multiply the colleges of the Society.*

With no less zeal did the Jesuits fulfil the other

---

* See the Hist. of the Council of Trent, by Pallavicini.

duties of their Institute, by devoting themselves to the functions of the holy ministry and the gratuitous exercise of works of charity towards their neighbors. On this account, they were received with enthusiasm in all Catholic countries. In a short time they had establishments in Spain and Portugal. In the latter kingdom, so highly were their labors appreciated and admired, that they received the name of Apostles.

With regard to the education of youth, no one will refuse to the Society the palm which it has so justly earned. Their success, in this particular, is unquestionable, and admitted by enemies as well as friends. The appearance of this order in the Church wrought a kind of revolution in education. Not that they introduced a novel method of literary teaching: they adopted the one then in use in the University of Paris, in which the "first companions" were educated, and, by their combined efforts, brought it to perfection. But they understood well, that instruction does not constitute the whole of education, nor is it even its most essential part. If it is important to a state that its subjects should be instructed, it is essential to it that they should be virtuous. The moral part of education, therefore, beyond doubt, demands the first attention: and that part, at the epoch of the foundation of the

Society, was most neglected. The greatest merit of the Jesuits was to establish a system of education on the basis of religion, without which there can be no solid virtue. This Christian education was one of the principal ends which St. Ignatius had in view, and occupies a considerable part of their constitutions.

But whilst they formed Christians, they, likewise, reared learned men. Should any one call this in question, let him examine any library, and he will there discover incontestable proofs of the capacity of the Jesuits as teachers, and of the learning of the scholars whom they have trained. Without exaggeration may it be affirmed, that a great portion of works in every branch of science and of literature that has appeared since the middle of the sixteenth century has been written either by the Jesuits themselves, or by their scholars. We know that, in Catholic countries, they were charged, if not exclusively, at least more than any other body of men, with the public education.

It is asserted that their system was defective, and that a new and better one has since been adopted. This surely cannot be meant in reference to moral instruction; and with regard to literary education, before the modern system can be pronounced preferable to theirs, it must have produced orators more eloquent, poets more perfect, philosophers more profound, literary men more accomplished, than those of preceding ages. At all events, this fact must be conceded : that, for the times, their schools were incomparably the best.

Bacon and Grotius—two unquestionable authorities—have borne testimony to their worth and excellence. The former, in his work *On the Progress of the Sciences*, writes in these terms : " When I consider their tact and ability to train up youth in the sciences and good morals, I remember the expression of Agislaus in reference to Pharnabazus : *Being what you are, would that you were ours.*"*

And, in another place, " As regards the subject of education, every thing may be said in a few words : Look at the schools of the Jesuits ; nothing can be better than their system."† Grotius speaks still more explicitly of their singular merit : " The Jesuits," he writes, " have great influence in the world, *on account of the sanctity of their lives*, and the manner in which they instruct youth in letters and the sciences ; without requiring any remuneration."‡ And again : " They govern with wisdom,

---

* Talis cum sis utinam noster esses.
† Pages 29 and 518.
‡ De Reb. Belg. p. 194.

and they obey with fidelity. The most recent of all, they have surpassed every sect in fame, and on this account are envied. They pursue a medium between crouching submission and haughty arrogance : they neither fly from, nor follow, the vices of the world."*

In this work, the reader will see some of the details of the missionary labors of the first Jesuits in the propagation of the gospel among infidel nations. It was not my object to write a long history, but merely to reduce into a small compass matter which would fill immense volumes.

In its very origin, the Society entered, with ardor, upon this salutary and sublime work. The name of St. Francis Xavier is familiar to every reader. His wonderful achievements in the propagation of religion in Japan and the East Indies are not less celebrated and praised by Protestants than by Catholics. His Apostolic career, the multitude of conversions effected by him, his unparalleled exertions, and his prodigious acts, have merited for him the glorious epithet of the Apostle of the Indies. He had noble successors in this magnanimous work : his companions, animated by

---

* Ibid. p. 273. Amsterdam, 1658. The original text will be found on the title-page of this volume.

the same spirit, labored with equal success in Africa, and in the wilds of the New World. The light of the gospel was carried by them among people who had never before heard of Christ, and millions of newly acquired Catholics compensated for the loss which the Church had sustained in Europe.

In conclusion, I earnestly hope that the facts which I have collected relating to the lives of the first companions of St. Ignatius may tend to show forth the real spirit of his order, and disperse some of the prejudices that prevail against it, at least in the minds of candid and sincere men. With Erasmus, I may add : " Abundè satisfactum est illis, si velint cognoscere. Si nolint, frustra tentemus eis satisfacere, qui calumniari malunt quam discere."*

---

* " If they desire to be informed, they will be abundantly satisfied ; if not, in vain may we hope to satisfy persons who prefer to calumniate rather than to learn."—Epist. 336.

ST. IGNATIUS.

CHAPTER I

ST. IGNATIUS.

IGNATIUS.—The proud knight converted to a great saint. Period of his birth. His family, character, sanctity. Book of Exercises. Pilgrimage to Jerusalem. His "Company." Its appellation. Its object. Its polity. He sues the approbation of Paul III. It is approved by Julius III. The General of the order: its various grades. Ecclesiastical honors repudiated. Why. No particular dress. Attack of the Sorbonne. Defence of Father Olauius. It is persecuted. Its efforts for the cause of education. Schools. Colleges. Ignatius' illness and death. His reputation for sanctity. Baronius prays at his tomb.

WEARIED and much agitated from a strange and recent apparition, a noble-looking cavalier, robed in the plain guise of a pilgrim, sat down to repose him on the banks of a gentle stream, not far from the village of Manreza.* The deep shadows

---

* The singular vision here alluded to is thus described by Orlandinus, in his History of the Society of Jesus: "A very comely image appeared to him in the air, the figure of which he could not clearly discern. It was lengthy, like the form of a serpent, bright, of various hues, and glittering with many eyes, like stars: which, while it appeared, rendered him happy, and when it vanished left him sorrowful." Lib. i. 22, p. 7. The conversion of Ignatius happened in 1521 He was in his thirty-first year.

were now falling from the neighboring hills: over the brow of Mount Serat, the dusk of the evening seemed already wreathing its sombre twilight, and the waters of the lonely river rippled beneath the breath of the solitude's breeze. There, in profound contemplation, with his dark-gray eyes fixed intently on the river, sat that wondrous stranger. His elegant mien, his broad, high forehead, his aquiline nose, his beautiful yet manly features, bespoke the high rank to which he belonged, and the magnanimous character with which he was adorned. He had recently fought, at the head of a chivalrous army, for the liberties of Spain, and had been wounded, in her glorious cause, on the walls of Pampeluna. He had been confined to his bed, suffering intense pain from the extraction of the ball which had entered his leg, and the amputation of a bone which protruded from the wound. During this period of lingering and solitary illness, he had sought to relieve his tedium, and engage his mind with reading. No works of fancy or books of chivalry being within his reach, he had recourse to a volume of the Lives of the Saints, in which he beheld depicted, for the imitation of great souls, their heroic virtues and sublime sanctity. The transition, in such a mind as his, from one species of chivalry to another, was very easy and natural: he had been trained up to that of arms and martial enthusiasm; he could, without difficulty, appreciate that of peace and religious glory. As he read on, his heart opened, as it were, to the divine influences of Christian heroism; his soul insensibly began to glow with an ardor more ennobling and inspiring than he had before experienced; a desire to emulate the splendid moral achievements of the examples before him, an irresistible admiration of their victories over themselves and their triumphs over the world, urged forward his generous ambition; and the grace of God, co-operating, meanwhile, with his natural dispositions, he determined to change the standard of war for the ensign of the cross. He had laid aside from his towering person the insignia of the knight, and taken upon himself those of an humble penitent, making a pilgrimage from shrine to shrine. Over the altar of the ever-blessed Virgin he had hung the sword which was still gleaming with the lustre of valor—a bright, a splendid trophy of the grace of God. For that brave spirit that knew not how to cower before the terrors of the cannon, was stricken down in profound subjection—not to any human power—and laid prostrate, by the "violence" of the love of God. Sweet violence, indeed, that gives no pain but contrition, and demands no subjection but a calm submission to the will of Heaven. Violence which, it is true, storms the citadel of the heart, but renders it, at the same time, a voluntary captive: which sometimes achieves its object by forcing the deep and silent tear from the fountains of some Magdalen's soul, and, at other times, by casting down headlong—blind and terror-stricken —on the sward, some Saul of Tarsus. That extraordinary personage, meditating, at this twilight hour, on the banks of the Rubricato, is the immortal founder of the Society of Jesus—Ignatius of Loyola.

Between the epoch of the birth of this defender of the ancient faith, and that of Martin Luther, its pest and scourge, a space of nine years occurred: the former having been born in 1491, the latter in 1482. God, whose providence could not but prepare a barrier against the calamities which he foresaw were about to desolate his Church, raised up Ignatius, as a host, in the Company which he was destined to establish, for her defence and edification. Guipuzcoa, a province in Cantabria, was the place of his nativity. His family was noble and renowned. His father and mother were both of illustrious origin. His youthful disposition tended to the study and the feats of arms:

and having, at a maturer age, embraced the military profession, he won the applause of his country and reaped no little glory on the field. This soldier-like character he impressed on the Company which he instituted. It appears in the celerity of obedience on the part of its members, in the enduring of labor, and the missionary exercises —all modelled on the exemplar of the camp. His soul, from early childhood, burned with inextinguishable ardor for renown, and human praise. which natural impetuosity, changed and chastened under holier influences, he carried with him into the ranks of religion, and infused into the breasts of his disciples. He was distinguished by grace, ease, and majesty of manners, and a singular love of elegance of dress; which qualities he afterwards hallowed, and transferred to sacred things, and made auxiliary to the discipline and spirit of his order. He possessed a sublime magnanimity in pardoning an offence, as well as in conferring a favor; an innate detestation of avarice, and-- the germ of all vices—cupidity. He exhibited a lofty daring in dangerous and difficult exertions; a singular prudence in the transaction of business, and an unwearied and patient perseverance and constancy of character. In the flower of youth he displayed the maturity of age; and in the first impulse of his conversion was raised, on a sudden, to the highest grade of perfection.

Hence the sublime ascetic character of his book of "Spiritual Exercises," written so soon after his retreat on Mount Serat, and his austere and penitential musings at Manreza. Hence his marvellous ecstasy, in which, wrapt in the contemplation of heavenly things, during eight days, he seemed dead to those of earth.. And hence, too, that solemn vow of chastity by which he devoted himself forever to the service of God, " following the Lamb whithersoever he went." This perfection displayed itself in all his actions. Whether we trace him to the isle of Cyprus, on his pilgrimage to the Holy Land; whether we view him, entering— an humble palmer—upon the consecrated soil of Palestine, prostrate, in tears, at the tomb of Christ, or partaking of the Redeemer's agony on the Mount of Olives; whether we behold him favored with celestial visions, or wrecked on the shoals near the coast of Cyprus, or, on his return to Europe, seized upon and contumaciously treated, as a spy, in France;—under all circumstances, and in every condition, there was a grandeur of soul, a sanctity of motive, and an enthusiasm of virtue, which stamped him, at once, with that transcendent character, which was afterwards so wonderfully developed in the course of his subsequent career.

The "Company" he established was destined to labor for the salvation of men, and to propagate the greater glory of Jesus Christ. Hence the motive for his styling it the "Society of Jesus:" deriving its name from Him, who is the only true salvation of the human race, and who promised to be "propitious to him at Rome.*

This appellation, therefore, seems to have been the effect of Divine inspiration, and was intended to exercise a universal sway over the motives and conduct of its members. They would be led to

---

* Christ, relates the same author, arrayed in light, appeared to Ignatius on his way to the capital of the Christian World, and addressed these words to him: *Ego vobis Romæ propitius ero.* (Lib. ii. 50.) "I will be propitious to you at Rome." This, perhaps, to some, may appear incredible, and unworthy a place in enlightened history: but I beg such to pause ere they pronounce, and hear the language of Mr. Stephens, a highly gifted and popular writer, in the Edinburgh Review for October, 1842: "As he (Ignatius) journeyed with Laynez, he saw a still more awful vision. It exhibited that Being whom no eye hath seen, and whom no tongue may lightly name, and with him the Eternal Son, bearing a heavy cross and uttering the welcome assurance: *I will be propitious to you at Rome.*" Critical Miscellanies, p. 323

understand that it was not into the "Company" of Ignatius, but that of the Son of God, they entered, to carry his cross, and to engage in conflict with Satan, and the vices and errors of the world ; to continue that work for which he descended from heaven and shed his blood ; to range themselves under his sacred banners, and to unfurl them to all the nations of the earth. Under the auspices and protection of Jesus, they could have confidence, undertake arduous labors, sustain difficulties, and overcome obstacles. With Him, they could fight, conquer, die : nor would they live or battle in any other manner, than after that model which their celestial Guide and Captain has pointed out by his precepts and example. Nothing could more efficaciously stimulate the faint-hearted, or encourage the timid, than the virtue and majesty of that most Holy Name. In adversity it would be the sweetest solace, in prosperity the purest joy, in darkness the brightest light, in fatigue the most perfect rest. In a word, all who range themselves under the standard of this adorable name, will ever bear in mind to what leader they belong, and should, under all circumstances, prove themselves to be worthy soldiers of Christ Jesus : and while they were designated by the most glorious name,—at which every knee must bend,—the founder, who was as humble in spirit as he was lofty in his heavenly purpose, was in the habit of styling it "the lowliest Society." *

The principal objects which Ignatius had in view in establishing a new religious order, at this critical epoch, were, first, the instruction of the people in a manner adapted to their comprehension and circumstances; the necessity of which became the more manifest on account of the Lutheran heresies which had begun to spread themselves abroad; and secondly, the missions, to which all its members generously devoted themselves by vow. He foresaw that unless they bound themselves together, and to their head, by Obedience, they could not continue according to the great plan which was meditated, much less could it be expected that it would be endowed with the principle of duration. And as he had chosen for their guide and model JESUS himself, and no other, they should imitate his detachment from all worldly goods, by the vow of poverty; and sacrifice

---

* "Quamquam Ignatius, ut erat modestissimus ... Societatem hanc volebat *minimam* appellare, ut ostenderet .. nostri ordinis homines ita de se deque aliis sentire debere .. ut sese pro omnium minimis ducant gerantque." Orland lib. ii. 63. How faithfully they have realized this sublime theory, as a body, impartial history has borne testimony.

all the pleasures of nature, by that of perpetual chastity. But this determination was not a mere prudential scheme: it was the result of mature reflection, fervent prayer, discreet consultation, and not without the inspiration of HIM, who was made obedient to the will of his heavenly Father, even unto the death of the cross.*

Having resolved on the character of his new institution—that of a regular religious order—Ignatius next directed his attention to its internal administration and polity. Over the entire "Company" a General was to preside, not during a term

---

* God, who is ever watchful over his Holy Church, has never failed to counteract the evil designs of great Heresiarchs, by the influence of great Saints and Doctors. Arius was opposed by Athanasius; Nestorius by Cyril of Alexandria; Vigilantius by Jerome; Pelagius by Augustine; and Luther by Ignatius. The triumph of the Divine power appears more wonderful in the last, inasmuch as, while those venerable Fathers were illustrious for vast learning and extraordinary eloquence, Ignatius possessed but little human acquirements, while his soul was enriched with the treasures of heavenly wisdom. In him, we behold a soldier contending with a Theologian, a Doctor in divinity, and an able writer. And yet, the result proves with what advantage that inspired soldier fought the battles of Truth and Virtue against the powers of Error and Vice. See Bartoli, Istoria della Compagn. tom. v. p. 10.

of years, but for life. That the novices, and all who desired to be enrolled under his banners, should be well tried by the performance of the spiritual exercises, by serving in the public hospitals, by pilgrimages, and other menial and onerous functions: and that all who were admitted to the solemn profession, besides the three ordinary vows, should add another, by which they promised to subject themselves to the spiritual orders of the Sovereign Pontiff; holding themselves ready to be sent, at his bidding, to any part of the world, and to any people, infidel or Christian, without demanding any outfit or emolument; moreover, to use every effort to instruct the young and ignorant, and watch over the morals of those committed to their care: and finally, to establish colleges, in which a remuneration might be received for the education of the alumni; and Professed Houses, which should depend for support on the charity and liberality of the public.*

The earnest desire of Ignatius now was to obtain

---

* Bobadilla, it appears, objected to the vow of educating children; which was afterwards modified, and brought under the general vow of Obedience: so that no individual could act according to the promptings of his own mind, but only as directed by the common wisdom of his brethren. See Orland. lib. ii. n. 64.

for this his new institute the approbation of the Holy See. To this end, he drew up a sketch—or rather made a clear and comprehensive abridgment—of the whole, which he presented in person to the Sovereign Pontiff, Paul III. It was a deeply interesting spectacle to behold the founder of one of the most illustrious orders in the Church kneeling at the feet of the Father of the Christian World, and begging his approval of an institute which has since been the admiration of all his venerable successors. This occurred amid the shady retreats of Tivoli, whither the pope had retired from the labors and summer-heat of the metropolis. The book was presented by the Cardinal de Contarini. Paul, having examined it, remarked : *The finger of God is here:* adding, moreover, that " this Society would prove an invaluable auxiliary and splendid ornament to the Church in those eventful times."* This verbal declaration of the sentiments of the Pontiff may be regarded as the first approbation of the Society.†

---

* Societatem hanc, id temporis . . . . afflictis Ecclesiæ rebus, non levi præsidio atque ornamento fore. Orland. lib ii. n. 83.

† "In his great and only extant work," writes the critic above quoted, "Ignatius Loyola is no dreamer. His mind resembled the body of his great disciple, Francis Xavier

But a few years later, his successor, Julius III., issued a solemn bull from St. Peter's, dated in August, 1550, by which, in a formal and public manner, he affixed his pontifical seal and approbation to

---

which, as he preached or baptized, rose majestically towards the skies, while his feet retained their firm hold on the earth below. The book, it is true, indicates a tone of feeling utterly removed from that which animates the gay and busy scenes of life ; but it could not have been written except by one accustomed to observe those with the keenest scrutiny, and to study the actors in them with the most profound discernment." Ubi Supr.

Concerning the book of " Spiritual Exercises," the reader will see more in the last chapter of this work. Mr. Stephens could not close his admirable essay on Ignatius, without atoning, in the eye of Protestantism, for all the true and good things he had dared to indite, by styling Xavier a " fanatic." Mr. Crane, however, likewise a Protestant, diametrically contradicts the former writer, by asserting that, " never did a *cooler head* keep time with a more enthusiastic heart," in his equally excellent (in many respects) article on the " Institution" of Ignatius. He also admits that " the enthusiasm of Loyola was in admirable keeping, and did not war with his *cold and clear intellect.* His was not a *fiery zeal ;*—there was a spiritual composure in his actions ; nor do we find wild imaginings and extravagant fancies, either of heart or mind, in his maturer days. There was evidently in him a singleness of disposition, that does not warrant the idea that his Society was instituted for those worldly objects which have formed the burden of the accu

the new religious order. This took place while the Catholic world, and especially Rome, were rejoicing under the celebration of the Jubilee: a period truly auspicious, in many respects, to the interests of religion, but in none more so, than in this memorable event.*

In the origin of the Society, the members naturally regarded Ignatius as their superior—for he was their master and parent in religion. And well were they convinced that they could not be governed more wisely than by him, whom God had chosen as the founder of their institute, and through whom his spirit was infused into the whole body. While they were scattered through various towns and places, Ignatius, with one or two companions, remained at Rome, making that city—the metropolis of Catholic unity—the centre, likewise, of the Society. With him—their spiritual head—all the members were intimately connected: to him all recurred for advice and consolation, which they never failed to derive from his wisdom and prudence.

---

sations against it."—Lives of Eminent Catholic Missionaries.

Why will great Protestant critics contradict themselves so egregiously, when treating of Catholic men and matters?

* See the opening of the Tenth Book of Orlandinus; and the bull of Julius III., which is given in full.

With them he felt himself completely identified, and so comported himself in their regard, that he seemed rather their servant and inferior, than their ruler and superior. He kept up a continual epistolary correspondence with them, informing them of the progress and increase of the Society, making them acquainted with every particular occurrence, whether favorable or adverse. The effect was admirable. Among all the members, of different nations, dispositions, languages, habits, and separated from one another by distance and time, there was but one heart and one soul : and this, too, in spite of all the difficulties, prejudices, and even persecutions they were doomed to undergo. Under every trial they were supported and united by the spirit of charity and of zeal, for the advancement of God's greater glory, and the salvation of mankind ; and by their pure and disinterested conduct rendered themselves beloved and esteemed by princes, dear to the people, and admirable even to those who were jealous of their success.

The wisdom with which the economy of the Society was regulated even from its incipiency, has been remarked by all writers. To all bodies there must be a head. But the mode of appointing that head varies according to the character of the community and the nature of its object. The enlightened policy of Ignatius, carrying out in practice the liberal disposition and generosity of his own soul, ordained that the first place should be conferred, not by favor or arbitrary appointment, but by election: thus impressing on the Society one of the essential attributes of republicanism, and, at the same time, the inflexible discipline of the camp. By the suffrages of the first Fathers, some of whom were far away, the general was appointed. Xavier, being on the point of departing into India, recorded and left behind his vote. Rodriguez did the same. Faber gave his by letter, from Germany, where he then was stationed. The reader will easily anticipate on whom the honor devolved, by unanimous assent. Ignatius had founded the order, and it was but just that he should preside over it in the capacity of General, especially as he presented in his own person a bright mirror, in which the virtues and perfection necessary for so exalted and responsible a station were admirably reflected.

The particulars of the manner of deciding on the choice of the General are minutely detailed by the author of the History of the Society.* They are as follows. During three days of mutual consultation and prayer, the subject, so important to

---

* Orlandin lib. iii. n. 5.

the whole community, was discussed ; on the fourth, the votes were all placed in an urn, and the doors were closed ; after which, three days more were consumed in devout supplication to Heaven. At the expiration of that term, the suffrages were examined, and Ignatius, without a dissenting voice, was declared the first General of the order.*

The original manuscripts by which their suffrages were expressed, were seen and consulted by the author of the History of the Society many years after, who records them in his faithful annals, for the edification and satisfaction of posterity.† In giving their opinions, they called God to witness,

---

* Ibid. n. 6. Ignatius was the only individual whose vote differed from the general voice : not actuated merely by the ordinary fitness of things, but from an infinitely higher motive. So humble was the opinion which he entertained of himself, that, in his own estimation, he was the least qualified among his brethren to hold the office to which they raised him.

† Hic ego continere me non possum, quin ex ipsis suffragiorum autographis velut e pulvere antiquitatis erutis, excerpam aliquid quod et exemplo sit posteris et voluptati. Orland, lib. iii. n. 7. The latinity of this famous author has been reputed among the most classic and eloquent productions of modern times. The entire work is worthy of its subject.

that they desired to raise to that high dignity him whom, in their consciences, they considered the most worthy and best qualified ; and whom, were they at the point of death, they would recommend. Cordurius, in nominating Ignatius, extols him in terms of praise as transcendent as they were deserved. He styles him the most ardent and zealous apostle of God's glory and man's salvation : as such he had always reputed him ; and the more readily did he deserve to be made their superior, towards whom he had ever comported himself with the humility of an inferior.* The entire declaration of Salmeron, which cannot fail to be regarded, at the present day, as fraught with interest, was couched in these words : "In the name of Jesus Christ, amen. I, Alphonsus Salmeron, the most unworthy member of the Society, having had recourse to prayer, and weighed the subject with all due deliberation, select, and declare as my superior, and the superior of the whole community, Ignatius, of Loyola, who, having begotten us, according to the wisdom imparted from above, and nourished us while infants, may now, that we have grown strong under the solid food of obedience, lead us into the

---

* Ibid. Next to Ignatius, Cordurius placed the **name of Faber**. So also did Xavier.

rich and pleasant pastures of paradise, to the fountain of life ; that when he shall be called to give back this little flock to Jesus Christ the great Shepherd, we may truly say, *we are the people of his pasture and the sheep of his hand:* and he, likewise, may be able to declare, *Lord, of those thou hast given unto me, not one have I lost.* Which may JESUS, the good Shepherd, vouchsafe to grant us. Amen."* Xavier specified, in his document, the three vows of religion to be made to him who should be elected General. Ignatius expressed no preference for any particular name, but was in favor of the one who should have the majority of votes, always excepting himself.†

When the result was made known to him, he evinced some unusual emotion, and made a long address to his companions, pleading a want of physical and mental vigor, and exhorted them to choose some other who might be equal to the task. For himself, he preferred to be governed rather than to govern ; and he trembled to preside over others,

---

* Ibid.

† Ibid. n. 8. Does not this conduct of Ignatius refute the assertion of many a prejudiced and shallow enemy of his order and his Church, that he was driven forward by fanaticism and ambition ?

when he felt he was unable to govern himself. Wherefore, he conjured them again to commend the affair to God during three days, and to reconsider the choice. The Fathers, having in vain protested against this measure, consented, at length, to comply with his urgent entreaty. But after the specified period, the result proved the same as before; the choice fell again unanimously on Ignatius. Still that great but humble man persisted in the wish to decline the honor, when Laynez, with the candor which distinguished him, assured Ignatius that either he should accept the office, or the Society must be broken up.* This extreme alternative overcame the modesty and dispersed the scruples of Loyola: from necessity — and, as is manifestly evinced — not from inclination, he yielded to the will of heaven; especially as he was warned to contend no longer against its manifestation, by a venerable priest of the order of St. Francis, who was his confessor and spiritual adviser. In the solitudes of the monastery on Mount Janiculum, he spent several days in retreat and works of penance; and, yielding with serene resignation to his lot, re-

---

* "Pater, munus accipe, quod tam perspicuè Deus tibi imponit, vel quod ad me pertinet, dirimatur Societas." Orland. lib. iii. n. 8.

turned, with new ardor and increased zeal, to the bosom of his companions.*

In the hands of the General, no little power was placed by the regulations of the Institute, and the approbation of the Holy See. All the offices of the Society were at his discretion; and not left to the zeal or disposal of individual members. He should, however, have his counsellors, without whose consent no new constitutions could be framed, no existing ones changed; no colleges or houses could be alienated or dissolved. In other things of less importance, the General, aided by the advice of his brethren, as far as he may see fit to be directed by it, shall have authority to order and command whatever he may deem most conducive to the glory of God, and the good of the community.† With regard to the members of the Society, they are bound to recognize a supreme authority and power in the General, in all things relating to the administration, correction, and government of the order: a

---

* He entered upon the office of General, on the 19th of April, A. D. 1541; and with his companions, having visited the seven churches of Rome, solemnly renewed his vow before the altar of the Blessed Virgin Mary, in the Basilic of Saint Paul. Tanner, Soc. Jes. Europ., p. 19.

† See the bull of Julius III., *Exposcit debitum*, &c. Apud Orland., lib. x. n. 5.

power that must be always tempered with benignity, charity, and mildness. They must not only evince a perfect obedience to him, but must contemplate in his person, and keep present before their eyes, JESUS, from whom they have derived their appellation.*

The Society was composed of various grades, among which are temporal coadjutors, whose duty it is to assist, by their manual labor and employment, the Fathers who are engaged in their sacerdotal and missionary avocations. The lot of these "Brothers" is pronounced "most happy," by the historian whom I follow.† For, they are participators of the treasures of merit earned by the spiritual fatigues and perseverance of the Fathers. They are removed from dangers and cares, an' they realize in themselves the promises which Christ has made to all who perform works of charity. The spiritual coadjutors were those Fathers, who stood ever ready to carry on, with greater security—not being subject to the nod of the Sovereign Pontiff—the local affairs of the Soci-

---

* Ibid. n. 20.

† Quorum multis nominibus beata sors est. Lib. vi. n. 1. Anno 1546. Many of the early lay-brothers were distinguished for their heroic virtues, but especially Rodriguez, who is, to this day, regarded as a shining model for his brethren of the same grade in the Society.

ety and of religion. They constituted by far the major part of the members. For, the "professed," or those who made the fourth vow to the Holy See, were liable to be sent, at any moment, to remote parts; and the qualifications by which it was essential that they should be characterized, necessarily rendered the number comparatively small. Exalted piety, prudence, and virtue, should be united to profound and general learning, superior talent, and mature experience.

It was the intention of Ignatius that his rising order should be illustrious more on account of the virtues of his religious, than of their numbers. For this reason, when postulants for reception made application to him, none were admitted whose dispositions, conduct, talents, learning, and reputation had not previously undergone a rigid scrutiny. Erudition was always a powerful recommendation, but not without piety and experience, so necessary at that calamitous epoch of the Church, when dissoluteness of morals in the clergy was made the ostensible cause of the religious revolution in Germany, and when, in the ranks of the Reformers, were reckoned not a few—apostates from the mother Church—who wielded great learning and fatal talents against the cause of truth.*

---

lib. v. n. 3.

He wished all, of every grade, to be strictly united together by the bonds of fraternal charity; and that virtue, which was the distinguishing characteristic of the primitive Christians, he longed to see the conspicuous prerogative of the Society. The name it bore should not be an empty decoration; but should be indicative of the spirit of Christ, which animated every heart. They should patiently endure each other's failings; the high in office and distinction should be lowliest in spirit, and when necessary, before the community: while the inferior in rank and qualifications, should be free from every sentiment of envy or jealousy, and serve God and discharge their respective duties to the Society with edification, submission, and humility. This "new commandment" of charity was, in effect, the foundation of the whole fabric of Loyola's institute.* The better and more securely to carry it into general effect, he determined to remove from his children all—and especially one—of the greatest obstacles to its consummation. This was the renunciation of all hope of ecclesiastical preferment and honors. The particular reasons which actuated him in this wise regulation are assigned by Or

---

* In the language of our historian: "Hoc, itaque, novum mandatum pro fundamento et radice sancta hæc Societas habet."—Lib. xi. n. 43.

landinus, and may be comprised in the following :*

1. Because the number of distinguished members, in a new Society, must necessarily be so small, that were they to be taken from it and raised to dignities, the Society would suffer from the privation of their services in her own advancement and welfare. 2. Because, when one is thus honored, the peace of others may be ruffled ; for, when the glare of glory surrounds the brows of one, others, who stand near, might be dazzled by it,—whereas, if seen only at a distance, and out of the precincts of their own order, it vanishes almost as soon as it appears upon their view. 3. Because, the means taken to obtain honors, might not always be compatible with the pure and simple spirit of a religious life : they might introduce party feeling and political feuds. 4. Because, precluding the hope of preferment, they who entered the Society must be influenced by no other motive than the love of perfection. 5. Because, by this arrangement, ambition—that pernicious serpent—would be kept aloof from this religious paradise. 6. Because, the members of the order could be more free in

---

* Lib. vi. n. 37, 38, 39, 40, 41, 42, 43, 44, 45, 46, 47, 48, 49, 50.

offering their services, and devoting their resources, to the prosperity of the Church, and the peace of governments. For they cannot but be regarded as disinterested; and will, on this very account, possess greater weight, and exercise a more salutary influence. 7. Because all were destined to labor with equal energy and perseverance: and it being impossible to reward all, some might deem themselves neglected; and there would be danger of creating contentions and complaints. For there can be no concert, where there is a striving after dignities. 8. Because the members would always keep before their eyes the rewards prepared for them in a better world; having here, in their trials, persecutions and missionary labors, no other object than the glory of God, the propagation of truth, and the salvation of the human race. 9. Because religious, who are debarred from rising to the eminence of the great, will not be regarded by them with the least sentiment of diffidence or suspicion. Great men are often jealous of inferiors in rank, who may have the chance of being raised to an equality with themselves. But, having no such chance, in the ordinary course of things, those inferiors will be loved and respected in their humble position in the Church. 10. Because they who are decorated with honors, if more friendly to some than to others, in the same order, will evince greater partiality to the former than the latter. Hence the wisdom of the Sovereign Pontiffs in appointing Protectors for religious societies, never select a prelate for that from which he was taken, in order to prevent such favoritism. 11. Because individuals raised from an order to the high posts of the Church, are sometimes most obnoxious to that very order, and, not seldom, interfere, to the disadvantage of the community, with its government and discipline. 12. Because Ignatius desired that his disciples should seek the shade of a retired life, and court the humility and the poverty of the Cross. In this he followed the maxims of the greatest saints in the Church ;* who contended not only in words, but, likewise, by their own example, that honors, far from being coveted, should be carefully shunned.

These, among others, were the motives which prompted Ignatius to close the doors of ecclesiastical dignity upon all the members of the Society. In such a manner, that no one was free to accept honors even when offered, unless by an express command of the Vicar of Christ: and, in such an

---

* *Apologetic* S. Greg. Naz. See also the opinions of Saints Dominic and Francis on this subject, in Orlandinus, lib. vi. n. 51.

event, the individual promoted ceased to belong to the body from which, even reluctantly and by obedience, he found himself separated.*

This feature of the Institute has been regarded by wise men as one of the most judicious and excellent character. And I cannot but entertain the belief that to it, in a singular degree, must be attributed the unity and powerful consistency by which the Society has ever been distinguished. It secured the talents, learning, virtues, and other qualifications of its members for its own use. The elements of greatness were not permitted to be scattered. They were blended and consolidated in one mighty and splendid mass, from which grew up the towering and magnificent whole, which, during three centuries, has stood a monument of wonder and veneration to the world.

Another remarkable provision of Ignatius was, that the members of the Society should not be designated by any particular dress, or any extraordinary system of life. Their habit was common

---

* Delatos autem honores nisi diserti præcepti vis adigat et Pontifex ipse compellat eadem voti religione recuset. Orlandin. lib. vi. n. 52. By this positive compulsion, several Jesuits, even in the early history of the order, were compelled to accept of the purple. Among those the most illustrious were Bellarmine, Pallavicinus, and Toletus.

to all the clergy—their mode of life conformable to the usages of the edifying secular clergy. Rigors, penances, mortifications, were to be left to the devotion and fervor of inferiors, regulated and approved of by superiors. So that, in the language of the historian, their offering to God should be "reasonable"—*rationabile obsequium*.*

The motive of this provision is given, with great freedom, by Olauius, in his answer to the Sorbonne,† who found fault with the Institute on this account. "That such learned Doctors," he writes, "should censure us for not being distinguished by dress from the secular clergy, is, indeed, extraordinary, when we know that this very circumstance has been approved by the Sovereign Pontiffs, and by the wisest and most venerable men. For all have judged it prudent that we, who have not chosen an idle, or monastic, or solitary life, but one of labor, and continual occupation in the welfare of our neighbors, should follow only the common laws of a Christian life: and that there should

---

* Lib. x. n. 25. Rationabile corporis obsequium, prout expediat, offeratur.

† The language of the Doctors of the Sorbonne against the Society is very strong and condemnatory. One would hardly be prepared to expect to find such abusive language from so refined a university. Orland. lib. xv. p. 45.

be nothing in our dress, and external deportment, to distinguish us from edifying secular priests, whose coadjutors we desire to be. No new rigor should be required, at least as a general rule, lest it might prove an impediment to the undergoing of great labors, to which the Society devotes her members. No peculiar distinction from the secular clergy, inasmuch as our founder meant to require of us nothing more than should be practised by all good priests. Hence Paul III., Julius III., and Marcellus II., were in the habit of styling us "reformed priests:" as also, at the present day, Paul IV., who, from the beginning, has been not only the friend, but the professed admirer, of our Institute...... It is our object to incite the secular clergy, with the Divine assistance, not to change their dress, but to discharge their ecclesiastical duties, with minds free from every temporal consideration, burning with charity towards their neighbors, directed by true humility, and perfect purity of intention. To this end, we have recourse, according to the requisition of our Institute, to frequent examination of conscience, assiduous mental prayer, imploring God that in all our thoughts, words, desires, and actions, we may have the grace to refer all to His greater glory. We understand well, that we have separated ourselves from the world by special vows, in order that, forgetting ourselves and our personal interests, we may live for Him alone, to whose service we have wholly and thoroughly consecrated our lives." *

---

* Ibid. n. 50. Olauius replies to the severe and uncourteous objections of the Sorbonne with dignity, candor, and eloquence. His address may be regarded as the first, and ablest vindication of the institute.

Others have been written at various epochs; the most recent has just appeared in France, from the pen of Father de Ravignan, entitled "De l'existence et de l'institut des Jesuites." From which, that the reader may become acquainted with some of the minutiæ of the order, I extract the following from the third chapter:

"THE DAY OF A JESUIT.

"At four o'clock in the morning the bell sounds for rising; the brother, named the '*Brother Excitator*,' passes through the chambers, and warns them to rise with the pious salutation: '*Benedicamus Domino*.' A quarter of an hour after he returns again, to see that punctual obedience has been rendered to this first duty of the rule.

"Thus an exact discipline ever comes in aid of personal good-will. Custom, then, calls the religious of the Society into the chapel, to the feet of the Most Holy Sacrament. At half-past four every one returns to nis cell, to devote himself to meditation for an hour.

"The *Angelus* Bell terminates the meditation; the priests say Mass in succession; and after the thanksgiving is finished, the course of daily occupations commences. Of these

From this exposition of one of the earliest Fathers of the Society, we can clearly perceive

there is an ample store ; and I may affirm, that time is a possession which, within our houses, is as much taken from the Jesuit, as honor and liberty are denied him from without, though from far different motives.

"Some hours are, however, reserved for solitary labor, and for study. Some, and by far the greater number, are required to apply to the laborious and slow preparations demanded for public preaching ; others devote their time to scientific and historic researches. All are employed in the active functions of the ministry of souls, which, in general, leave little room for peaceful leisure. Moreover, unless imperious necessity of the rule should require the religious strictly to interdict access, his poor cell is almost constantly besieged. And there men, of all conditions, and of all opinions, are allowed freely to present themselves ; misfortune in every shape, affliction under every form, come to excite our compassion and our zeal. The statistics of the visitors of a single day to any one of us, would often form a very curious history. The police, not unfrequently, takes its share ; busy schemes of worldlings seek to have theirs , the larger portion will remain for the unfortunate who come with confidence to ask from us consolation and truth......

"Is this obedience, slavery, or freedom ?

"'O slavery! which the insolence of man is not ashamed to call liberty!' said Fenelon ; and it was the exclamation of a noble heart and a splendid genius.

"Thus the religious is no longer a slave ; he no longer makes use of human caprice, the senses, pride, nor the

the object of Ignatius in not designating his disciples by any extraordinary or particular habit. But, though they resembled the secular clergy in dress, they were distinguished from them by rules of seclusion and silence to which the same venerrable writer refers, in these terms : " With respect to retirement, we have this rule, that no one can go out of the house without notifying the Janitor that he has permission, and this we observe with great severity. In regard to silence, these are our rules : we not only have times specified for conversation, but also the subject of conversation, and the persons with whom we are to converse. No one is allowed to discourse of merely secular things, particularly of war which may be carried on among Christian princes ; in praise or condemnation of nations, or provinces, or rulers; but of those topics only, which may conduce to piety, edification, and mutual charity. Moreover, no one

---

passions : he treads his tyrants beneath his feet. He is at full freedom, in sure paths ; truth and prudence regulate his steps. He is free : for he obeys the wisdom of God ; and obeys for the purpose of devoting himself to useful labors, to all the labors necessary to promote the eternal well-being of humanity. 'Soldier, go plant thyself at the head of that bridge : thou wilt remain there ; thou wilt die there, we shall pass on.'—' Yes, General.' "

can speak with any but persons of the house, without the Superior's permission: nor can the younger members speak with all, but with those only, from whose conversation it is believed they can derive the greatest fruit. Nor can they converse at any time, but only one hour after dinner, and another after supper. Once a week, and on festival days, a somewhat greater license is granted. Whoever transgresses these rules, is severely dealt with."*

It was the fate of the Society—as it was that of Christianity—to be persecuted in its very origin. Not only in France, by the most famous University of Paris, but likewise at Salamanca and Toledo; and in Portugal and elsewhere.† This persecution was waged, as Father Olauius remarks,‡ by three kinds of adversaries (excepting, however, the Doctors of the Sorbonne.) First, by heretics, or men of suspicious faith, with whom there was an incessant war, especially in Germany. Secondly, by men of loose morals, who could not endure the reproach and condemnation which the rigid morals of the Jesuits constantly pronounced against them

---

* Id. Ibid. n. 52.
† Lib. viii. n. n. 43, 44. xi. n. 57. xii. n. 54.
‡ Orland. lib. xv. n. 58.

Thirdly, avaricious schoolmasters, priests, and monks, who loudly complained, in the name of their "craft," because the gratuitous education conferred by the Society was detrimental to their pecuniary interests : or because the duties of the ministry were discharged without any expense to the faithful. "The persecution carried on by the two first classes," adds Olauius, "we consider as contributing to our gain and glory; those of the other, we will endeavor to bear with constancy and patience, rendering always good for evil."* A noble sentiment! and worthy of the Society which is named after the founder of a religion of charity and peace.

The diffusion of education, after a long period of comparative ignorance, throughout the world, was, as I mentioned above, one of the main objects of the institute of Ignatius, and an object which lay very near his heart.† The rays of intellectual

---

* Ibid. n. 58.

† This most arduous, but, certainly, most useful ministry engaged, in a peculiar manner, the attention of Ignatius for it was the best calculated to stay the evils of the times, and root into the young mind the hallowed principles of truth. Hence Bartoli well remarks: "Dove questo del ben 'alevare la groventù fin da' suoi piu teneri anni, sommamente necessario, e in ogni tempo, e in ogni luogo ha dati

light had, some years before, again appeared, breaking with renovated splendor over Italy. That light was first ushered in by the agency of the Church, in whose bosom had been perpetuated and preserved the spark of science, which, kindled by the magic breath of Leo X., burst forth into a flame that has since spread itself over all the civilized earth. But in order to give this flame a proper and successful impulse, the aid of prudent and enthusiastic minds was necessary. Among these, Ignatius stood em-

---

all compagnia, piu collegi egli solo che forse tutti gli altri insieme." The greatest men of the times united in paying a just tribute to the schools of the Society. The famous Navarro (Miscell. 69, de Orat.) declared that *Studiorum Pietatis et litterarum conjunctione, maximam orbi Christiano, præsertim circa pueros, et adolescentes, utilitatem importarunt, et important*. The Cardinal of Augsburg, and the Electors of Treves and Mentz, adopted in their States the system of the Society. *Super institutione juventutis et norma institutionis, quam servat Societas et ab omnibus, licet nomini Societatis non multum addictis, fuit judicata melior magisque proficua Reip. et accommodatior vitæ Christianæ.* Henry IV., king of France, acknowledged that the primitive glory of the University of Paris was restored by the Society: *Nunc, ex Jesuitarum, discipulorum æmulatione, ad suum pristinum florem tota universitas revocata est.* All these references will be found verified in the fifth volume of Bartoli, chap. xiii. Second book, p. 136 et seq.

inently prominent: and posterity will have no difficulty in acknowledging, that to him the republic of letters owes vastly more than to any other individual of any age. In this admission, the enemies of the Society cannot but unite their reluctant testimony with the testimony of its devoted friends. As early as the year 1556, schools under its direction were called for, in all parts of the world. To mention only a few cities in Italy: Brescia, Arezzo, Ancona, Spoleto, and Mazzara were loud in their entreaties, although, on account of the paucity of members, they could not be responded to. Rimini, Sienna, and Catanea in Sicily, were more fortunate.* And so great was the reputation of the Jesuits as teachers of youth, and directors of seminaries of learning, that no less than a hundred colleges were established in the old and new worlds, before the death of their venerated founder. Of these the principal were at Paris, Padua, Louvain, Lisbon, Goa, Cologne, Bologna, Tivoli, Venice, Palermo, Vienna, Rome, Florence, Naples, Ferrara, Modena, Cordova, Syracuse, Prague, Sienna, and two in Brazil.† The

---

* Id. lib. xvi. n. 2, 3, 4.
† Id. lib. x. n. 108. lib. xiii. n. 53. lib. iii. n. 92. lib. iv. n. 10. lib. iv. n. 104., etc., etc. It would be going far beyond the object I have in view to enter into the particulars of the

Roman college, from its conspicuous position, in the metropolis of the Catholic world, and under the eyes of the Pontiffs, was naturally the object of greatest solicitude and interest in the mind of Ignatius. This he desired to be a model for all the others, and placed over it as superintendent the celebrated FATHER OLAUIUS, to whom I had occasion to refer the reader above ; a personage whose eminent talents and profound erudition imparted a splendid reputation to the famous Institution over which he presided.* As an appurtenance to this college, Ignatius, always actuated by munificent plans, and though poor, never distrusting the favor of Divine Providence, added a beautiful villa. This edifice he erected near the baths of Antoninus, not far from the church of St. Balbina, as a retreat for the sick, and a place of relaxation for the students, during the season of vacation from study.† To the quiet shades of this villa he himself withdrew, just before his death: the details of which are faith-

---

foundation of these various colleges. I have enumerated a few, in a general way, merely to show how widely extended was the system of education adopted by the Society, during he lifetime of Ignatius ; and how much he contributed to the cause of letters and religion.

* Vid. lib. xiii. n. 5.
† Lib. xv. n. 6.

fully described by Orlandinus. "Three things our blessed Father desired to see accomplished before his departure from this world : the Spiritual Exercises approved by the authority of the Holy See, the Society confirmed, and the Constitutions finished." Having obtained these, he longed to be dismissed in peace. His health had now declined : worn down, not so much by the weight of years, as by extreme mortification and wasting labors In the month of June, 1556, he began to grow weaker than usual, and unable to attend to his ordinary affairs. Feeling that the hour was approaching to lay aside his tabernacle of flesh, he intrusted the administration of the Society to Fathers John Polanco and Christopher Madridio. The city, at this juncture, presented an image more of ancient warlike Rome, than of the Holy Capital of Christianity. For a fierce war was raging between the Pope and the Catholic king. Day and night the loud and promiscuous clamors of the soldiers and populace were heard ; the clangor of trumpets rang ; the roar of cannon, the noise of drums, and the peal of bells, thundered and echoed over the seven hills. To get rid of this tumult, which he deplored and loathed, he sought the solitude of the villa, which, though within the walls, was, nevertheless, remote from tne scene of arms.* It was, at first, apprehended that an edifice not yet entirely finished or dry might not be salubrious: but a decision to the contrary was given, after strict examination, by Alexander Petronius, an eminent physician. Amid the calm shades of this place his strength daily failed. The Fathers, becoming alarmed, caused him to be removed to the Professed House, where, a few days after, having received the holy Eucharist, he called to his bedside Polanco, and, with a placid spirit, requested that Father to repair to the Sovereign Pontiff, commend to him the protection of the Society, and ask his benediction upon it. "Has it, then, come to this, Father," replied Polanco, "that we are to lose thee in so short a time?" "God hath so willed it," answered Ignatius. "Go to the Holy Father, and bring back his blessing or indulgence, not only for myself, but for all our brethren." Polanco inquired whether he might not defer it until the next day. "Do as you please,"

---

* Multas enim Romana mænia solitudines includunt, observes Orlandinus, lib. xvi. n. 94. This was the case nearly three hundred years ago; and even now, the walls of Rome embrace within their compass many places which are uninhabited and solitary. If I am not mistaken, the villa mentioned above is still in the possession of the Society, and is called *Macao*.

rejoined Ignatius. Polanco became seized with terror, and immediately, in conjunction with Turriano, the ordinary physician of the house, called in Petronius, another, of high repute. Both, after consulting together, decided that they feared no instant danger; but, on the day following, they would be enabled to pronounce with greater certainty. When the physicians withdrew, Ignatius took a little food, as usual; and then passed a great part of the night in conversing on subjects connected with the Roman College: after which, he was left alone. Unable to sleep, he communed, during those weary and silent hours, with God, after whom his soul panted with incessant aspirations of love. How many varied reminiscences then broke upon his memory; how many thoughts of glorious achievements, mingled with sentiments of deep humility! What wonderful things has not this dying priest effected—not only for his own times, but for every succeeding age! The interval between that memorable evening, when we found him habited as a poor pilgrim, meditating on the Rubricato, and this eventful night—lying, in his last extremity, on his solitary bed—has been filled up with deeds and projects of immortal usefulness. The palmer from Mount Serat has established in the Church an order of religious men, whose zeal, learning, sanctity, and fame will spread over Europe, and be bounded only by the limits of the habitable globe. There, in his expiring attitude, he lies, placid, resigned, grateful—full of merits, of glory, of hope. The luminary which has enlightened the earth, is now waxing pale and tremulous: it flickers, then brightens again for the last time, and is extinguished. With the adorable name of Jesus trembling on his dying tongue, Ignatius breathed out his saintly spirit into the hands of his Creator.*

It is not difficult to imagine the sensations of Polanco, when, on entering the chamber where, the previous night, he had watched by the holy man, he found him dead. How despondingly his eyes, streaming with tears, riveted themselves upon those features, grateful and noble still in death: and how endearingly he embraced, with the grief of a child, the venerable remains! There--on that silent couch—lay the body of his Father, his Founder, his Superior. The Society, deprived of her Head, was now reduced to widowhood; and who could be worthy to supply his place? Over

---

* He had attained his sixty-fifth year: his death occurred fifteen years after the establishment of the Society. Vid. Orlandin. lib. xvi. n. 94, 95, 96, 97, 98, 99.

his death, the whole Church mourned, as for a public and general calamity. The voices of the greatest and noblest characters of the age were raised in deploring the melancholy event, and in commemorating and blessing the memory of the deceased. "Under his guidance," exclaims the Superior of the Barnabites,* "the faith, religion, and doctrine of Christ were so widely propagated, that they penetrated to the very antipodes. Wasted with many cares, and borne down with the solicitude for the churches, he fell a martyr in retirement. He was the common Father of all. He soothed the mourner's heart with words of tender sympathy, poured into the afflicted soul the balsam of consolation, and extended aid and protection to the needy and forlorn. . . . May God bestow on him a reward for his good works! We will not cease to offer the Holy Victim at the altar for such a soul. While others scatter over his tomb the purple flowers. These mysteries are the lilies of the priests, more fresh and acceptable to God, though offered for a soul enjoying, as

---

* In a letter written from Milan on the occasion of the demise of Ignatius. Id. ibid. n. 124. This epistle is admirable, as well for its eloquence as for the tribute it pays, in the name of an entire religious order, to the virtues of Ignatius, and the excellence of his Institute.

we believe, the infinite bliss of immortal life. For we cannot but evince by these offerings our undying veneration for him, no longer among us, whom, while in life, we venerated and loved."*

John Vega, governor of Sicily, who had witnessed the incalculable good effected in that island by Ignatius, wrote, in a strain of military eloquence, extolling "the trophies raised by the Society, which would defy the power of time, and resist

---

* The Society had been established only sixteen years, but was spread through the whole world. Her members had preached the gospel in all languages, had rescued nations from idolatry, and united them to the Church. One hundred colleges had been established. All these things Ignatius had the happiness to witness before he was taken away to his heavenly reward. He had, besides, seen one of his children lay down his life—dying a martyr for the faith —Father Anthony Criminali. He had beheld prodigies wrought by their hands; he had witnessed their sanctity and merits, which won the admiration of emperors, popes, kings, and princes; by whom they were honored as apostolic nuncios in various parts, as orators and theologians in the Council of Trent and other synods: and, having enjoyed all these accumulated consolations, and commend ng his dear Society to the ever-vigilant care of Divine Providence, he sweetly closed his eyes to this mortal scene, and slept in the Lord. See Tanner, Soc. Europ. p. 23.

the elements themselves. Trophies erected not by earthly ambition, nor by vainglory, but by heroic zeal and disinterested exertions."* Sentiments not less laudatory, nor less expressive of admiration and sorrow, were uttered by John III., king of Portugal,† and by the illustrious Cardinals Otho Truchses, and Bartholomew a Cucua.‡

Polanco declares, that, though he had never read of mortal as much beloved as was Ignatius, by the whole Society, and though he believed that in the annals of history no parallel could be found, still none of his children were overcome with grief. On the contrary, a new vigor seemed to spread itself through all, a new love of labor and perfection, and a new confidence and hope in the welfare and augmentation of the body. For the spirit of their holy founder was still with them, and his intercession in heaven would constitute an ægis of protection and safety, under which they would survive, and flourish, and be perpetuated. Three hundred years have confirmed these primi-

---

* Ibid. n. 128.

† He was accustomed to say that Ignatius ought to be Pope. n. 129.

‡ Ibid. n. 131 and n. 132.

tive hopes, which have been more than realized The glorious achievements of the Society are blended with the archives of universal history, identified with the civilization, learning, conversion, and prosperity of innumerable countries. She has had her alternations of adversity and triumph, she has passed through the deep shades of night as well as the bright beams of day. She has had friends—devoted and true—in every class and grade of life ; she has encountered, too, the fiercest and most formidable enemies, in the same. She has been entirely suppressed in Europe, and that with the concurrence of a pope ; but she has been restored to being, and covered with favors, by his successors.* The memory of Ignatius is in benediction ; his name stands enrolled, conspicuous and effulgent, on the catalogue of saints. Of his rare merits and heroic virtues, it is not my province to speak at length. And, indeed, it would be an act of supererogation, if not of temerity, in me, to attempt the panegyric of him in whose praise the

---

* Since its restoration, the Society has spread itself abroad anew with extraordinary celerity. Stripped of most of her ancient houses and colleges, she provided others with an energy and success worthy of her earliest days : and her members are again proving themselves to be "**the stoutest oarsmen in St. Peter's bark.**"

noble eloquence of Bellarmine was employed, and before whose shrine, in prayer and veneration, the great Baronius knelt.*

---

* In the year 1599, Cardinal Cæsar Baronius, one of the most learned chroniclers of modern times, went, with Cardinal Bellarmine, on the anniversary of the death of Ignatius, to the Professed House. After a discourse delivered by the latter, over the tomb, Baronius fell upon his knees, with profound respect, and ordered the image of the saint, for the first time, to be exposed to public veneration. For all the particulars, consult Orlandinus, lib. xvi. n. 136.

"Loyola was a soldier to the last breath he drew, a general whose authority none might question, a comrade on whose cordiality all might rely, sustaining all the dangers and hardships he exacted of his followers, and in his religious campaigns a strategist of most consummate skill and most comprehensive survey. . . . To conquer Lutheranism, by converting to the faith of Rome the barbarous and half-civilized nations of the earth, was among the earliest of his projects. . . . It was necessary that he should select men superior not only to all the allurements of appetite and the common infirmities of our race, but superior also to those temptations to which an inquisitive mind, and abilities of a high order, expose their possessor. . . . Long he weighed and most sagaciously did he decide this perplexing choice. It fell on many who well fulfilled these conditions."—Stephens, *ubi supr.*

PETER FABER.

CHAPTER II.

PETER FABER.

PETER FABER.—How gained over by Ignatius. Performs the Exercises. Is ordained Priest. Teaches in the University of Rome. Is sent to Parma; and to Germany. His mission at Ratisbonne. Goes to Spain. Returns to Germany. His labors at Spires; and at Mentz; at Augsburg, and Cologne. Is called to Portugal. Thence to Liege. Returns to Cologne. Defends the Catholic Faith. His manner of treating with heretics. Is sent back to Portugal. Goes to Castile. Distinguishes himself at Salamanca. Goes to Valladolid. His influence at the Court of Philip. Traverses Madrid and Toledo. Is deputed to the Council of Trent. Sickens at Barcelona, and dies at Rome.

THE first individual who associated himself with Ignatius was Peter Faber, born among the wild mountains of Savoy, of parents more conspicuous for their piety, than distinguished by their lineage; and educated in sentiments of devotion under the care of Peter Vegliardo, an exemplary and holy man;—"Who," as Faber himself informs us, "in his teachings, made the pagan poets and profane writers so many heralds of gospel morality, and rendered them all subservient to the cause of Christian education.* Fostered by the tuition of such an instructor, the ardent and susceptible mind of Faber became inflamed with the love of letters and religion, in such a manner, that in his twelfth year, wandering alone over the silent fields, and musing under the broad canopy of the heavens, he devoted himself to the Lord of the universe, by making a vow of perpetual chastity ; a vow, which he was enabled the more easily to observe, on account of the enthusiastic ardor with which he pursued the study of literature and the sciences. From a simple shepherd-boy, as he originally was, he became, by the dint of his great talents, and the elevation of his noble soul, an aspirant after the highest attainments of learning : and, bidding adieu to his native valleys, he resolved to seek his fortune in Paris, where, in a short time, he mastered the abstruse philosophy of Aristotle, which, with astonishing ease and correctness, he read and understood in the original Greek.†

---

* Orlandinus, lib. i. n. 76. He was born in 1506, on Easter Sunday.

† Bartoli asserts that, after having studied nine years under Vegliardo, Faber became master of the Greek and Latin tongues, and so deeply versed in scholastic theology, that he composed a Commentary on the " Master of Sen-

It was in this gay metropolis of France, that Ignatius first became acquainted with this extraordinary man. They lodged under the same roof; and, in return for some kind offices rendered him during that period, Faber, who had now taken the degree in philosophy, offered his services to Ignatius in aiding him towards the prosecution of the studies in which he was then engaged. Gradually there grew up between their congenial hearts a confidence and affection, which rendered them mutually happy and emulous in the performance of holy deeds. Faber beheld with admiration the heroic virtues of Ignatius, and Ignatius was charmed with the candor, ingenuousness, and ardent piety of Faber, who, casting aside all personal considerations, or vain-glorious ideas, resolved, though a master in human philosophy, to become,

---

tences," before he went to the University of Paris. Tom. v. p. 87.

Ignatius and Calvin were at Paris at the same time; where each selected his disciples and companions: and it is a remarkable fact, that their first disciples were of the same name—Faber. "The one," in the language of Florimund Remond, "destined to be, by his learning and virtue, the scourge of heresy; the other, its advocate and defender.' Tanner's Soc. Europ. p. 11.

in spiritual wisdom, the disciple of Ignatius.* Nothing could be more in conformity with the desire of Ignatius ; nor did he hesitate to undertake the task of directing and forming to a religious life so eminent a scholar. He taught him to watch over his heart, by the use of a daily examination of conscience : to have recourse to the tribunal of penance, and receive the blessed Eucharist every week, and to struggle incessantly against his predominant passion.† Having laid this foundation, it was not difficult to raise upon it that tower of perfection, which will afterwards astonish the beholder. Faber dedicated himself to the service of the Church ; and having gone through the usual course of theological studies, with the advice of Ignatius, he embraced the clerical state. Before, however, receiving orders, he performed the spiritual exercises, with a loftiness of soul and generosity of purpose which are rarely to be met with. During the winter, which, that year, was so in-

---

* Ibid. n. 78. The elegance of style and fidelity of details with which Orlandinus treats of this admirable union between Faber and Ignatius, are as pleasing to the classic scholar, as they are edifying to the pious Christian.

† These rules of a spiritual life were taken by Ignatius from the ancient fathers of the desert, especially the Abbot Serapion, as the historian remarks; *ubi supr.* n. 80.

tensely cold that coaches might safely cross on the frozen waters of the Seine, he undertook this career of penance.* Glowing with fervor while all was cold and bleak in nature, he spent hours in the open air wrapt in sublime contemplations; and several days without tasting any food. After this, in the twenty-eighth year of his age, he was ordained priest, A. D. 1534,—the first-born, as it were, of the great parent of the Society, and through whose influence and example two distinguished doctors in theology, John Cordurius and Paschasius Broëtus, were induced to range themselves under its standard. Having acquired no ordinary renown by publicly lecturing in the college of the *Sapienza* at Rome, he was appointed by the Pope one of the companions of Cardinal Ennio Philonardo Verulano, in his legation to Parma; in which city he not only won golden opinions for erudition and wisdom, but preached the word of God with incredible success. Multitudes gathered not merely for the purpose of admiring the surpassing eloquence of the orator, but also—excited to compunction—in order to confess their sins. With indefatigable zeal, he instructed the ignorant, animated the secular clergy to the

---

* Ibid. n. 81.

more faithful discharge of similar duties, and instituted an association of pious ladies, whose office it was to go from house to house for the purpose of teaching the catechism to young girls.* The admonitions which he left in writing to the noble sodality of Parma, when on the point of quitting that city, are fraught with maxims and rules of devotion and piety.† The daily mode of life he proposed to them was : at night, before retiring to rest, to reflect, upon their knees, on their last hour, on judgment, on the punishment of hell, and the joys of heaven. On each point they were to meditate for a few minutes only. This was to be succeeded by an examination of conscience, with a hearty sorrow for all the sins committed during the day, and a resolution to confess them at a specified time. Finally, the blessing of God should be invoked upon themselves and all the faithful living, that their sleep might be pure and tranquil ; and on the dead, that they might find solace and mercy beyond the tomb. The same exercises were to be repeated every morning, with the addition of a chapter of the life

---

* Lib. ii. n. 76.
† They are given in full by our faithful historian, and will richly compensate the attentive perusal of the learned reader Vid. lib. ii. n. 108, 109, 110.

of Christ, (if time and circumstances would permit,) and assisting at the Divine Sacrifice. Every week he recommended them to approach the Holy Table. With regard to the necessities of life, they were instructed to moderate their desires, and refer all their labors and secular occupations to the glory of God and the salvation of their souls. Blessed and holy maxims, which, if observed, would do more for the happiness and virtue of a community than a thousand utopian speculations of theorists and philosophers. With what efficacy these admonitions of the saintly man were received and cherished, there is abundant evidence in the fact, that sixty years later, as Orlandinus testifies, that sodality continued in a flourishing condition.*

Having labored so successfully at Parma, Faber's next destination was Worms, in Germany. The heresies of Lutheranism had now taken deep root on that doomed soil, and it required an apostle of no common character to appear on an arena of religious conflict against the combined and powerful adversaries of the ancient faith. The more so, as he was the first of the new order of JESUS sent to face the hydra in its own kindred realm. Here, it was necessary to be armed with a twofold en-

---

* Lib. ii. n. 112.

ergy—one, to be wielded against the errors of the country, the other in vindication of the dogmas of truth. Each did Faber possess, and each did he exercise, in an eminent degree, under the special influence of Moroni, then Bishop, but afterwards decorated with the Cardinal's hat.* Many Lutherans were, by his assiduous and convincing discourses, brought back to the fold, and innumerable Catholics were confirmed in their faith, and converted from their evil ways, by attending the spiritual exercises, and frequenting his ascetic instructions.†

His stay at Worms was not of long duration. At the request of the Emperor Charles V., he accompanied the apostolic legate, Gaspar Contarini, to Ratisbonne.‡ Whithersoever he travelled, he

---

* Ibid.

† Melancthon, "*Ieri Grammatico, oggi Teologo,* yesterday a grammarian, to-day a theologian," writes Bartoli, was present at the Diet of Worms, with Faber; he had ten years previously drawn up the famous Confession of Augsburg and he now held a high rank among the Lutherans. But, despite his popular character, and exaggerated meekness, the Catholic faith was preserved in Germany by the exertions of the Sons of Ignatius.

‡ Lib. iii. n. 26. "Quocunque autem vestigia posuit," writes the historian, "eundem se præbuit Fabrum, navum videlicet hominem et operarium."

proved himself a laborious and indefatigable man, assisting the curates in their parochial duties, and preaching the word of God. At Ratisbonne, he was honored by the Duke's son, in whose dominions that capital was situated, and by him chosen as his Confessor. At that Court, which was composed of Germans, Italians, and Spaniards, he was venerated as a common father. He extended his missionary solicitude throughout the country, imparted spiritual aid and consolation to the living and the dying, and left such deep and lasting impressions on his converts, that none of them was ever known to relapse into the habits of vice, or the wiles of heresy.*

From Ratisbonne, Faber was ordered to proceed to Spain. Before his departure, he made his solemn profession in the Church of the Blessed Virgin,—before the grand altar of "the ancient chapel,"—on the feast of the Visitation. The formulary of vows, signed by his own hand, he sent to Ignatius;† after which, he departed from Germany.

---

* This is related, and justly, as a remarkable fact, by Orlandinus, lib. iii. n. 26. Among his converts were two Moors. From Germany he addressed a letter of admonition to his brethren at Paris, which breathes the most fervent piety, and is stored with heavenly wisdom. Ibid. n. 27.

† Ibid. n. 29.

Entertaining a peculiar devotion to the angels, he committed himself, on his journey, to their guardian care, and on entering any town, he was accustomed to recommend its inhabitants to the particular protection of their angels, and their patron saints. Everywhere did he preach and exhort: in the churches, in the streets, on the highways, in public and in private: complying, thus, with the admonition of St. Gregory the Great, who advised the ministers of the word of God to season every opportunity with the salt of eternal life.* He dissembled nothing; but, on all occasions, discoursed of virtue, of truth, of God; not, indeed, producing disgust by excessive rigor, but rendering palatable, by the sweetness of his manner, duties the most severe, and practices the most repugnant.

In passing through France, he was arrested, with his companions, and confined in prison. But, even in chains, his spirit and zeal were not to be manacled. With such unction and power he spoke of heavenly things to the commander and guard of the castle, that they were excited to repentance, and humbly confessed their sins. Contrary to the public expectation, he was not only humanely treated, but honorably set at liberty:† whence, having

---

* Hom. 17, in Luc. 10.   † Lib. iii. n. 32.

resumed his journey, he arrived safely at Madrid. From this capital, the rays of Faber's zeal diffused themselves far and wide through Spain. He conciliated and attached to his person all orders and classes. But these efforts were only, as it were, in passing through a country, which obedience soon rendered it necessary for him to quit, to return to Germany, where a wider field extended itself for his labors. His excessive disinterestedness is apparent from the circumstance of his having made a vow of peculiar poverty—never to accept of any remuneration for preaching, celebrating Mass, or any other function. Having thus perfectly detached himself from all earthly objects, it is not to be wondered at, if he devoted his heart to celestial and divine things. His ordinary prayer, with which he was in the habit of sanctifying his actions, was this: "Heavenly Father, give me a good spirit."* Frequently did he call upon the adorable name of JESUS, and the holy name of Mary: and practising the memorable counsel of St. Basil to his monks, always to remember the presence of God,† he appeared, at all times, as though he was walking, and acting, and living, in Him, and by Him, and through Him.

---

* Ibid. n. 35. † Reg. Br. Q. 21.

Having no companions, on his return to Germany, he besought the Almighty to join with him some strangers, at least, with whom he might tranquilly and happily pursue his journey. His prayer was heard. For, two individuals not only became his associates in travelling, but most unexpectedly united themselves with the Society. These were John Arragonius and Alvarez Alphonsus, priests, and chaplains of Maria and Joanna, the daughters of the Emperor Charles, who sacrificed the splendor of the court for the humility of the cross. Accompanied by these new brethren, he journeyed, during three months, through imminent dangers and pressing difficulties. Safe, at length, and sound, he arrived at Spires, having escaped from the grasp of robbers on the confines of Spain, from the gloom of a prison in France, from the insolence of the soldiery in Swabia, and from the insults of heretics in Germany.* At Spires, the harvest was white, and boundless. By his daily exhortations and indefatigable perseverance, he brought back thousands to the ways of righteousness, and reformed, in a great measure, the rather lax morals of some of the clergy.† The rigid measures of the bishop with regard to the latter,

---

* Lib. iii. n. 65. † Ibid. 61, 67

instead of producing the desired effect, only increased the evil. But the mild, candid, and yet firm and uncompromising conduct of Faber brought them to a sense of duty. By his prudence and singular probity he won the esteem of all, even the Cardinal, who afterwards showed his benevolence and affection for the Society. As a mark of his kindness to Faber, he offered him a silver vase of great value, which, however, the humble Jesuit, ever mindful of his vow of poverty, begged respectfully to decline receiving. On the following day, the Cardinal, in shaking hands with him, threw into the case of his breviary, which was suspended from his girdle, a hundred golden florins. Finding himself compelled, out of respect for the illustrious donor, to receive the gift, he sent part of it to his brethren at Paris, and the rest he distributed among the poor.*

Returning to Spires, he resumed his catechetical instructions in that city with great usefulness. On one occasion, when attacked by a minister on the impropriety, as he termed it, of venerating sacred images, and invoking the saints, Faber replied with this home-thrust argument: "If you

---

* Ibid. n. 71

deny that we should honor God only in his own person, and not in his saints, why should we be bound to venerate the king, not in his person only, but in that of his representative?"—a plain, but convincing retort: a powerful *argumentum ao hominem*, which silenced the Lutheran caviller on the spot.*

From Spires, Faber was called to Mentz, at the solicitation of the archbishop, who, knowing his prudence and erudition, intended him to assist, with some other illustrious and learned men, at the

---

* This reply of Faber contains in brief the whole of the doctrine touching the nature of the veneration of images and the invocation of saints. All the respect is merely relative—all tending to the supreme worship of God, by whom the saints are rewarded, and through whom alone their intercession can avail the faithful on earth.

† Before the General Council of Trent, several provincial synods had been held for the purpose of defending the Catholic faith, and reforming morals. In Germany, the most remarkable were those of Cologne, Mentz, and Treves. The heretics, not satisfied with their decrees, appealed to an œcumenical council. But no sooner was that convoked, than they protested against its authority, on the ground that it should be celebrated, not at Trent, but in Germany, as it was against the Protestants of that country it was intended. But this was a frivolous objection—a mere subterfuge. For, they must have known, that although the Arian heresy

Council of Trent.† But this mission the Holy See had reserved as a pledge of its own esteem for his

---

sprang up at Alexandria, in Egypt, the council that condemned it was held at Nice, in Bithynia; the same may be said, also, of the Nestorian heresy, which was broached at Constantinople, but anathematized in the Council of Ephesus.

Moreover, the Lutherans themselves, in the Diet of Spires, in 1542, had assented to the proposition of convening the council at Trent, which is conterminous with Germany, convenient for the Germans, and affording no suspicions to other nations.

Another objection was, that the council was convoked by the Sovereign Pontiff, who, they argued, could not preside on this occasion, as no one should be a judge in his own cause. This, too, was a mere sophism. For, it is well authenticated, that no œcumenical council had ever been celebrated, either in the East or West, at which the visible head of the Church, the Sovereign Pontiff, did not preside, if not in person, at least through his legates. In contemplating the conduct of the Reformers, I am forcibly reminded of the following memorable language of St. Vincent Lerins, in speaking of Nestorius: "Invecti sumus in Nestorii sceleratam præsumptionem, quod sacram scripturam se primum ac solum intelligere, et omnes eos ignorâsse jactaret, quicunque ante se magisterii munere præditi, divina eloquia tractavissent: totam postremo etiam nunc errare, et semper errasse ecclesiam, quæ (ut ipsi videbatur) ignoros, erroneosque doctores et secuta est, st sequeretur."

"We have inveighed against the audacious presumption

great qualities, as we shall hereafter relate.* In the mean time, the archbishop kept him near his own person as an adviser and friend. What was the state of his mind, and with what heavenly gifts he was replenished, a letter written at this epoch to Laynez clearly testifies. "I cannot, brother James, express," these are his terms, "the favors which God has bestowed on me, since we parted at Placenza: he has healed all my infirmities, and effaced my iniquities. To Him be glory, praise, honor, and benediction, from every creature. With all my heart do I say, Amen! and I entreat you also to bless and praise him for me, your brother, and for all the Society."†

Here, as usual, he stood forth the intrepid and powerful vindicator of the faith, and excited universal admiration, and produced incredible good, by

---

of Nestorius, who boasted that he was the first and only individual that ever understood the sacred Scriptures, and that all others were ignorant of them, who, before him, endowed with the office of teaching, had explained the divine revelations; that the whole Church, in fine, was in error, and always had been in error; because (as he pretended) she was following, and had followed, ignorant and erring teachers." *Commonitor. adv. Hæres.*

* Orland. lib. iii. n. 73.
† See the whole epistle, apud Orland. lib. iii. n. 74.

his frequent discourses, especially by an explanation of the Psalms, in a series of lectures. By his amiable virtues, he attached all orders of citizens to him, and reformed abuses, especially among the clergy. All seemed honored by going through the spiritual exercises under such a man, or by having him as their confessor. His success was so far beyond his own most sanguine anticipations, that he could not but give vent to his astonishment in a letter to Ignatius.*

The Cardinal, who, from his first acquaintance with Faber, esteemed him as an extraordinary and holy man, witnessing the immense fruit which his labors produced in Germany, conceived a still more vehement admiration for him, and desired to know more concerning the Society to which he belonged. No one could be better fitted to discharge the task assigned him than Faber : insomuch, that having finished it, the Cardinal declared that he believed the Society to have been divinely instituted, to counteract the calamities of the times.†

Whilst thus engaged in reviving discipline and virtue among the clergy and laity, he was suddenly

---

* Ibid. lib. iv. n. 32.

† Ibid. " Ut Societatem sibi videri diceret propè divinitùs ad ea tempora tam difficilia, tamque aspera reservatam."

called to Cologne, where the Church was in danger of being infected with the Lutheran heresies.* On his arrival in that city, he found the Archbishop, Hermannus, tainted with them, and no one resolute enough to oppose so powerful a prelate. He did not shrink from the task: but, after recommending the step to God, went to the palace, gently warned the Archbishop of his error, and, by his prudence and moderation, effected a manifest change. The Pope's legate, John Poggius, a very learned and experienced man, who was afterwards raised to the cardinalate, being informed of the condition of that Church, would not suffer Faber to be removed from it. Whilst intent upon the study how to rescue that ancient portion of the kingdom of Christ from the calamity that menaced it; whilst he labored, with assiduous care, to raise Religion from her fallen state, and preserve unimpaired the glory of the archiepiscopal chair, Heaven gave him a powerful auxiliary in the person of the venerable Peter Canisius, who burned with a desire to propagate the true faith, and to defend it against its enemies.†

---

* Lib. iv. n. 33. The historian does not conceal the vices of many of the clergy of Germany, at this period; which, no doubt, facilitated the spread of errors.

† Lib. iv. n. 54. With what profound arguments he asserted the cause of faith, his Catechism will convince any

He was the first German who joined the Society. Attracted by the reputation of Faber, he sought after him—"and found that man, or rather angel," in his own language; "nor have I ever seen or heard a more learned or profound theologian, or a man of such eminent and shining virtue."*

Meanwhile Faber received a letter from Ignatius, directing him to quit Cologne, and proceed with Alphonsus and Arragonius into Portugal, as a companion to the daughter of the king. This was done at the request of the monarch himself.† Without delay he set out for Louvain, thence to embark for Portugal. Hardly had he arrived at that city, before he was attacked with the tertian fever, by which he was prostrated upon his bed. Having lingered for a long time, the Sovereign Pontiff, deeming it proper to defer, on that account, his mission to Portugal, commanded him, on his recovery, to go back to Cologne. He there met Alphonsus: but Canisius, whose father had died, had gone to his native country, for the purpose of arranging his domestic affairs. Faber wrote him

---

reader. The canonization of this servant of God is now in process.

*Id. ibid.—"Si tamen Vir est, et non potius Angelus Domini."

† Lib. iv. n. 35.

a letter of condolence, entreating him, at the same time, to return as soon as possible.*

Affairs of vast magnitude now occupied the mind of Faber; a task of infinite importance was placed in his hands: no other than that of supporting again the tottering faith of Hermannus, who, during his absence, wavered from the standard of truth, and inclined to the errors of the times. The unfaithful prelate had invited to Cologne, Bucer, Melancthon, and other renowned doctors of the Reformation, from whom he derived the fatal poison of heresy, and permitted it to be spread, far and wide, through his diocese.† Faber saw, with horror, the lamentable evil, and strained every nerve to save at least the people among whom the contagion had not yet been caught: he held daily conferences, to which the learned doctors, academicians, and others—ecclesiastics as well as laics

---

* Ibid. n. 87.

† This unfortunate prelate, who, in the early progress of the Reformation, had convened a synod at Cologne, in which many excellent and wholesome decrees were passed, was, at length, led astray, by Bucer and Melancthon, and joined their ranks, in which he continued till his death. Had not Faber been on the spot to stay the spreading evil, Cologne, no doubt, would have fallen, beyond the hope of rescue, into the power of those bold heresiarchs.

—flocked incessantly. Such was their efficacy, that, at the request of thousands of the principal personages of that city, the Emperor banished Melancthon and Bucer, who, under the specious appellation of Reformers, were infecting the country with the spirit of schism and disorder. Before their departure, however, Faber, the more solemnly to refute their novelties, challenged them both to a public disputation, in which, with immense erudition and resistless arguments, he exposed the fallacy of their pretensions, and annihilated the daring sophistry of their system.* His adversaries, as may easily be conceived, were far from yielding : they clung, with desperate obstinacy, to their darling errors, which emancipated the human mind from all ecclesiastical authority, and, under the glorious name of Liberty, gave free scope to boundless license. But if their hardihood was not overcome, their audacity was repressed. They were condemned to be silent while Faber was at Cologne; and justly has it been conceded by contemporary writers, that, had it not been preserved by his exertions, religion would have perished in that city.†

---

* Lib. iv. n. 90.

† Ibid. "Ut meritò qui recte sentirent assererent, nisi

In a letter addressed, at this juncture, to Laynez, Faber has left upon record certain sentiments touching the manner of treating with Lutherans, which deserve the attention of the reader: "It becomes all," he writes, "who desire to do good among them, to evince the greatest charity towards them; to love them truly; to disabuse their minds of every thing that might tend to lessen us in their estimation. We should seek to conciliate their good-will, and gain their confidence. This will be effected by gentle intercourse with them, and conversing only of those points concerning which we all agree; carefully shunning any altercation..... We should, in the next place, teach them first what they should practise, and afterwards what they should believe: acting, **in this** particular, differently from the custom of the primitive Church, at a time when the minds of men were to be imbued with faith, which is 'from hearing,' and then to be gradually led to the consentaneous practice of good works. We should, therefore, strive to recall them from their evil ways before we speak to them of their evil doctrine. If Luther himself could be persuaded to lead a virtuous and pious

---

Fabri vigiliæ intervenissent, perituram funditus fuisse Coloniam."

life, it would be no difficult matter to bring him back to the bosom of the true Church."*

These were the principles which he expressed and followed in laboring for the conversion and salvation of the Lutherans at Cologne; whence, having confided to Canisius the business of erecting a college in that city, by order of Ignatius, he departed for Louvain on his way to Portugal, and arrived safely at Lisbon, on the feast of Saint Bartholomew. Thence he proceeded to Evora, where he fell sick; and, on recovering, proceeded to Coimbra, to overlook the laying of the foundations of a college in that town.† This being done, his next destination was Castile: and at Salamanca, where he passed some time, he fanned the flame of piety which had already been enkindled by Araozius, and let slip no opportunity of aiding in the cause of religion. The Society now began to be favorably known, and colleges, at the suggestion of the noblest men, were founded.‡ There flourished, at this era, at Salamanca, two illustrious characters, Alphonsus de Castro, of the order of St. Francis, and of that of St. Dominic, Francis Victo-

---

* See the whole document, ubi supr. n. 91, 92, 93, 94, 95.
† Lib. v. n. 43.
‡ Ibid. n. 59.

ria, whose names were renowned in the schools, and whose piety shone brightly in the Church. By them Faber was received with every demonstration of benevolence, and the Society was so highly extolled before the public, that an effort was made to retain him in that famous capital : but, having merely sowed the seed of future good, he pursued his journey to Valladolid, then the seat of the empire.* He was graciously received by Philip and his queen, Mary, through whose kindness a vast field was opened to his zeal in Spain. Wherefore, he began immediately, both in the churches and public places, to harangue the people, to instruct the young and ignorant. He visited the hospitals, in which he often spent entire nights, and penetrated into the cells of the prisons. By this devotedness and generosity, he converted thousands, and shed the light of virtue and faith into the deep gloom of vice and error. The fame of these apostolic deeds soon spread throughout all Spain ; and Faber was the topic of universal conversation. By Charles, he was invited to Madrid ; whence he proceeded to Toledo, where, three years before, he had won the admiration of the people by his labors and virtues ; and after a brief visit, retraced his steps to

---

* Ibid. n. 60.

Valladolid. To the court and nobility he was peculiarly dear, and their influence extending itself to the lower classes, he became the idol of all; insomuch that he seemed to experience some emotions of fear at the unprecedented prosperity that attended him.* But no; this was the wise disposition of Providence, who, having filled the chalice, which Ignatius was destined to drink at first, with the bitterness of adversity and suffering, changed it now, for the welfare and glory of the Society, into sweetness and joy. And this consideration, which Faber founded on the writings of Blessed Mark the anchorite, dispersed the cloud of his misgiving.†

The crown of all his merits was to have been placed upon his brows by the Sovereign Pontiff, who had chosen him to assist as one of his Theologians at the Council of Trent.‡ But Divine Providence had other views over his good and faithful servant. Fatigued with his labors, and exhausted by acts of mortification, which he practised in the midst of the luxury and pageantry of the Court, he was seized with a burning fever at Barcelona, where he was reposing a few days, on his

---

* Ibid. n. 78.

† B. Marc. Anach. *Tractat. de pœn.* Quoted by Orlandinus, ubi supr.

‡ Lib vi. n. 19.

way to Rome. It was midsummer, and the heat was excessive. Ignatius did not, under those circumstances, advise his continuing on his journey; but the other Fathers thinking differently, it became him to make the attempt. Actuated by the spirit of perfect obedience, he summoned all his energies, and succeeded in reaching the capital of the Christian world. A few days elapsed after his arrival, at that unwholesome season, before he was attacked again, and laid prostrate upon his bed, from which he never rose. He died: and when he died, one of the grandest and most conspicuous pillars of the Society fell to the earth, the loss of which was mourned and deplored by his brethren, and by all the faithful. Ignatius wept over the grave of his first companion and beloved friend; while the whole Church was deprived of an Apostle whose heart yearned for the propagation of the faith, the conversion of heretics and sinners, the greater glory of God; and whose life was a continual exemplar of the purity, piety, zeal, and perfection of the gospel. His conversation was always in heaven. Amid all the contingencies of life, his confidence in God was unwavering, and his gratitude unbounded. His virtues were heroic: renowned for all, he was particularly remarkable for prompt obedience unrestricted poverty, and spiritual recollection.* His devotion to the Blessed Virgin, mother of God, was most tender; to her, after the example of the primitive fathers of the Church, he was accustomed to recommend his wants and those of the Society and his fellow-mortals; and guided by the same venerable authority, he paid due honor to the angels and saints, offered his prayers to them, as the especial friends of the Most High, who, in the infinite enjoyment of the beatific vision, do not fail to experience a never-ceasing and universal interest in the welfare and happiness of the poor pilgrims of earth. The Lutherans, among their other numberless errors, attacked, as unmeet, nay, even as idolatrous, this practice, which loses itself in immemorial ages. The whole progeny of the Protestant Reformation, in succeeding times, have followed their example—and not only continue to reject in spirit and in truth "the communion of saints," but distort the ancient doctrine, and calumniate the millions of Catholics who cling to it, not, as it is said, with

---

* Vid. lib. iii. n. 71. Ibid. n. 33. 34. lib. v. 48. lib. vi. n. 86. Faber's death occurred in 1546. The historian exclaims: "Cecidit præcipuum Societatis columen, et cunctos Socios mœror ingens invasit. Ipse vero B. Pater quo putas animo carissimi Sodalis occasum tulit?" See also Tanner, p. 38.

morbid superstition, but with vigorous, enlightened, and primeval devotion.

The grave where Faber's mortal relics reposed was a hallowed and venerated spot, in the estimation of all who knew how to appreciate the sanctity of that spirit which so recently animated and consecrated them. Among others, one of the most distinguished members of the early Society, Father Oviedus, did not hesitate to burn over it a blessed taper, beseeching "the Saint" to obtain for him, by his intercession, spiritual light from the "Father of Lights." This private veneration, evinced by such a man, will speak more eloquently than my pen can describe, the odor of sanctity which the name of Faber diffused through the Society and the Church.*

---

* This practice Oviedus continued yearly, with the approbation of Ignatius. Orlandinus relates this fact with his wonted precision and elegance of style. "Oviedus quidem singulis deinceps annis candidum in Urbem cereum misit, rogans B. Patrem ut ardentem tumulo Fabri juberet imponi, quo sibi ille spirituale lumen a Patre luminum impetraret," etc. Lib. vi. n. 87. This he did as an act of private devotion, cherishing the hope that, at some future time, his name would find a place among the servants of God who are publicly venerated by the Church. His death occurred on the first of August, A. D. 1546.

ST. FRANCIS XAVIER.

St. Patrick's Church,
Huntington, L. I.

CHAPTER III.

ST. FRANCIS XAVIER.*

FRANCIS XAVIER.—Converted by Ignatius. Rejects a canonicate. Is sent to the Indies, as Apostolic Legate. His labors at Mozambique, Melinda, and Scotora; on the Fishery-coast; at Goa; at Cape Comorin; at Travancor; in the Island of Manaria; in Ceylon. Visits the tomb of St. Thomas at Meliapor. Goes to Malacca; Amboina; Maluco; to the Isle of Moro; meditates a mission to Japan. Returns to India; to Goa. Departs for Japan. Arrives at Gangoxima. Traverses Japan. First Japanese Christians. Goes to Firando, and to Meaco, and Amangouchi. Disputes with the Bonzees. Conference with the King of Bungo. Returns to the Indies. Departs for China. Arrives at the Island of Sanchin. Dies in the midst of his glory.

FROM the midst of the most flattering worldly hopes and affections, the second companion of Ignatius was drawn into the bosom of the Society by the persuasive influence of that wonderful man. He saw in Xavier a magnanimous disposition, a

---

* " It was in the year 1506, that Francis Xavier, the youngest child of a numerous family, was born in the castle of his ancestors in the Pyrenees. Robust and active, of a gay humor and ardent spirit, the young mountaineer listened with a throbbing heart to the legend of his house,

soul expanding with the natural energies of greatness and ambition; and could he only succeed in directing them to the cause of religion and virtue, no imagination could conceive how boundless would be their extent, how tireless their operation. To this end, Ignatius suggested to Xavier's mind profound considerations on the inconstancy of all human things, the vanity of the world, and the briefness of time. The seed took root—deep root, in his susceptible and noble heart. God's grace accompanied the hand that planted it; and, after long and severe struggles within himself—struggles of passion against virtue, pride against humility, human reason against faith—a perfect and glorious victory was achieved. Xavier resolved to dedicate himself to the altar, and to associate himself with the holy man to whom he was indebted,

---

and to the inward voice which spoke of her days to come, when his illustrious lineage should derive new splendor from his own achievements." Stephens, *ubi supr.*

He owed his conversion especially to that solemn admonition of our Saviour, repeated by Ignatius in the midst of the frivolities in which he delighted, or in the studies which he was pursuing. Whatever was the theme of conversation between Ignatius and him, it was always closed by the same awful inquiry: " What doth it profit a man, if he gain the whole world, and lose his own soul?"

under God, for his rescue from the snares and vices of the world.* This memorable event occurred in Paris, in the year 1535.

Hardly had he entered upon his theological studies before he was nominated canon in the Cathedral of Pampeluna, his native city: the dignity, however, he refused to accept, preferring the humility of that order which closed the door of honors against its members.† After going through all the preliminary stages of the Spiritual Exercises and necessary retirement, and in all giving proofs of perfection and sanctity, which might render him worthy to undertake any project no matter how arduous, how uninviting, the vast regions of the East were spread before his mind, and he was admonished by Providence to prepare himself for a mission which would open the gates of the Church and of Heaven to a far-off world that then lay buried in the darkness of Idolatry. The Indies had been penetrated by the spirit of adventure; they were now to be explored by the spirit of religion. When this great project was proposed to Xavier by Ignatius, he clasped it to his heart with incredible alacrity and ineffable delight, and incontinently set out to Rome with the ambassador

---

* Ibid. n. 105.   † Orland. lib. i n. 85.

of the king of Portugal.* At the request of that monarch, he was invested with the dignity of Apostolic Legate, in order that he might exercise a greater authority and influence over those distant missions.† Obedience alone induced the humble man to accept the dignity. But he refused all presents, with the exception of a few books; nor would he consent to have the services of an attendant, saying, as long as he had the use of his hands and feet, he did not require any waiting upon. In taking a last embrace, on board the ship, of Simon Bobadilla, Xavier thus addressed him: "Do you not remember, Father, when we were together in the hospital at Rome, how you were, one night, aroused from sleep by my cries of *more, more, more?* Since now the dream is about being realized, I will inform you that those cries were forced from me by the prospect of innumerable sufferings and dangers which Heaven seemed to tell me were soon to be my painful but blessed portion." ‡ Eager to seize upon that chalice, of which, his subsequent history tells how

---

* It must not be concealed that Bobadilla was the first person selected by Ignatius for the mission of the Indies, but could not undertake it, on account of illness. Thus, by the wise interposition of Providence, the lot fell on Xavier.

† Lib. iii. n. 42   ‡ Lib. iii. n. 43.

cheerfully and deeply he was destined to drink, he sailed for the Indies, in April, A. D. 1540, accompanied by Martin Alphonso, governor of India, and two brethren, Paul Camerte, a priest, and Francis Manilla, not yet in holy orders ; but did not reach Goa until thirteen months later. The cause of this was their detention for nearly six months at Mozambique, an island inhabited by Portuguese and Saracens, and subject to the crown of Portugal. The interval which he spent there, was filled up with works of zeal and usefulness, not only among the Christians, but likewise the infidel portion of the inhabitants. Thence they sailed for Melinda, a Saracenic town, in which, however, many Portuguese merchants resided, who came out in a body, bearing in their front a marble cross, to greet the arrival of the holy missionary ;* and, after a short detention, they continued to the island of Socotora, lying on the eastern coast of Africa. The heat in this region is excessive ; the soil uncultivated, sterile, and dried up, and produces no sort of fruit ; so that the inhabitants have no other food than milk, meat, and herbs. They called themselves Christians, and traced back to the days of St. Thomas, whom they held in the

---

* Ibid. n. 86.

highest veneration,* by whom, they affirmed, their ancestors had been baptized; but of the nature of baptism they were, nevertheless, entirely ignorant. Among them many vestiges of Christianity continued. Their temples were well built, with crosses on the altars, and lights perpetually burning; and a cacique, like a parish priest, attached to each. But the caciques were utterly ignorant of the elements of instruction, and no monuments whatever of learning, no books, no teacher, could be found among them. All was wrapt in profound darkness, and so dense were the clouds of Saracenic and pagan superstition, that not a single ray of Christian light could be discerned.† On quitting this singular place, Xavier wrote the most touching letters to the king of Portugal, commending to his attention these wandering sheep, whose hope and happiness depended on their emancipation from the tyranny under which they were ground down by the Saracens. His appeal was successful. The king

---

* Ibid. n. 78.

† The description of this island, and of the manners, customs, and religion of the people who inhabit it, as well as the tradition of their having been visited by the Apostle St. Thomas, are all fraught with exciting interest, especially as narrated by the very eloquent and judicious historian whom I follow.—Orlandinus, *ubi supr.*

ordered a fleet to Socotora, took possession of the island, expelled the infidels, and restored the people, so long oppressed, to freedom.*

Passing by the coast of Arabia and Persia, Xavier reached Goa, the capital of the Indies. That this region had been visited by St. Thomas, and watered by the blood of that holy apostle, no doubt can be entertained; but, as was observed above, except some places which still bore his name, and some faint traditions of his labors, no vestige of Christianity survived.† The first missionaries in these parts were Franciscans; but they were few in number; and the converts to the faith were so persecuted by the pagans, that little hope existed of propagating the Christian religion. The Portuguese, long deprived of the benefits of the Church, had ceased to live, in great measure, like Christians; and vice, superstition, and immorality reigned triumphantly. Such was the condition of Goa when Xavier landed in that capital. His great sanctity conciliated, at once, the veneration of the bishop, Alberquercque. He selected as his residence the public hospital; where, day and night, he ministered to the spiritual and temporal wants of the sick. He preached as-

---

* Ibid. n. 87, 88. † Ibid. n. 89.

siduously, taught the elements of the catechism, and held daily conferences; gathering together the people by the sound of a bell which he himself rang through the streets for that purpose, evincing thus the lowliest humility and the most ardent charity.* A seminary, under the name of St. Paul,

---

* The strange levity with which the otherwise philosophic genius of Mr. Stephen treats the miracles which were wrought by the Almighty Power through the ministry of Xavier, would, were it to be applied to others, admitted by himself, destroy the entire veracity and divinity of the Christian religion. That Xavier performed miracles is no article of our faith: the facts, like all others, depend upon testimony and authority. The pontiff, Urban VIII., therefore, by whom he was canonized, did not, according to Mr. Stephen's language, "pledge his papal infallibility" in their behalf. Infallibility pertains to the Church not in matters of ordinary facts, but in transmitting from age to age, unimpaired and unadulterated, the deposit of truth, committed by Christ to her sacred keeping. Mr. Stephen would fain make us believe that Xavier scoffed at the idea of the virtue of performing miracles by his agency, or that of any other mortal man. "Two persons revealed to him a tale of his having raised a dead child to life, and pressed him to reveal the truth. *What,* he replied, *I raise the dead? can you really believe such a thing of a wretch like me?* Then smiling, he added: *They did, indeed, place before me a child: they said it was dead, which, perhaps, was not the case. I told him to get up, and he did so. Do you call that a miracle?"*

was established, over which Xavier placed his companion, Father Camerte.

Having restored discipline in the church of Goa, he departed for the coast of Malabar, a pearl fishery, more than a hundred and fifty leagues distant, so named from the pearls with which the waters abound.* The inhabitants styled themselves Chris-

---

The "*perhaps*," uttered by the humble apostle, sufficiently indicates that of his own nothingness he conceived so debased an idea, that he desired others not to think differently of him. If Mr. Stephen had called to his mind an almost parallel case in the sacred Scriptures, he would have paused ere he pronounced so biting a sarcasm. When Christ was conjured by the ruler to raise his daughter from death, did he not reply, *she is not dead, but sleepeth?* and yet she was dead, and the bystanders laughed at him. (Matt. chap. ix.) Does it follow that because the Saviour expressed himself in this manner, that he did not look upon the resuscitation of the damsel as a miraculous act? Let not the Protestant say there is no logic in this argument because one reputed prodigy was effected by a man, and the other real one by the Son of God. Both the one and the other were the works of Omnipotence. The apostles, all concede, were made the agents of that Omnipotence; and who will dare say that the arm which was extended in prodigies and wonders from the beginning of the world, was, in the incredulous age of Xavier, or is, in our own, no longer clad with the same glorious and awful attributes?

* Ibid. 94

tians, but possessed the name merely. On his arrival, Xavier hastened to baptize a multitude of children, and to announce the kingdom of heaven to the pagans. In order to convince them of the divinity of the doctrine which he proclaimed, several miracles were here wrought through his agency; of which the most astounding—but well authenticated—was the restoration to life of two dead persons.*

One of the most important duties of a missionary, is the teaching of the catechism. Upon this Xavier devoted his assiduous attention. And as the inhabitants of the fishery and Cape Comorin were ignorant of the Portuguese tongue, he selected a number of individuals of that nation, by whom the catechism might be translated into the vernacular language. He then collected the children, at the sound of a bell, and taught them the elements of Christian doctrine. Through the children he communicated instruction to their parents and friends. On Sundays and holy-days he convened all, and invoking the Most Holy Trin-

---

* Ibid. n. 98, 99. For the particulars, see Orlandinus, as also, the Life of St. Francis Xavier, by Père Bouhours, translated by Dryden. In these miracles, we contemplate the fulfilment of Christ's promise : *In nomine meo demonia ejicient,* &c.

ity, recited (the whole multitude repeating it with him) the Apostles' Creed, the Decalogue, the Lord's Prayer, and the angelical salutation. He then asked whether they firmly believed each article of the creed ; to which the entire multitude, with deafening vociferation, responded : We believe.* They then united with him in this prayer : " Jesus, Son of God, give us the grace to believe firmly, and without doubting, every article of faith." The fruits produced by the zeal of the holy missionary were incredible. Morals were reformed ; vast multitudes of both sexes and all ages were baptized ; the idols were thrown down with every mark of ignominy, and a complete triumph of Christianity was achieved. His sanctity not only shone out in his heroic virtues with such brilliancy as to attract the admiration of all, but it was rendered wonderful by the many prodigies which he performed in the name of Christ.†

---

* Lib. iv. n. 62.

† The following beautiful extract from Mr. Carnes's article on " Francis Xavier," will be read with delight. So eloquent a tribute, emanating from a Protestant pen is invaluable indeed :

" When a commanding spirit is let loose on its chosen destiny, how swiftly and richly it can people its own exciting world ! His head reclining on the rock, his eyes fixed on the ocean, which he peculiarly loved. Francis often saw

The Brahmins saw with jealous indignation, the inroads which he made upon their influence and

with a prescience that to his friends seemed like a familiar spirit, the veil of the future withdrawn—the chequered, the wild and terrible future. He saw it with a kindling eye, for he panted for the struggle. There was another quality of his mind, that was of inexpressible avail; namely, its wild sublimity, its insatiate reaching unto the things that are before, that first awoke within him when Ignatius pointed to the thrones of heaven, and never afterwards forsook him. 'Eternity only, Francis, is sufficient for such a heart as yours: its kingdom of glory alone is worthy of it: be ambitious, be magnanimous, but level at the loftiest mark.' This passion, as it may be called, was as absorbing as that of ambition to the successful statesman or warrior, filling every faculty, haunting him when asleep or awake, ever expecting great events—as in the vision in Lisbon, when islands, empires, and deserts were presented to him, and he cried out, 'Yet more, O God! yet more!' If it had been possible, he would have kept his eyes from slumber, and his thoughts from oblivion; he literally 'murdered sleep,' allowing himself only three hours' repose. 'He often,' it is said, 'passed the night in the open air; and nothing so much elevated his soul to God, as the view of heaven, spangled over, and sowed as it were with stars;' in that ineffable beauty of an Eastern night, when sea and sky, island and grove, seem like a fairy vision, arrayed in a light that is not of this world. It was to the missionary a season of silence and quiet: no sooner did the morning break on the waters, than he surrendered every hour and moment to the

superstitions. These priests were, at the same time, of royal descent, and exercised an unbounded sway, as well by the position they held, as also by the knowledge of the magic art, and their skill in the interpretation of omens. Among the Indians they were regarded as the Haruspices of old by the Romans. They were sagacious, but not refined by mental culture; actuated in their measures by avarice, and wielding over the public mind an irresistible power of deception. To the vulgar and simple they appeared gifted with supernatural wisdom and adorned with eminent virtues. They affected great abstinence and devotion to their pagods. Some of them even professed perpetual celibacy.

---

calls of others: the Paravas quickly gathered round to be instructed, or talk with him; numbers crowded to the chapels: the day did not pass without two or three sermons or exhortations; and when night came again, the soul panted to be alone: how welcome, when the clash of tongues, and importunate demands, and hurrying footsteps paused at last, and he heard no sound save the plaintive song of some lonely fisherman, and the low dash of his oar as he hastened to the land! In these solemn moments, he was like the prophet, intensely looking forth, and calling from on high, 'Watchman, what of the night? Watchman, what of the night? and he answered and said, The graven images of her gods he hath broken to pieces; within a year all the glory of the heathen shall fail.' "—*Lives of Eminent Catholic Missionaries.*

These men, extremely austere, abstained from the pleasures of the body for a certain term of years: after which, raised, as they imagined, above the level of mortals, they obtained unrestrained license for sensual indulgence, were bound by no laws, and indulged in all manner of crimes with impunity. Among these people the ape was an object of divine adoration, and the elephant and the ox were worshipped.* To expose the fraud, hypocrisy, idolatry, and vices of the Brahmins, was no inconsiderable undertaking. Yet Xavier did not shrink from it. In a public disputation with them, he put this question: "What form of life do the gods require to constitute human happiness?" The question took them by surprise: they sought to evade answering it; and, after wrangling among themselves, at length they referred the matter to one of their priests, a Brahmin of extreme old age, who, attempting to escape from the difficulty, retorted the same query on Xavier: "What does *your* God require?" he asked. Xavier, however, perceiving his cunning, urged and

---

* Ibid. n. 69, 70. Fanum est Simio dicatum. Elephantis etiam religionem numinis tribuunt: Bobus autem eo majorem quod mortuorum animos in eam maximè belluam migrare opinantur. Even here we find the far-spread system of Pythagoras teaching the transmigration of spirits.

repeated the interrogation. Compelled to betray his ignorance, the Brahmin answered: "All who wish to possess the gods, must be governed by two laws: first, to abstain from slaying calves, under the form of which the gods are worshipped; secondly, that all worshippers bestow a portion of their goods and fortunes upon the Brahmins."*

The zeal of Xavier being excited by this reply, he began, incontinently, to explain, with a loud voice, the Decalogue, and to recite the Apostles' Creed, in their vernacular language. He then instructed them concerning hell and heaven, and concluded with an animated exhortation. He had hardly finished, when the Brahmins rushed into his arms, acknowledging that there was no other God than the God of the Christians, whose law was so conformable to natural reason; and which, after due preparation, they were permitted to embrace, through the sacrament of regeneration.†

Amid these cares and labors—on which, however, the favor of Heaven so copiously descended—the heart of Xavier was replenished with consolations, and seemed already to anticipate its blessed reward. In a letter to Rome, he affirms that so excessive was his joy in the arduous and fatiguing

---

* Ibid. n. 70. † Ibid.

ministry in which he was engaged among these barbarous nations, that it sweetened and gladdened his existence. Often, overpowered with celestial delights, he would exclaim: "Lord, do not lavish upon me such joys in this life :—rather, if I must be favored with them, translate me hence to those happy realms above. For, to him who has once tasted thy joys,' this life must be bitter indeed. If such be exile, what will our country be?"*

Having reaped an abundant harvest at Cape Comorin, he returned to Goa, in order to transact with the Governor some important business regarding religion. He took with him several youths of the highest families, to be educated in the college which had been founded in that city. By all the citizens his return was greeted with a general welcome. As was his wont, after paying his respects to the Bishop and Governor, he took up his lodgings in the public hospital. The affairs which brought him to Goa, being speedily arranged, he hurried back to Cape Comorin, with three priests,

---

* Domine, noli me tantis obruere in hac vita deliciis ... vel transfer me hinc ociùs in istas sedes, regionemque beatorum. Qui tuam semel dulcedinem gustavit, is necesse est acerbam prorsus vitam sine te agat... Quæ si tanta in exilio, quanta tandem erit in patria. Ibid. n. 74.

with whom he divided the province. His presence at the Cape, at this juncture, was most auspicious. For the people of Badaga, a wild and lawless banditti, incited, at once, by the lust of gain and the hatred of the Christian name, had made a descent upon that entire region. But they were repulsed by the faithful and shut up in rocks and precipices, where they would have perished with hunger, thirst, and misery, had not Xavier come to their relief, and rescued them from their impending fate.* He then passed over to Travancor by land, a journey of about eighty miles. The inhabitants were fishermen, partly Saracens, and partly pagans, and all vehemently opposed to Xavier on account of the conversions he had made. Disregarding, however, their fury, and in spite of the solicitations of his friends to the contrary, he boldly dared to appear amongst them. Nay, he forced his way even to the tyrant himself, whom he succeeded in conciliating by bland conversation, insinuating religious truth, dissuading him from the superstitions of his country, and enforcing the necessity of the adoration of the true God. If the earnest exhortations of the apostle did not convert the tyrant, they, at least, had the effect to allow his subjects to embrace

---

* Lib. iv. n. 141, 142.

Christianity.* A decree sanctioning this toleration having been extorted by the persuasive power of Xavier, more than ten thousand persons ranked themselves under the banners of salvation.† The labor of instructing and baptizing this immense multitude he bore almost single-handed, but with so much cheerfulness and rapture, that he declared himself, in a letter to Ignatius, unable to give expression to it in writing. Among the people, who beheld, with amazement, his boundless energy, and incomparable zeal, he acquired the appellation of the "Great Father." At first, he preached in the open air, on the wide field, in the valley; and sometimes, the better to command the view of his numberless hearers, from the very branches of some lofty tree. Before chapels were erected, he offered the holy mysteries on a rustic altar under a spreading tent. But as soon as possible sacred edifices were built: of which, in a short time, not less than twenty dotted and consecrated the land.‡

In planting the tree of religion on this bleak and barren soil, miracles, as we have seen, were wrought; but it was necessary that it should be watered, too, by the blood of martyrs. This glorious boon was not refused by Providence. In the

---

* Ibid. n. 145, 146. † Ibid. ‡ Ibid. n. 149, 150.

island of Manaria six hundred Christians were put to death for their faith.*

From the island of Macazaria, (about fifty miles distant from Cochin-China, where he had passed the preceding year,) Xavier sailed to Ceylon, in company with Mansilla. His first conquest there was the king's son, who was privately baptized, together with his cousin and several noblemen.†

On quitting Ceylon, Xavier stopped at Meliapor, with the view of making a pilgrimage to the tomb of St. Thomas. This was a large and flourishing city of the Portuguese, about a hundred and fifty miles distant from Comorin and equidistant from Goa, situated in a region called Coromandel. The shrine of the apostle had originally been a pagan temple, which he himself, however, had rescued from the rites of idolatry, and dedicated to the worship of the true and only Deity.‡ It was re-

---

* Ibid. n. 151. The spectacle of primitive Christianity was here, in the sixteenth century, presented to the admiration of the world. An apostle of Christ performing signs and wonders, and Neophytes in crowds, stooping their necks, in vindication of their faith, to the sword of the executioner. That apostle was a Jesuit,—those martyrs were Catholics!

† Lib. v. n. 84.

‡ Ibid. n. 86.

nowned and celebrated far and wide, and attracted crowds of pilgrims, not only among Christians, but likewise of pagans. It was near this fane, on the declivity of a super-impendent hill, that St. Thomas was martyred and interred; and the very stone that was sprinkled with his blood, was still exhibited.* Over the tomb of one of the twelve, who, after the dispersion of the apostles, came into these distant lands to proclaim the resurrection and religion of Christ, Xavier, his successor, bent in rapturous contemplation. What wondrous associations did not these sacred scenes excite in his ardent soul! What devotion, zeal, and hope did they not awaken and inflame! He comes to rekindle, amid the "shades of death" that had gathered, during nearly fifteen hundred years, over these regions, the sacred torch of life: to call up the spirit of truth and faith which had been sleeping, as it were, with the ashes of the venerable dead. A follower of JESUS—to succeed, in the work of "evangelizing good, evangelizing peace," the disciple of Christ, who had reared, in ancient days,

---

* Orlandinus relates some marvellous circumstances connected with this stone, which, as they are merely given upon local traditional authority, will not be interesting to the general reader. Consult his history, *ubi supr.*

the cross of Redemption among the nations afar off, and, like his adorable Master, had shed his blood for the "flock." That blood was not shed in vain; the soil once watered and fertilized by it, required but the labor of the spiritual husband man to quicken into life the germ of a rich harvest, which still lingered under the rugged surface. And he was here—a self-devoted and heaven-directed missionary—ready to consume his days in the heat and toil of the field: and prepared, if necessary, to imitate the heroic example of the apostle near whose tomb he knelt, by laying down his life for the propagation of the gospel, and the salvation of his fellow-creatures. The flame of his own piety and sanctity seemed to glow more intensely, fed at this hallowed shrine. And his zeal devoured, as it were, all the abuses and vices which prevailed among the faithful, and which resisted and set at defiance the authority of the clergy and prelate. But, from the dreadful assaults of the evil spirit he did not escape; by incessant prayers, however, during the day, and habitually at midnight also, he spurned the Tartarean foe, and vanquished his power and temptations.*

---

* Ibid. n. 87, 88. "Even around the tomb of the apostle," writes the above-quoted critic, "malignant demons prowl

This holy pilgrimage being accomplished, Xavier set sail for Malacca. This city was a populous and flourishing emporium, situated beyond the Ganges, and lying under the pole, almost six hundred leagues from Goa. The showers fall almost daily, by which the heat of the sun is tempered, and the fields are covered with perpetual verdure. The Christians, though professing the faith, had assumed the depraved habits of the infidels, and seemed not desirous to accept of the blessings which were offered to them through the ministry of Xavier. He did not despair. With redoubled energy and assiduous perseverance, he preached and exhorted, persuaded and menaced, soothed and terrified, in such a manner, that the longed-for im-

---

by night, and though strong in the guidance of the Virgin, Xavier not only found himself in their grasp, but received from them blows, such as no weapon in human hands could have inflicted. . . . Baffled by a superior power, the fiends opposed a still more subtle hindrance to his design against their kingdom. In the garb, and in the outward semblance of a band of choristers, they disturbed his devotions by such soul-subduing strains, that the very harmonies of heaven might seem to have been awakened to divert the Christian warrior from his heavenward path. In vain their fury and their guile. He found the direction he implored.—*Stephen*.

pression was, finally, made. Reflection took the place of dissipation, the gospel-maxims prevailed over the suggestions of the passions, and, in a few months, the entire face of society was changed; morals were reformed, the practices of piety resumed, and a complete victory of grace was obtained.* His catechetical instructions were uninterrupted, except by other arduous duties, amidst which he found time to translate the elements of the Christian doctrine into the language of the natives of the country. Of these, many were induced to forsake their idolatrous worship—a worship which they paid to the sun, under the bright expanse of the heavens, having no fanes nor altars—and to join the standard of JESUS, which now gleamed on the temples of Christianity under the divine rays of the "Sun of Righteousness" and Truth. In the middle of January he embarked for Molucca, an island nine hundred miles from Malacca, thickly populated by natives and strangers, and filled with handsome towns, of which seven were occupied by Christians, but deprived of the benefit of clergymen. The pagans were ar-

---

* Ibid. n. 91. Orlandinus relates, that, at this epoch, Xavier raised a dead girl to life, and performed other signal miracles. Ibid. vid. *ubi supr.* n. 92

rayed in deadly hostility against the Mahomedans, who compelled the former either to embrace the Koran, or else to be held in subjection. For seventy years the superstitions of Mecca had here prevailed: but the people were rude and ignorant, and not ill-affected towards the teachings of Xavier.* Through all the Christian settlements, he rapidly passed, baptizing infants and children, and affording means of spiritual aid to adults, and exercising a charity which no opposition could subdue or check.† He extended his labors to Amboina, whence, after three months of unceasing exertion, he proceeded to Molucca, an island under the equator, rich in spices, with which it supplied the whole world. There might he be seen, day and night, devoting himself to the instruction of the people; and the more effectually to imprint the Lord's Prayer, the Creed, and the Hail, Mary, upon their memories, he rendered them into rhyme, which, like so many familiar canticles, were sung by children on the house-tops, by fishermen in their boats,

---

* Lib. vi. n. 105.

† Ibid. n. 104. Many of the newly baptized, our author relates, expired immediately after having been regenerated in the saving waters; as though they had been reserved merely to receive this grace.

by laborers in their fields. Among his converts, the most illustrious was the daughter of King Almansor, formerly a Saracen; a woman of a lofty and acute mind, and well versed in the superstitions of her country. Her name, while an infidel, was Neachiles; in baptism she assumed that of Elizabeth.*

Being informed that in the island of Moro many Christians were settled, without any priests, Xavier determined to go to their assistance. The distance from Molucca was sixty leagues; the soil barren, productive neither of wheat nor wine, but abounding with wild-boar. The palmetto-tree supplied a species of bread, and its bark was used for raiment; the inhabitants were ferocious, inhuman, and stupidly ignorant, and not only cruel towards strangers, but barbarous in their treatment of one another.† From this wild and dreary solitude, in the midst of Moors and Tartars, with dangers and hardships frowning upon him on all sides, the magnanimous Xavier, towering above all natural terror, and calmly confiding and reposing in the goodness and protection of Providence, addressed a letter to his companions at Rome. "These islands," he wrote, "it seems to me, should be

---

* Ibid. n. 105. † Ibid. n. 106.

styled *Divine Hope*, rather than *Moro:* for, in them i feel an unalloyed and perpetual bliss." This region was subject to frequent earthquakes, horrid murmurings, and subterranean fires : noises more formidable than the sound of the loudest can non often shook the rocks to their centre, hurling down huge trees, while the air was filled with clouds of ashes that strewed the scathed fields, and blinded both man and beast.* But what were these terraqueous occurrences in the estimation of an apostle, whose existence was consecrated to the salvation of his race? What recked that holy man of clime or element, whose whole being was but a fulfilment of the declaration of Christ : "Whosoever would save his soul must lose it?" Many of his friends entreated him not to risk his life among these barbarous tribes, whose thirst for human blood was innate. But their importunities could not avert him from performing what he believed to be God's will.† He flew to the wretched Christians who were dwelling among them, desolate and lorn.

---

* Ibid.

† Ibid. n. 107. Our historian expresses, in splendid language, the glorious change which, in so short a time, was effected: "Cessit denique," he says, "Christo Satanas, tenebræ luci, et omnis illius regionis tartarea dominatio venerandæ crucis imperio."

During three months he hurried from town to town, bringing back to a sense of religion those who still bore the name, but long since had forgotten the virtues and duties of Christians: baptizing the young, instructing the adult, converting numbers of the pagans, and thus shedding over this darksome region the brightest rays of religion and civilization.

He so divided his labors as to preach to the Portuguese in the morning, and the Neophytes in the evening. He paid frequent visits to the King Aërius, who appeared to delight in his conversation, and gave some hope of conversion. The Saracens were not strongly attached to their sect, and the pagans showed less repugnance to the pure doctrines of Christ, than to the sensual code of Mahomed. Of the latter, many received the gospel, among whom by far the most distinguished and conspicuous were the king's two sisters.*

Duty now calling him to Malacca, he revisited the Amboinians, from whose compassionate and endearing embraces, tearing himself away at midnight, he set sail for that island. There he entered again, with increased energy, upon his arduous duties. At night he could be seen with a lan-

---

* Lib. vii. n. 85.

tern in one hand, and a bell in the other, going about the city, admonishing the faithful of their obligations, and menacing sinners with the vengeance of Heaven;* commanding universal veneration by the manifest disinterestedness which inspired his conduct, and admiration by the power which he received from above of working wonderful deeds, and predicting future events. To the vast aspirations of his zeal for man's salvation, no limit could be set. They extended as far as there was a fragment of habitable earth; and the more distant the object and the more difficult to be reached, the more irresistible was its force, and the more glowing its unquenchable fire. Upon the vast vision of his mind a new star now appeared— a bright hope amid the boundless desolation and darkness of the night through which it twinkled.

It chanced that he fell in, at this conjuncture, with a certain man whose name was Anger, a native of Cangoxima in Japan, who there had become a Bonzee.† In embracing this course of life, he was actuated by the hope of obtaining peace of

---

* Ibid. n. 81, 82, 83.

† The Bonzees were men devoted to religion. Vid. Or. land. *ubi supr.* n. 90. Tum demum in spem venit viam sibi in eas insulas per hominem Japonem apertum iri.

conscience. But, disappointed in this hope, he resolved to seek among strangers for the boon which he could not procure at home. Having received some information concerning the Christian religion from the Portuguese merchants, and heard through them, likewise, of Xaxier, he longed to have an interview with that holy missionary. To this end, he did not hesitate to commit himself to the perils of a long and tedious navigation. He arrived safely at Malacca, and found, as he had anticipated in Xavier, a teacher, a consoler, and a friend : by whom he was instructed in the principles of the Christian faith, relieved of the keen anguish which hitherto had preyed upon his conscience, and conducted into the ways of spiritual peace and heavenly content. Anger spoke to Xavier of Japan; told of the interminable field that stretched out to his as interminable zeal, in that great country, and kindled in his heroic soul those glorious desires which were afterwards so wondrously and so magnificently accomplished in the Empire of Japan. From this most hazardous project his friends used every persuasion to deter him, on his return to Goa. But to no purpose. Having created Antonio Gomio Rector of the College, and Paul Camerte Superior of the Province, he waited a favorable opportunity to depart, to carry the gospel to a people gifted with genius and judgment, and peculiarly adapted to the reception of the doctrines of Christianity.* He sailed from Cochin-China in the month of May, and, after a perilous voyage, arrived at Malacca. Here two circumstances were made known to him, that sharpened, if possible, yet more keenly his hopes for Japan. One, that that nation having heard of the Christian law, had dispatched ambassadors to the governor of India, requesting that some priests might be sent among them. The other, that the holy cross was already held in veneration by them, its virtue having been taught them by the Portuguese, who placed it, as an ornament and a protection, in the vestibule of their houses.† Xavier burned to be among this well-disposed people : and not finding any Portuguese vessel bound to Japan, he intrusted himself to a Chinese ship, styled "The Robber." On the feast of St. John the Baptist, he quitted Malacca, confiding his fate to the protecting care of Heaven, and ever mindful of the maxim which he had learned from the mouth of Ignatius, namely : "that the members of the Society must endeavor to conquer themselves, must throw far from them all fears, must fix their hopes on God

---

* Lab. ix. n. 161, 162. † Ibid. n. 170.

alone, whose grace will never be wanting under any trying circumstances."* These generous dispositions he not only cherished in his mind, but carefully practised in his conduct. After many adventures, and great delay, on the festival of the assumption of the Ever-Virgin Mary, his eyes rested on the island of Japan, and he landed at Cangoxima, a very powerful city of Saxuma. Nothing could have happened more opportunely; for this was the home of his convert Paul, through whom he was received with public demonstrations of welcome by the governor and the nobility.†

It would be foreign from my design to enter into a lengthy description of Japan and its inhabitants, of the magnitude of the country, of its form of government, of its soil, of the character and manners of the people, of their love of glory and nobility, of their morals, their superstitions, and their literature. I cannot, however, omit to state, that besides

---

* Ibid. n. 171.

† Ibid. n. 177, 178. It seems to have been by mere accident that the vessel was driven into this port. Divine Providence thus disposing sweetly all events by which to facilitate the accomplishment of the great design in view. There are many curious incidents connected with the voyage which are accurately described by the historian, but which are not necessary in a mere synopsis.

the gods called Cames, and Fotoquez, and Xaca, by some the devil was worshipped, and to his infernal majesty altars and temples were erected.* The ministers of religion were nominated Bonzees, men of flagitious and impure lives; among whom there were many sects, distinguished by various forms of superstitions and worship. They professed celibacy, and to marry was reputed a capital crime. They shaved their heads and harangued the people at their pleasure, on festival days, of which many were prescribed throughout the year. They were generally selected from high families. They had, in various places, academies richly endowed, where their doctrine and discipline were taught; and acknowledged a supreme head, who was chosen either on account of his rare birth or great wealth. His dominion was universal, and his income so large, that it often did not yield to that of the king's. His residence was at Meaco; under his roof there were more than three hundred and sixty-six idols. He was considered by the vulgar as most holy, and was venerated as a divinity, while in reality he was revelling in the most shameful vices.†

What a field of battle here expanded to the

---

* Ibid. n. 195. † Ibid. n. 198, 199, 202.

view of Xavier, the reader can have no difficulty in imagining. A field on which the virtues of Christianity must enter upon a dreadful conflict with the crimes of paganism ; and the doctrines of truth with diabolical errors. But the more terrible the struggle, the more glorious will be the triumph. And, under the guidance of Heaven and the ægis of the cross, what has the apostle of Christ to fear? Nothing ! He who had already won such signal victories over the legions of hell, felt a strength and a confidence which nerved him for the issue. He began by opposing the Bonzees with their own weapons. They affected extraordinary frugality and abstinence : he practised still greater.* They were distinguished—especially their Superior—by urbanity and elegance of manners : he surpassed them even in these ; which in him were so much admired, that he insinuated himself into the favor of Ninxit, then at their head, and the most venerable among them, as well on account of his reputation for learning and wisdom, as of his extreme old age. With Ninxit he disputed on the immortality of the soul, and the na-

---

* In such a manner, that he himself declared that he was sustained during that time, less by natural food, than by the nourishment of charity. Ibid. n. 207.

tuie of religion; and though he silenced the proud Bonzee, and thereby excited all the envy of a vain and self-conceited heart, still so gentle were his manners and so polished and winning withal, that he could not but extort its admiration. It was evident, that by no other motive than that of philanthropy and virtue could he have been prompted to pass such boundless oceans, and expose himself to such countless perils and pains. Permission was given him to preach the gospel in Japan. This permission was granted by a solemn edict of the king; and no sooner did he commence his heavenly task, than his undertaking was sealed by the omnipotent stamp of the King of kings. Like his Divine Master, he healed a leper, cured a boy afflicted with a mortal malady, and even raised a deceased maiden to life.* Many converts immediately enrolled themselves under the cross, among whom were the wife and daughter of Paul.

By the Bonzees, the miracles of Xavier, which they did not deny, were attributed to the power of the devils and the effects of incantation and charms; and could they have prevailed with the king, his head would have paid the forfeit of his success.

---

* For the details, see Orlandinus, *ubi supr.* n. 113, 114, 115, 116.

But the king spurned them from his presence, and exhibited still more admiration of the apostle and his doctrines. Encouraged by these tokens of royal benevolence and favor, he resumed his labors with tenfold enthusiasm, proclaiming Christ and the gospel in the public streets, and confuting and confounding the sophistry and errors of the priests of idolatry. So profound were the convictions, so firm the constancy, so pure the morals of the first Japanese Christians, that the king of Saxuma wrote to Father Anthony Quadrio, the Provincial of India, conjuring him to send to his dominions some other missionaries, by whom the Christian law might be spread throughout the entire region, and the morals of his subjects might be made conformable to its holy standard.*

From Cangoxima, Xavier pursued his way to Firando, where he was received with every demonstration of respect and welcome by the Portuguese inhabitants, and the king himself, who granted him license to announce the gospel to his subjects. He converted many, and erected a church, which leaving to the charge of Father Cosmo Turriano, he proceeded to Firando, and thence to Mecao, a large and flourishing city,

---

* Ibid. n. 222.

whose king possessed immense wealth and power Here Xavier met with many distinguished families desirous of learning the Christian law, in consequence of his great fame, which had already preceded him. He was followed by thousands, though not treated by all with the same respect. But the admirable patience and meekness he displayed in the midst of the insults which he frequently was subjected to in the public streets, won the admiration of the more reflecting and better disposed. The king listened to the sublime maxims which he taught, and heard, in wondering silence, during the space of an hour, the explanation of the word of God contained in the holy Scriptures. He wondered, and was silent, but did not yield to the grace which was offered. He continued in his superstitions, and his obstinacy encouraged that of his subjects, of whom few were induced to range themselves under the banners of Christianity.*

From Mecao, the untiring apostle cast his eyes back upon the expanding fields of labor at Meaco, and resolved to visit again a capital soon to

---

* Lib. x. n. 135, 136, 137. De Meacensis Urbis magnitudine, collegiorum celebritate, cœnobiorum multitudine varietateque cognôrat; et jam tum in animum induxerat eo recta contendere.

be covered with abundant fruit: to be distinguished for its numerous churches, prosperous colleges, and extensive charitable institutions.* He occupied two months in the journey, each moment of which added a fresh leaf to the crown of his merit in heaven. For, besides the roughness of the roads, which were covered with deep snow, they were, moreover, infested with robbers. The season was extremely cold, and his feet were ulcerated with frost, being obliged to cross frequent streams, and wade through torrents, without shoes, carrying his baggage upon his shoulders, and passing entire days without eating. Add to all these complicated miseries, the insults and contumely he underwent in the towns and villages through which he passed. To every humiliation as well as hardship he cheerfully resigned himself, and lost no opportunity of announcing the name of Christ, and showing the folly of idolatry. At length, after innumerable sufferings, and the conquest of some converts made on the way, he arrived, worn out and emaciated, at Meaco.† In this splendid metropolis and seat of empire, Xavier had long but vainly struggled to obtain an interview with the proud emperor; every avenue to the throne he found closed against his

---

* Ibid. n. 138.   † Lib. xi. n. 100.

efforts. He, therefore, turned his attention towards his subjects, who, unfortunately, agitated by the expectation of an impending war, sealed their ears likewise to his preaching.* Not to lose his precious time on that ungenerous soil, he hastened to Amanguchi, reciting as he went the Psalm of David : *In exitu Israel de Ægypto.*† There he was received with distinguished favor by the king, who offered the illustrious stranger a quantity of gold and silver. Xavier, with his wonted disinterestedness, refused the present, requesting the monarch to grant him merely one privilege : namely, that of announcing the gospel of Jesus Christ to the people under his dominion. This greatness of mind and contempt of riches excited the admiration of the king. A house of the Bonzees was assigned him as a place of residence, and a decree issued authorizing him to proclaim in public the law of God and the tidings of salvation. Day and night he continued the holy work of preaching, and disputing with the learned men of the place. His house was constantly besieged by crowds of curious persons of all orders, and ages, and dispositions ;

---

* Ibid. n. 101, 102.

† Psalm cxiii. 1. When Israel went out of Egypt, the house of Jacob from a barbarous people.

and thousands, finally, yielding to the force of truth, forsook their false gods, and abjured their absurd superstitions.* Again the seal of the Omnipotent was impressed on the dogmata which Xavier taught. Contemporary evidences show that by the sign of the cross, he effected sudden and marvellous cures, and performed other indubitable miracles.† The consequence was, that ten thousand Amanguchians became Christians, and models of the virtues which constitute the ornaments of the Christian name.

The joy of Xavier on account of this his unexampled success, was increased by the receipt of a letter from the king of Bungo, couched in terms of affection and respect, and expressive of an ardent desire to see him. Though the distance was four hundred leagues, the apostle set out immediately. By the Portuguese, he was advised to make his appearance at that capital accompanied by a magnificent retinue, and in splendid attire.‡ The vessel in which he embarked was decorated with silken sails and gorgeous pennons : and he entered the port amid the clangor of trumpets and the

---

* Ibid. n. 104.
† The details are given, *ubi supr*, n. 110.
‡ Ibid. n. 116.

sound of music. On the shore, he was received with great ceremony by a deputation assigned by the monarch, and conducted to the palace. The effect which his instructions produced on the king's mind was most beneficial to morals and religion, and a happy change was soon perceptible in the city. The infamous rites of the Bonzees were suppressed, the sacrifice of infants prohibited, and the lewd and dissolute practices which had hitherto prevailed in their superstitious functions entirely abolished. This mutation, it is evident, could not be brought about without exciting the rancor and vengeance of the Bonzees. The most noble and renowned among them, accordingly, undertook to dispute the subject with him, in presence of the king and nobles. The dispute resulted in the solemn humiliation of the priest of Satan, the glorious triumph of truth, and the conversion of thousands of citizens of Bungo.*

After planting religion in these strange regions, Xavier prepared to return into India, taking with him, like some victor after the conquest of a distant land, two captives—not, indeed, to the yoke of an earthly hero, but to the grace of heaven—two Neophytes, Matthew and Bernard, whom he intended

---

* Ibid. n. 118, 119, 120, 121, 122.

to send to Rome as specimens of the natives of Japan. The king of Bungo wept at his departure, and mingled his sorrows with the hearty regrets and lamentations of the Portuguese and converts. A period of two years had elapsed since he first put foot on the shores of Cangoxima, and, after a tempestuous voyage, he arrived at Cochin, hailed and greeted by the unanimous acclaim of all. Having during his sojourn there edified and animated the faithful by his sanctity and exhortations, he continued his way to Goa ; where, no sooner had he disembarked, than he hastened, as was his custom, to the hospital, and imparted consolation to the sick and suffering, and then proceeded to the college.*

But it was not to rest long, much less to spend the remnant of his years under the shades of retirement and quiet, that he repaired within its peaceful walls. No ; his insatiable zeal was never satisfied. His mind seemed vast as the universe itself. His aspirations owned no bounds but eternity. Reposing like a wearied soldier after a wasting but glorious campaign, it was only to gather new strength for other fields, fresh energies for other conquests. Not content with the mighty

---

* Lib. xii. n. 78, 79.

conquest of the Indies and Japan, his vision turned to another and still a mightier one. China must be entered. That region, hitherto inclosed and protected from the stranger by adamantine walls, must open its gates to the messenger of JESUS. Having made all the necessary arrangements for the domestic economy of the Society, and appointed Father Barzeus Provincial of the Indies, he sailed from Goa in the month of May for Malacca, where he embarked again, and, favored by the winds, soon reached the coast of China.*

The great question now was, in what manner he could effect an entrance into that sealed country, into which to admit a stranger, was a crime liable to be punished with the severest penalties. Sometimes he seemed resolved to force his way, and brave the danger: for, anhelating after the salvation of the people, his magnanimous spirit spurned the menace of punishment or death. At other times, having consulted with his brethren and some enlightened Portuguese, his ardor was checked by his prudence. Meanwhile he was seized by a fever, under which he suffered during fifteen days. On his bed of sickness he had time leisurely and calmly to consider the enterprise so near his heart.

---

* Ibid. n. 86, 97.

The language of our Divine Master seemed to ring perpetually in his ears: "He who putteth his hand to the plough, and looketh back, is not worthy of me." Not, indeed, that the words could, in any wise, apply to him, who had forsaken all things, and devoted his whole existence to the service of the Lord, but his humility and zeal referred them to the project which he had commenced, of penetrating into China. He arose from his sick-bed confirmed in his first determination: and though he saw no means of accomplishing it, according to human appearances, still he did not despond. But God, in whose presence the ardent desires of the apostle were as meritorious as their consummation, was satisfied with the labors of Xavier. His life had been spent in fatigue, peril, and labor: it is now time for him to be taken into rest. He had succeeded in landing upon the Chinese soil,—the task of entering into the interior must be left to other missionaries. He relapsed into the fever from which he had temporarily recovered. Upon a heap of straw, under a wretched cot, he lies in a bleak and inhospitable land. The rude winds moan through the crevices, in the cold and dreary month of December. One only companion attends him—a poor but faithful Portuguese. There, in utter destitution, without the necessary diet or

proper offices of care, without a murmur, rapt in divine contemplation and enjoying the anticipated vision of JESUS, whose name he bears—Xavier struggles in the agonies of death. Broken passages from the Psalms occasionally escape from his lips—then they essay to utter the humble invocation, "Jesus, Son of David, have mercy on me!" and frequently, too, to call upon the intercession of his holy mother: "Mother of God, remember me!"* To his heaving heart, clasped in his cold and attenuated hands, he pressed the crucifix, which had been his inseparable companion in all his journeyings and missions, and persisting in fervent prayer to the last moment, he breathed out his noble spirit in the sweet odor of sanctity, on the feast of St. Bibiana, the second of December, A. D. 1552.†
The following day, robed in the sacerdotal vest-

---

*Lib. xii. n. 108, 109. Nunc e psalmis pium aliquid suave recinens, et eas subinde voces suæ salutis ingeminans: Jesu fili David, miserere mei, Mater Dei, memento mei.

† Ibid. He was in the forty-seventh year of his age; ten years after his departure from Europe. "During his residence in India, he had maintained a frequent correspondence with Ignatius. On either side, their letters breathe the tenderness which is an indispensable element of the heroic character—an intense though grave affection, never degenerating into fondness; but chastened, on the side of Xavier, by filial

ments, the venerable body was placed in a wooden coffin, and then conveyed to the grave with as much ceremony as the solitary and barbarous land whereon he expired would allow. Afterwards, just before the mourners began to throw the clod upon the mortal remains, it was thought more expedient to lay the body in an open coffin covered with live lime, in order that the flesh might be con-

---

reverence; on that of Ignatius, by parental authority..... He traversed oceans, islands, and continents, through a track equal to more than twice the circumference of the globe; everywhere preaching, disputing, baptizing, and founding Christian churches. There is at least one well-authenticated miracle in Xavier's story. It is, that any mortal man should have sustained such toils as he did; and have sustained them, too, not merely with composure, but as if in obedience of some indestructible exigency of his nature." Stephen, *ubi supr.*

Would not a good translation into English of Xavier's letters be an invaluable acquisition to sacred literature, the Society, and the Church? Would it not afford infinite delight to the pious and curious reader, to muse over the correspondence of "Xavier, the magnanimous, the holy, and the gay: the canonized saint, not of Rome only, but of universal Christendom?" These are the terms in which even the cold spirits of the north must indulge, when warmed by the contemplation of that primeval ardor, which was animated and directed by a power more than human. The frozen bigotry of Mr. Stephen melts under its influence.

sumed, and the bones be translated into India. It was done: and two large rough stones were raised nigh, to indicate the spot to which the sacred deposit was consigned.*

Does any thing remain to be added by me concerning the character, virtues, and sanctity of this man of God, this perfect disciple of Ignatius, this true follower of JESUS, and one of the greatest of missionaries since the days of the apostles? His mind was lofty and vast, adorned with Christian greatness—that greatness which is founded on the humility of the gospel—seeking the lowliest place himself, while, for God's glory, undertaking the most arduous and magnificent projects, relying not on his own energies, but on the Divine aid. In the accomplishment of these, he reckoned as naught, labors, injuries, vigils, hunger, thirst, fatigue. In a word, if it be true that by its fruits the tree will be known, the Catholic Church and the Society of JESUS can point to Xavier, in whom the virtues of the former and the spirit of the latter were purely and thoroughly exemplified and carried out. And, with such a glorious model of both,

---

* Ibid. n. 112. With what solemn rejoicings and celebrations the precious remains of the apostle were received at Goa, will be found, lib. xiii. n. 89.

the calumnies and misrepresentations of one and the other must be shamed into eternal silence.*

---

* There is extant a hymn composed by St. Francis Xavier, which contains, as it were, the embodiment of all his lofty and heavenly aspirations; in which he breathes forth his inspired strain of Divine love, and perfect detachment of heart from all the vanities and pleasures of this life. The following translation, by an anonymous writer, is faithful, and not inelegant:

> "My God! thou art the object of my love;
> Not for the hope of endless joys above,
> Nor for the fear of endless pains below
> Which those who love thee not must undergo:
> For me, and such as I, thou once didst bear
> The ignominious cross, the nails, the spear.
> A thorny crown transpierced thy sacred brows;
> What bloody sweat from every member flows!
> For me, in tortures thou didst yield thy breath;
> Nailed to the cross, thou savedst me from death.
> Say—can such sufferings fail my heart to move?
> What, but thyself, can now deserve my love?
> Such as then was and is thy love for me,
> Such is, and shall be still, my love for thee.
> That love, O Jesus, may I ever sing,
> O God of love, kind Parent, dearest King."

JAMES LAYNEZ.

CHAPTER IV.

JAMES LAYNEZ.

JAMES LAYNEZ.—Unites himself to Ignatius. Enters Rome barefoot. Teaches in the Roman Academy. Is sent to Parma. His labors at Venice; at Brescia; at Padua; at Bassano; at Rome. Refuses the purple. Is sent to the Council of Trent. His zeal at Bologna; Florence; Perugio; Monte Pulciano; Sienna; Venice; Naples. Is sent to Sicily. Accompanies Vega to Africa. His labors. Is called to Pisa. Is again sent as theologian of the Pope, to the Council of Trent. Is made Provincial of Italy. Preaches at Genoa. Writes a compendium of theology for the use of the schools of the Society. Is sent back to Germany to the Diet of Augsburg. Returns to Italy. Rejects the Cardinal's hat. His great merits, talents, and actions.

WHILE Ignatius was pursuing his studies at Paris, there arrived in that metropolis a young gentleman, a native of Almazan in Spain. He was in the twenty-third year of his age, the cherished child of parents distinguished not less by wealth than piety, by whom he had been trained to the study of wisdom and the ardent love of religion. Already had he obtained the degree of Master of Arts in the university of Compostella, where he had endeared himself to all the inmates by the suavity of his manners, and the excellence of his talents: and as he destined himself to the Church, he resolved to enter upon the study of theology in the most celebrated school in France. This was James Laynez.* One of the principal causes that directed his course to Paris, was to become acquainted with Ignatius, of whose admirable fame he had heard in his native country. By accident it happened,—or rather by the disposal of Providence,—that he took up his lodgings in the very house where Ignatius dwelt, in that city. Immediately he communicated to that wonderful man the object which had led him thither, and a strong and mutual friendship seemed to bind their hearts together instinctively, upon the spot. He placed himself under the guidance and government of Ignatius, and, after some days of prayer and retirement, easily consented to become his disciple with Faber and Francis Xavier.

The first destination of Laynez was Rome. Quitting Paris, under the direction of obedience, he departed as a penitent, clad in sackcloth, for the capital of the Christian world. Though suffering under no trifling illness at the time, he seemed

---

* Orlandin. lib. i. n. 87.

to forget his debility and pains, in the anticipation of treading upon that sacred soil, venerable for the graves of innumerable saints, hallowed by the blood of myriads of martyrs. On entering the gates, he made his way directly, barefoot, to the tomb of the apostles, where he prostrated himself in fervent prayer, and dedicated his whole being to the service of the Church which was built on the rock of Peter. It was to defend that Church against the powers of darkness—the schisms and heresies of the times—that the Society sprang into being: and whither could her earliest members go to imbibe deep draughts of the spirit of truth and zeal, but to the fountain-source? The memories of the ancient dead who slept in their venerated tombs within the walls of Rome, came up, with all their influences, before the contemplation of Laynez, and inspired his generous soul with a nameless enthusiasm in the cause of the Catholic Church. At first he lodged in the hospital of his countrymen; but was, afterwards, persuaded by some wealthy and noble Spaniards to accept of a more becoming hospitality under their roof.*

---

* "Negantes," writes the historian, "suæ dignitatis nationisque comittere, ut tales tantique viri tota urbe precario cibum quotidie quæritent." Idem. lib. ii. n. 8. In this cir

The original design of the first disciples of Ignatius was to perform a pilgrimage to Jerusalem, and, like the pious Palmers of olden days, to kneel before the sepulchre of their Lord in devout and penitential meditation. Before setting out on this long and perilous journey, Laynez presented himself to the Sovereign Pontiff, Paul III., and implored his benediction. "It affords me infinite pleasure," the Pontiff said, "to see united in your person so much learning and so great humility, and if you have any favor to ask, I shall willingly concede it."* To this gracious speech, Laynez calmly replied: "Holy Father, I crave your benediction, and the privilege of visiting Jerusalem." The Pontiff immediately assented, but added: "I do not think you will ever start for the Holy Land."† Whether he made this assertion because he was aware that the Venetians were about turning their arms against the Turks, or whether by Divine inspiration, it is not my province to determine. He,

---

cumstance, we see with what a spirit of poverty and humility the Society began. Its most eminent and distinguished men were always, at least in its early period, (no matter how its enemies may misrepresent its after-character,) the purest examples of both these virtues.

* Id. n. 10.
† Id. ibid.

however, afforded Laynez and his companions every facility, and, of his own accord, supplied them with money, which, added to that bestowed by the liberality of the Spanish people, amounted to more than two hundred golden florins. This sum Laynez expended in making a votive pilgrimage to Venice, living, while at Rome, upon charity collected from door to door, not without the admiration of those who had been present at his learned disputations. Shortly after he returned to Venice in poverty, where he was received with paternal affection by Ignatius, and spent his time in the hospital to the great advantage of the inmates, and the edification of the city.* Here he was promoted to holy orders, on the festival of St. John the Baptist, and looked anxiously for an opportunity to sail to Palestine. No such opportunity presented itself: for, since the war that had broken out between the Republic and the Turks, all intercourse between the two countries had been suspended. This was an event worthy to be remarked—as a clear manifestation of the will of Heaven, that the meditated pilgrimage should, from necessity, be set aside, and Laynez should, thereby, be liberated from his vow. He did not, however, leave Venice, but spent the re-

---

* Id. n. 12.

mainder of that year in devoting his services to the hospitals, and performing other good and heroic deeds. After that period, he was sent in company with Faber to Vicentra, with the understanding, that if there should be an opening into Palestine, he should forthwith retrace his steps to Venice.*

Meanwhile, he was appointed to one of the chairs in the Roman University, which he filled with magnificent eclat. Thence he was sent to Parma, where he taught in the schools, delivered lectures explanatory of the sacred Scriptures, and preached with extraordinary success to the people, among whom—as well as among the nobility—he wrought a general and manifest change of morals. From that city, at the solicitation of the Republic itself, he was again sent to Venice by the express command of the Pope.‡ His exertions in that great capital did not prevent him from extending his influence and zeal to other places. Under his auspices the College of Padua was founded, to obviate

---

* Id. n. 14. All the other Fathers were distributed throughout different places by Ignatius, with the same understanding. See their destinations in Orlandinus, *ubi supr.* Their dispersion among the cities resembles that of the apostles through the whole world.

† Lib. iii. n. 55.

the errors which had begun to be spread throughout that city by the industry of depraved men. The evil was the more formidable, as the fautors and leaders of it were "wolves in sheep's clothing."* To check the growing calamity, Laynez incessantly vindicated in his public discourses and harangues, the cause of religion, to which an immense concourse of citizens were attracted by his eloquence and erudition. His explanation of the Gospel of St. John, which formed a series of conferences, he delivered in the church of the "Holy Saviour;" and it is not easy to imagine the infinite good they effected in suppressing error and confirming truth. So universally were they admired, that he was requested, by the most illustrious and learned citizens, to continue them thrice a week. He consented: and such was the persuasive and convincing character of his oratory, that he rescued many from the fatal errors with which they began to be imbued, and induced others to abandon their evil ways and devote themselves to the practice of virtue and acts of charity. By his means, the hospitals, which had been left neglected and badly supported, were sustained and endowed anew by the ample contributions of the

---

* Id. Ibid.

faithful; and, in a word, awakened by the zeal of the spiritual exercises, piety, which had long languished and decayed, again began to revive and flourish amidst the gratulations of all orders of the republic.*

Encouraged by the fruits of his labors at Padua and Venice, Laynez next betook himself to Brescia. Here, although he devoted his attention to the hospitals and monasteries, as also to the instructing of children and the ignorant in the catechism—an exercise far more useful than ostentatious—nevertheless he commenced on Quinquagesima Sunday, in the cathedral, a course of sermons, which he continued, always attended by a numerous audience, every day during the season of Lent: besides which, he preached thrice a week in the other churches, and heard innumerable confessions. Nor did his efforts cease with the Lent. Urged by the bishop, he consented to explain the sacred Scriptures on three days in the week, and likewise to preach to the nuns in three monasteries. The character of this city was soon changed for the better: certain heterodoxical opinions, which for some pre-

---

* Idem, n. 56. Quâ in re adeo eloquens Lainii pietas fuit, ut mille amplius ipsis ex auditoribus affirmarent paratos se pro veritate Catholica jugulum ac cervices offerre.

ceding years had glided into the minds of thousands, were entirely eradicated: and so deeply did the eloquence of Laynez impress the doctrines of truth in their stead, that numbers were heard to declare that, should it be necessary, they would not hesitate to lay down their lives for the faith.* Challenged to a public disputation by a nobleman who denied the existence of purgatory, he argued with such power upon that article of the ancient faith, that the individual who had the temerity to enter the lists with him, was not only silenced, but acknowledged his defeat. This triumph induced several others who were tainted with the Lutheran heresies, to abjure them and adhere most firmly to the doctrines of their forefathers. The majesty of divine worship was renewed, piety resumed its ancient sway over the public morals, and the practices of religion reflourished.† So great and unusual was the change effected, that in a few months Brescia could hardly recognize herself.

Nor was he less successful at Bassano, a city which, from its contiguity with Germany, was fearfully exposed to the contagion of the errors that had spread over that fated country. By his assiduous exhortations, and solid discussions, he so strength-

---

* Lib. iv. n. 79. † Id. n. 79.

ened the minds of the citizens against them, that they persevered, after his absence, in maintaining the Catholic faith. He divided his labors with his companions in such a manner, that every morning and afternoon a discourse was delivered in the church of St. Lawrence *in Damaso*, to a noble and approving audience. His reputation for learning and sanctity daily and justly increased; and so enthusiastic was the public admiration in his regard, that wreaths and flowers were often scattered on his person while he announced and defended the word of God.* The dignity of bishop was offered him; but he rejected it, in conformity with the spirit of his order, and still more from a spirit of personal humility.

Meanwhile the dispute between the King of France and the Emperor of Germany having been adjusted, the Sovereign Pontiff turned his attention to the General Council of Trent, which had been interrupted during the space of three years. As his legates, he deputed the Cardinals, John Maria de Monte, Marcellus Ceruinus, and Reginald Pole.† These were followed by a hundred and

---

* Lib. v. n. 16.

† One of the most classic and finest histories in the English language, is the life of Cardinal Pole, by Canon Phil

more Bishops from Italy, and a large number from Spain, Portugal, and France ; besides representatives of all Catholic princes, and the most learned theologians, secular and religious. To the apostolic legates were added two divines, selected from a society devoted to the service of the Holy See, and the defence of the Catholic Church against the assaults of heresy. These were Laynez and Salmeron, men of profound erudition and well tried virtue. The former was in his thirty-fourth,

---

ips. In point of style, felicitous and beautiful narrative, accuracy, and eloquence—all combined, or each in particular—it will dispute the palm with Roscoe's Leo X. Why does not some enterprising Catholic publisher give us an American edition ? The account which the author presents of the Council of Trent, is by far the best and most detailed in our language.

"He was," writes Dr. Lingard, "the son of Richard Pole, a Welsh knight, and of Margaret, Countess of Salisbury; and a kinsman of Henry VIII., who had taken on himself the charge of his education." He could not assent to the divorce of the king : Lord Montague waited on Henry to deplore the infatuation of his relative. "I love him in spite of his obstinacy," was Henry's reply : "and were he but of my opinion, I would love him better than any man in the kingdom." Such was the Pope's legate to the Council of Trent, and with whom Laynez was so intimately associated. *Hist. of England,* vol. vi. chap. iv. p. 223. *Philad*

and the latter in his thirty-first year. Ignatius, in consideration of the jealousy which this extraordinary honor might excite against his infant Institute, and, likewise, of the youth of the individuals selected for the high station, used every effort to free them from it. But, finding it in vain to contend against the fixed determination of the Pontiff, he drew up for their direction certain admonitions, which I cannot refrain from abridging for the edification of the Reader.*

"In discharging the duties alloted to your care, there are things which I desire you particularly to observe. First, in the Council, seek only for the greater glory of God, and the common good of the Church. Secondly, when not engaged in the Council, continue your customary functions among the people. Finally, at home do not neglect your private duties and devotions; but, by your diligent and assiduous practices of piety, take care to render yourselves better fitted for the arduous task that is devolved upon you.

"In the business of the Council, it will become you to be slow in speaking, and very considerate and benevolent in giving your opinions. In listening, be attentive and sedate, and see clearly the

---

* Lib. v. 24, 25, 26.

mind and drift of those who are speaking; in order the more easily to reply directly, if needs be, or silently to assent. In the disputations that occur, wait for the arguments to be adduced on each side before you form a judgment of your own, always studying to be impartial and just in your decisions. If it be necessary for you to express your opinions, you will do it modestly and calmly, never omitting the clause: *to the best of my judgment.**

"Out of the Council, let no opportunity pass of doing good to your neighbors; by hearing confessions, preaching to the people, exciting them to fervor and prayer, instructing children, and visiting hospitals. In your sermons, never touch on any point controverted between Catholics and Protestants: but, labor to reform the public morals, and enforce obedience to the Church. In explaining the catechism to children, accommodate your style to their comprehension and understanding; and conclude with a brief prayer for the prosperity and happy termination of the synod.

"As regards your own conduct, you will set aside an hour at night for the purpose of examin-

---

* Ibid.

ing your actions of the day, and conferring on the affairs which will occupy your attention on the next: this you will do by private deliberations. And the more firmly to bind yourselves together, by humility and mutual charity, you will advise, freely reprehend, and, if necessary, even correct, one another."*

Guided by the wisdom that breathed through this masterly admonition, Laynez proceeded to the Council, where he was affectionately received, with Salmeron, by the Cardinal legates, who offered them a princely hospitality. But, acting in conformity with the proper spirit of their Institute, they preferred an humble residence which had been prepared for them near the church of St. Elizabeth.† The fifth session had been convoked for the seventh of June, 1546.‡ Before taking his seat, Laynez devoted his

---

* Id. n. 26. † Lib. vi. n. 21.

‡ The Council opened the year previous, convoked by the authority of Pope Paul III.; and with some interruptions, continued until 1563, when it was brought to a happy termination under Pius IV. It consequently occupied the long space of eighteen years. Twenty-five sessions were held, at which the Pope's legates duly presided; a hundred and twenty-seven canons were issued.

Of this famous Council, a false and ridiculous history was composed by Fra Paolo Sarpi, which is solidly and learnedly

time to the duties of the hospital, teaching the Christian doctrine, and other works of charity, by which he, at once, gained the affection, and confidence, and veneration of all.

In the august assemblage of dignitaries and legates, he made his appearance clad in an humble and worn-out habit, in such a manner, that he was regarded, at first, as an object of contempt, and of especial disgust to the Spanish prelates. But it was not long ere the fact was made evident, that the most splendid talents, profound erudition, and admirable eloquence, were hidden under the garb of poverty.* Unbounded confidence was placed in his opinions, which he sustained with such a depth of learning, and accuracy and perspicuity of language, that in all disputed points his sentiments were the first to be heard by the Fathers, before entering promiscuously upon the debate.† The most weighty responsibilities were laid on him; as was evinced by the circumstance of the

---

confuted in an authentic one, compiled by Cardinal Palavicini, formerly a Jesuit, from the original acts, preserved in the Vatican.

* Id. n. 23. "Tum demum intellectum est sapientiam interdum sordido latere sub pallio."

† Id. n. 25.

task of drawing up the decree on justification having been committed to his prudence and that of his companions.* A compendium of all the Lutheran errors—a work of immense labor and delicacy—likewise emanated from their hands, for the use of the Council.

During the recesses of the Synod, Laynez returned to the customary offices of zeal : he preached, catechized, visited the sick, attended in the confessional, and labored for the aid and solace of the poor and wretched. Considering the assiduous attention which the affairs of the Council required, it is difficult to realize the amount of usefulness and solicitude which he accomplished among the faithful, as it were by snatches. For the duties of the Council were incessant and absorbing. Each day two meetings were held : that of the morning treated of the reformation of morals ; that of the evening, of the dogmas of faith. One hour was allotted to each speaker : Laynez, as he states in a letter to Canisius, was heard three hours at a time.† And to his industry was assigned the task of selecting from the Councils and Fathers of the Church, and from the decrees of the Popes, monuments and proofs condemnatory

---

* Id. n. 27. † Lib. vii. n. 23.

of the various errors of the Reformers. And, nevertheless, from these momentous studies and investigations, he passed with incredible facility and celerity to the practical avocations of the pulpit and the confessional.

In the eighth session, held in March, 1547, it was determined, on account of the inclemency of the climate, and for other causes, to transfer the Council to Bologna.* Thither Laynez repaired, with the legates and Salmeron. The question now to be agitated and decided was *De Penitentia*, (on Penance.) In this weighty and abstruse dogma, his attention was entirely wrapt: during three successive hours, he delivered his sentiments on it, which were heard with intense attention by the Fathers, who assigned to him the development, likewise, of the other sacraments.†

The hours of interstice which were snatched from these accumulated and onerous occupations, he devoted to the instruction of the people and the attendance in the confessional.

With the approbation of the legates, he obtained permission to visit Perrugio; where, as he never failed to do, he first paid his respects to the bishop and leading personages, and afterwards betook

---

* Id. n. 24. † Id. ibid.

himself to the poorhouse, in which he lodged.* Multitudes of the citizens rushed to his discourses. Conversions were numberless : and in such general veneration was he held, and such wonderful fruit did his labors produce, that he was entreated to remain during the season of Advent in that city. But he had promised to spend that time at Florence. In return for his usefulness in Perrugio, the Archbishop of Milan addressed two letters, one to Ignatius, the other to Laynez himself, breathing the most grateful sentiments, and hoping to see the good work, begun so auspiciously, rendered durable by some permanent foundation of the Society.

On his route to Florence, Laynez was invited by the Bishop of Eugubio to tarry some time in that city : thence he continued to Monte Pulciano, where he preached to the faithful three days in succession. At Florence, his exertions in the pulpit and the tribunal of Confession, knew no bounds. Wonderful was the result. The field of his zeal was covered with fruit. Morals were reformed,

---

* Id. n. 28. " Pauperum ad hospitium suo more divertit," writes Orlandinus. What a grand spectacle, to contemplate the light and ornament of the Council of Trent, passing from the admiring view of that august body, into the abode and communion of the poor and humble!

alms-deeds were practised to an unprecedented amount; and penitents, as well among the military as the citizens, flocked to the sacred tribunal. With the spirit of Christian virtue, he aroused also that of letters. He was a pattern of both: and in order to unite both in an indissoluble connection, the Florentines proposed the immediate erection of a college. He was offered the choice of six or seven sites in the city. Of none of them did Laynez deem it expedient to accept. Still the city persisted in the determination to found such an establishment. They urged the duke to place it in his dominions; and obtained a promise that in a short time it should be commenced at Pisa.* He preached the Lent, in the great cathedral, beginning from Septuagesima, to more than eight thousand auditors.† At the end of the season, regretted by all whom he left behind, he quitted Florence, and repaired again to Venice; whence, after having fortunately brought to a termination a trying question relating to the college of Padua, he was

---

* Id. n. 30.

† One of his sermons, "On the Tears of Magdalen," delivered, according to an immemorial usage, to dissolute women, converted many of them. For the particulars, see lib. viii. n. 18.

called to Rome.* But a short time was given him to repose amid the venerable retreats of the Holy City. He was ordered to Sicily, at the request of Cardinal Alexander Farnesius, and Vega, the governor of that island. On his way, he was detained at Naples over the space of a month, during which he never ceased from preaching, and exhorting, and instructing; whilst he had the opportunity of enjoying in the quiet monastery of Benedictine monks, where he made his abode, much solitary repose. By the viceroy he was most humanely received. And so great was the enthusiasm of the people to hear his sacred eloquence, that it became necessary for him to address them twice, and often thrice, on the same day. In the chapel of the convent, he entered upon an explanation of the sacred Scriptures; and was always ready to receive and advise numbers who flocked to consult with him in their doubts and difficulties, spiritual and temporal.

In February, 1549, he arrived in Sicily, and, at Palermo, was greeted with every token of welcome and kindness by the viceroy, Vega, and the nobility.† He was invited to preach the Lent in a church near the palace, which was thronged with

---

* Id. n. 20, 21, 22. † Lib. ix. n. 23.

a distinguished and numerous audience. In the midst of these labors, he was suddenly prostrated by illness, and was removed from the turmoil of the capital to the calmer retreats of Mon-Reale: No sooner had he recovered his strength, than he hastened back to the arena of his zeal, and resumed his sermons with unequalled eloquence, and unprecedented effect.*

The anxious yearnings of these holy disciples of Ignatius were not bounded by any quarter of the globe. Xavier had passed returnless seas, and enkindled the light of the gospel in the interior of Asia. Laynez is now chosen to do the same in the gloomy and barbarous regions of Africa. Vega, who was intrusted with an expedition into that country which lies opposite to Sicily, prevailed on Ignatius to permit Laynez to accompany him. This expedition was ordered by Charles V., in consequence of the irruptions which were made by the pirate Dracutus, who had infested the maritime coasts of Italy and the Straits of Gibraltar; and the command of this was assigned to the viceroy himself. They departed not only with a strong Sicilian fleet, but aided also by the Pontifical, Florentine, and Maltese; and reached, after a fa-

---

* Ibid.

vorable sail, the island of Ægates, anciently renowned for the slaughter of the Carthaginians, and recently styled Fauagnana. Four days later, they landed on the continent of Africa, and selected a place for their encampment. Laynez, meanwhile, diligently occupied himself in constructing a hospital for the soldiers, who soon began to sink under these torrid heats and insalubrious skies. He, with his own hands, prepared and administered their medicines, washed their linen, tendered their diet, watched, frequently the entire night, over their beds, heard their confessions, offered up the Divine Sacrifice daily, exhorted them to patience, resignation, contrition, prepared them for death, and consigned their bodies to the earth. In such numbers were they carried off by the plague, that two or three hundred lay heaped together, which, regardless of the loathsome and pestilential atmosphere, he strove to cover with the sod, and compose with decency and religious care.* For the success of this expedition, Ignatius ordered the holy mysteries of the altar to be celebrated by all the Society : and the Sovereign Pontiff, moreover, imparted the blessings of a jubilee to all the troops engaged in it. These joyous

---

* Lib. x. n. 88, 89, 90, 91, 92.

tidings were announced to the camp with the sound of the trumpet, and Laynez exhorted all to profit by the favor, especially as their lives were exposed to the twofold danger of the climate and the enemy. The rush to the holy tribunal was immense : whole nights were spent in the confessional, and the army presented the appearance of one great school of virtue and self-victory. Their souls being thus purified and strengthened, their valor necessarily became intrepid and fearless, sustained, as it seemed to be, by the propitious favor of Heaven.* They laid siege to and captured the city on the tenth of September ; and four days after—the festival of the Exaltation of the Cross—the sacrifice of the Mass was celebrated in one of the mosques of the Mahomedans, which had been duly dedicated to the true God, under the patronage of St. John the Baptist ; and some Moors were solemnly baptized.† The victorious troops embarked, and the fleet returned to Sicily in triumph, amid the congratulations of

---

* "Haud obscurè in exitu auxilium cœleste cerni potuerit," writes our historian. Why not believe in the interposition of the omnipotent God of battles now, as well as in the history of the wars of the Hebrews?

† Id. n. 93.

the people. Laynez was especially covered with honors, as having been—they well knew—the life and soul of the army. But no part of the spoils would he consent to accept. One who evinced so noble a contempt for suffering or death, whilst the danger lowered, was not to be dazzled by success, or corrupted by booty. He preserved, under every circumstance, the same stern love of poverty, and the same imperturbable detachment from the glory and fortune of the world.*

---

* Laynez' exhortation to the soldiers, when on the point of engaging with the enemy, deserves to be recorded. It is manifestly the expression of a patriotic and, at the same time, apostolic heart: "It behooves you to remember, soldiers, how different are our weapons from those of the enemy:— they fight for booty, and vain-glory, and the extension of their dominion: whilst we have taken up arms from the pure love of Christ, prepared to brave every danger, and even to shed our blood in defence of our altars and hearths. And although great achievements are performed by valor and strength, we must not confide in them, but in the protection of God, on whom victory depends. You must fight, indeed, and bravely; but, in the camp, your conduct must be pious, and worthy of Christians. It would be criminal, whilst fighting against the enemy, to wage war against the Omnipotent. By your virtue and piety, united with fortitude, you will render God propitious. Wherefore, it is not for the spoils and booty that you should contend, as the barbarians

From the noise and business of the camp, he knew how to pass, with a wondrous transition, to the calm and *otium* of the college. With him, it was no difficult matter for "arms to yield to peace,"* or peace, if necessary, to arms, when the voice of obedience bade him mix in either. In the year 1551, we find those hands which on the desert shores of Africa were employed in raising a temporary hospital for the sick and wounded soldiers, now employed, with no less earnestness, in erecting a magnificent college in Etruria. Eleonora, the wife of the Duke of Tuscany, caused the Sovereign Pontiff to recall Laynez from Sicily to Pisa. Here, on Sundays and festivals, he preached in the church of the Benedictines; and such was the charm of his urbane and conciliatory manners, that he attracted to the confessional numbers of distinguished persons, and thousands of the various classes of society. To the catechetical instructions, he drew the children

---

are accustomed to do, but for the glory of God, which you should always have before your eyes: so that the peace of the empire and the common safety of our citizens may be effected by your arms." Ribadeneira, de vit. Layn. lib. i. p. 26.

* Cedant arma togæ, &c.

and poor, by giving little presents to the former, and alms to the latter.*

Meanwhile, the services of this extraordinary Jesuit were again required in the Tridentine Council, to which the Sovereign Pontiff called him, knowing well, as Polancus expressed in a letter written to him at this period, that he was qualified not merely to teach the Lord's Prayer to children, but to instruct, by his incomparable erudition, the whole Christian world. On his arrival at Trent, he was received amidst the gratulations of the legates and the prelates, and the first place among the theologians was assigned to him, as having been deputed immediately by the Holy See.† In giving his opinion, he modestly prefaced it by remarking, that in the all-important subjects relating to the orthodox faith, his reliance was not on human judgment, which was fallible, but on the Divine assistance : that every doctrine should be made manifest by the testimony of the sacred Scriptures and the authority of the holy Fathers. He declared, moreover, that not a single Father would he quote, whom he had not read from the beginning to the end.‡ When the august sacra-

---

* Lib. xi. n. 9. † Id. n. 36.

‡ Nullum se pro suâ sententiâ Patrem aut Doctorem in

ment of the Eucharist was brought under discussion, he cited no less than thirty-six Fathers in confirmation of the Catholic dogma: all of which, according to his own declaration, he not only had read, but had, likewise, reduced into an admirable abridgment. When he arose to speak, a deep silence prevailed, and loud applause was often elicited, by the singular learning and splendid talents which he displayed, during three hours at a time.* Being seized with a fever, probably brought on by his incessant application and fatigue, the Council, unwilling to be deprived of his invaluable aid, held private sessions, in which, despite his illness, he and Salmeron assumed the heaviest burden. Ægidius Foscari, Bishop of Modena, bore testimony of their combined and admirable usefulness. In one of his letters, written at Trent, he asserted that Laynez and Salmeron discussed the venerable dogma of the Eucharist, against the Lutherans, in the most splendid manner. "I deem myself truly happy," he added, "to be a contemporary of such learned and holy Fathers."†

---

medium allaturum quem non ipse totum a capite ad calcem pervolutasset. Id. n. 37.

* Id. n. 28.

† Et re verâ, me felicem duco, quod in hæc tempora tam doctorum, quam sanctorum Patrum inciderim. Ibid.

The Council of Trent having been again suspended, in 1552, Laynez, hardly yet recovered from his quartan fever, repaired to Padua,—but not, indeed, to rest. A new burden was imposed upon his shoulders by Ignatius, who made him Provincial of Italy. This honor, he, at first, strove to refuse, on many grounds, but on the one particularly suggested by his extreme humility—namely, that he himself had not learned to obey.* But he sacrified his own will to the designs of Providence, made known through his Superior, and submitted to them with resignation. To the letter, however, installing him in that responsible and distinguished office, he replied in these terms: "On receiving your Reverence's epistle, I had recourse to prayer, with copious tears, (which I rarely shed,) and my desire ever was and is yet—which I adjure you through the bowels of Christ to take into consideration—that you would free me from the duty of governing, of preaching, and from all literary pursuits; leave me only my breviary. Order me to retire to Rome as a poor mendicant, and there place me in the kitchen, or refectory, or garden, or any other humble position: or, if I be not fit for such occupation, let my office be to

---

* Lib. xii. n. 20.

teach the lowest class of grammar, until my death."*

And still, when the unchangeable determination of Ignatius was made known to him, with prompt obedience and child-like simplicity, he bowed to the yoke of preferment which was laid upon his neck. A noble example of heroic self-abnegation, which how much more easy it is to admire than to imitate, few of my readers have yet to learn.

The happy effects of his administration soon began to manifest themselves. At Genoa, a college was founded by the liberality of the citizens, aroused and inflamed by the powerful and exciting eloquence of Laynez,† who, with his peculiar versatility of mind, and wonderful faculty of dividing his abilities, at the same time, among various occupations, compiled, at the desire of Ignatius, a summary of dogmatic theology, for the use of the schools of the Society.‡ And so unbounded was the sway which his sacred oratory exercised over the public mind, that frequently the appeals which he made in his Lenten sermons in aid of the poor and friendless produced, at each time, not less than a thousand—and once as much as two thousand— golden florins.§

---

* Id. n. 22.   † Lib. xiii. n. 11.
‡ Id. n. 18.   § Lib. xiv. n. 31.

In the year 1555, he was again selected by the Sovereign Pontiff to accompany into Germany the Legate, Cardinal John Moroni: but the inopportune demise of Julius hastened his return to Italy. This melancholy event was bitterly deplored by the Society: in Julius, it was deprived of a Father, by whom it had been munificently confirmed, and endowed, favored with many privileges, and adorned with numberless titles of his highest favor.

Marcellus, who succeeded to the tiara, succeeded, in like manner, to the benevolence of Julius towards Ignatius and his order. When the latter went to pay his homages at the feet of the new pontiff, "Go," Marcellus addressed him, "gather soldiers and warriors; we will make use of them."* He then selected as his theologians, Laynez and Olauius. But—such is the uncertainty of human events—the hopes awakened by the friendship of Marcellus were soon destined to wither away. A few days later he was precipitated, by a sudden stroke of death, into the tomb, followed by the regret, and bewailed by the lamentation, of all good men.†

---

* Tu milites, inquit, collige et bellatores, nos utemur Lib. xv. n. 3.

† Id. n. 4.

But the auspicious elevation of Paul IV. to the throne of the Vatican compensated for the recent calamity, and dried the tears of the Church. His partiality to the Society yielded, in no respect, to that of his predecessor. When Ignatius presented to him in person the congratulations of his whole order, he was received with every mark of regard, kindness, and affection : not suffering him to remain upon his knees, but allowing him the unusual honor of promenading, while conversing, through the hall of reception.* The confidence reposed by the venerable Pontiff—he was eighty years old— in the Society, was unbounded : but of all the renowned Fathers then living, Laynez was most dear to him. In a conversation with some of his brethren, Ignatius did not hesitate to affirm, that unless the hand of God should interpose, they should soon see Laynez adorned with the Cardinal's hat. To confer this eminent distinction on him, Paul, indeed, had intended : and the apprehension of the event excited, at once, all the anxiety of Ignatius, and all the terror of Laynez. Day and night did this humble man implore the mercy of God to avert such a destiny from his head. He had passed the better portion of his life in the retired spirit of his Insti-

---

* Lib. xvi. n. 4.

tute: how could he, in its decline, consent to plunge into the splendid turmoils and distractions of a court? He had vowed to shun all honors in the Church; he had coveted the lowliest offices in the Society,—what desire could he now entertain to be raised to the pinnacle of ecclesiastical and princely glory? And yet, he was commanded by Paul to take up his residence in the Vatican. Not to appear to disregard the will of the Sovereign Pontiff, or to be deficient in the due obedience which he owed the Vicar of Christ, he instantly obeyed. There he remained but one day. On the next, he returned to his brethren, and drew up the following schedule, which he signed with his own hand:

"Whereas, from grave authority, I have learned that the Sovereign Pontiff has some design upon me, I call God to witness, and declare, in his presence, with all the candor and sincerity of my heart, that I am utterly unfit for any office which may be destined for me; and that, with my whole mind, I shrink from it. For, having examined myself, and seeing my utter want of the necessary qualifications, I would deem it ridiculous for me to accept it, and altogether abhorrent from the character of the Institute to which I belong; an Institute, in which my labors will be far more useful to the Church, and more congenial to the vow that I have taken. Of this I will strive, by every possible argument, to convince the Pope."*

In short, if the Pontiff should persist in his determination, Laynez had resolved to fly, and, after the example of some other holy men, hide himself from the world. Paul, viewing in his sudden disappearance from the palace, the interposition of the finger of Providence, did not recall him, much less force upon him the honors from which he fled. Laynez saw the danger pass away: his joy was incredible; his thanksgiving to Heaven unceasing and intense.†

---

* Lib. xv. n. 7.

† Id. n. 8. "Quo depulso periculo," writes Orlandinus in his classic style: "Laynius incredibili perfusus est gaudio, nullum ut gratulandi Deo finem faceret." This was not the only occasion in which he had to struggle against high honors in the Church. While General of the Order, the Cardinals in conclave assembled, after the demise of Paul IV. thought seriously of raising him to the pontifical throne He, however, escaped the splendid burden of the tiara, which fell to the lot of Pius IV. I cannot here omit an interesting circumstance that occurred at Paris, whither he was deputed by the Pope, with the Legate, Cardinal Hippolyto, as theologian, to the Synod of Passy. At that Synod were present the King and Queen of Navarre, five Cardinals, fifteen Bishops, the Prince of Conde, and several

But, escaping one dignity, he was only reserved for another: a dignity, however, compatible with his vocation, and which he afterwards filled in a

---

other princes, twenty Doctors of the Sorbonne, and the two standard-bearers of Lutheranism, Peter Martyr and Theodore Beza. The object of this Convention was to put an end, if possible, to religious disunion. Laynez spoke at length on the necessity of yielding to the authority of the Church, when Peter Martyr urged not a few objections against several dogmas of faith, and especially against the sacrifice of the Mass. He argued that Christ cannot be really offered on the altar, as there the sacrifice of the cross is merely represented. But, he insisted, if the thing itself be present, there is no representation of that thing; consequently, according to the admission of Catholics themselves, Christ is not truly present. To this specious sophism—which has been repeated a thousand times since—Laynez gave this triumphant reply: Suppose a king desired to institute an annual commemoration of some great victory; this he might effect in three different ways: 1. By merely causing the fact to be narrated. 2. By causing it to be represented by actors. 3. By being present at it himself, and thus representing the scene in which he himself had personally been engaged. No one could doubt the reality of the king's presence, although the past victory is merely represented anew. This clear and original position he supported, to the conviction of all candid minds, by the holy Scriptures, and the ancient Fathers of the Church. See Tanner, p. 98.

manner that added new lustre not only to his own person, but to the entire body of the Society. On the demise of Ignatius, Laynez was raised, by the suffrages of his brethren, to succeed their saintly founder as General of the Order. In which capacity, during the space of seven years, all the treasures of his erudition, the qualities of his mind, the magnificent attributes of his character, were displayed, to the admiration of the world. The history of his administration would fill a volume with splendid conceptions and glorious achievements. But to write this would be straying from my object: which is, to show forth to posterity the picture of these wonderful men, merely as they stood in conjunction with Ignatius, as his first companions,—that the spirit transfused by him into their conduct and character may be properly understood; and that the grandeur with which it was carried out, in their persons, may be justly appreciated and admired. With this view, I will close the life of Laynez: and, in so doing, I take farewell of one of the most admirable men who, in any epoch—but especially that of the sixteenth century—flourished in the Catholic Church.*

---

* Laynez died in the year 1565, at Rome.

ALPHONSUS SALMERON.

CHAPTER V.

ALPHONSUS SALMERON

ALPHONSUS SALMERON.—Called to the Society. Teaches in the *Sapienza*, at Rome. Is sent to Ireland. Seized as a Spy at Lyons. Is called to Modena. Is persecuted. Is sent to the Council of Trent. Draws up a Summary of the Errors of Luther. Goes to Bologna; to Verona; to Germany, at the command of the Pope. Labors at Ingoldstadt. Is recalled to Verona; is sent to Naples; afterwards to Poland; then to Belgium. His labors forever appreciated by that nation—his immortal name.

THE desire of making the acquaintance of Ignatius having attracted Laynez, as the reader saw in the preceding chapter, to Paris, he was accompanied, with the same view, by a young Spaniard, a native of Toledo, whose name was Alphonsus Salmeron. He was born in the year 1515. His parents were not of the highest order, but, what is more valuable, they were honest and virtuous; and perceiving in their son extraordinary talents, a heart disposed to goodness, and a mind ornamented with many gifts of nature, they trained him up to letters, as far as their means would permit, at Toledo and Compostella, where he applied to the study of the Greek and Latin languages, and the various branches of philosophy. The suavity of his manners did not yield to the excellence of his genius. He acquired the degree of Master, and having determined to pursue a course of theology, set out, with this intent, to the metropolis of France, where, as above described, he became, with Laynez, the friend and afterwards the disciple of Ignatius.* With the other companions, after severe fasting, penitential austerities, and sacramental confession, he made his vows, on the feast of the Assumption, (1534,) in the chapel of the Blessed Virgin Mary, and sealed the solemn act by receiving, immediately after, the holy Eucharist from the hands of Faber.

After his ordination, his first destination was Rome ; where he commanded universal attention and respect by his eloquent discourses, and his public disputations in the famous university of the Sapienza.† He was next selected for a mission of a very arduous, but extremely interesting characacter. Henry VIII., king of England, having repudiated his lawful wife, Catharine, had espoused, contrary to justice and right, the famous Anne Boleyn. These nuptials could not be approved by the Sovereign Pontiff. On the contrary, he con-

---

* Lib. i. n. 87. † Lib. ii. n 80.

demned and annulled them as a violation of conscience, and a contempt of the majesty of Charles V.* Henry, hurried on by the impetuosity of his lust, and forgetful of the distinguished stand he had before taken in defence of the Catholic faith, was driven to fatal extremes. Rather than forego the charms of Anne, he embraced the errors of Luther, which he once had combated with his own pen, and dared to separate from the Holy See.†

---

* The reader will remember that Catharine was the aunt of that emperor.

† When Luther first began to dogmatize, and before Henry had yielded to the violence of his own beastly passions, he wrote in the following terms against the German apostate:

"I wonder more, O Luther, (wrote Henry VIII. to him,) that thou art not, in good earnest, ashamed, and that thou darest to lift up thy eyes either before God or man, seeing that thou hast been so light and so inconstant as to allow thyself to be transported by the instigation of the devil to thy foolish concupiscences. Thou, a brother of the order of St. Augustine, hast been the first to abuse a consecrated nun; which sin would have been, in times past, so rigorously punished, that she would have been buried alive and thou wouldst have been scourged to death. But so far art thou from correcting thy fault, that moreover, shameful to say, thou hast taken her publicly to wife, having contracted with her an incestuous marriage and abused the poor and miserable . . . . . to the great scandal of the world, the re-

Nor was he satisfied with this: but maddened by his brutal passions, he even arrogated to himself the title and prerogative of head of the Anglican Church, which he required all his subjects to acknowledge, under the penalty of most cruel enactments. This sacrilegious tyranny one portion of his dominions had the courage and the virtue to resist. Ireland could not be bribed or persecuted into heresy and schism. She was doomed to op-

---

proach and opprobrium of thy country, the contempt of holy matrimony, and the great dishonor and injury of the vows made to God. Finally, what is still more detestable, instead of being cast down and overwhelmed with grief and confusion, as thou oughtest be, at thy incestuous marriage, O miserable wretch, thou makest a boast of it, and instead of asking forgiveness for thy unfortunate crime, thou dost incite all debauched religious, by thy letters and thy writings, to do the same."

It was this vindication of the ancient religion that obtained for Henry—and it is unjustly retained by his successors—the glorious title of "Defender of the Faith," granted by the Sovereign Pontiff, Clement VII. See Lingard, Henry VIII., chap. ii.

Henry did not throw off some of those practices which have since been stigmatized by Protestantism as idolatrous: in his last illness, he was constantly *attended by his Confessor*, the Bishop of Rochester, *heard Mass daily*, in his chamber, and received the communion *under one kind.* See Lingard, *ubi supr.* page 275.

pression, and terrible visitations of the tyrant's vengeance ; but the purity of her faith could not be debauched, nor her constancy to the Holy See be crushed by despotism. "That faith," writes Orlandinus, "remained intact, and that constancy sincere."*

But the faithful fold was lamentably deprived of shepherds, while, in every direction, wolves without number were prowling, and lions going about seeking whom they might devour. With paternal sympathy and solicitude, the Sovereign Pontiff, Clement VII., contemplated the forlorn condition of that part of Christ's heritage. In order to place within their reach the aids of religion, by which their spiritual wants might be supplied, and their hitherto unshaken adherence to the faith of their ancestors be more and more confirmed, with the apostolic vigilance becoming his position, he cast his eyes upon Salmeron as a fit instrument, in the hands of Providence, to effect this twofold object. This eminent Jesuit, together with his companion,

---

* Intactam tamen Catholicam fidem, et sincerissimam erga Romanum Pontificem obedientiam animo ac voluntate servabante. Lib. iii. n. 45. For the particulars of the king's divorce, his marriage with Anne Boleyn, and his rupture with Rome, see Lingard, Henry VIII., chap. iii.

Paschasius, was designated for that mission, and invested with ample powers from the Holy See. "Without sack or sandal," in the primitive style of the first followers of Jesus, he set out for that beautiful but blasted island. He went, moreover, invited and expected with cordial veneration by the Primate Robert, of Armagh: and the protection of his heavenly Father was with him.* Accompanied by a third associate—not, however, yet of the Society—whose name was Francis Zapata, he started, in the month of September, from the city of Rome, upon a long and difficult journey, taking with him, as their common guide, the following salutary admonitions of Ignatius: "In their intercourse with men of every grade, but especially their inferiors and equals, they were instructed to be reserved and moderate in their language: to listen with patience, and gentleness, and attention; and reply with brevity and precision, so as to cut off all necessity of persistence in the argument: to imitate the benevolence of the apostle, who became all things to all men for the sake of gaining them over to Christ: to remember that nothing conciliates so effectually as conforming, as far as proper, with the customs and prejudices of others:

---

* Id. n. 46.

to adapt themselves, therefore, with due discretion and wisdom, to the manners of the people : to oppose Satan with his own weapons, and make use of every art to insure their salvation which the infernal enemy exercises for their eternal ruin ;—this was the maxim of Saint Basil ;*—for, when Satan sets about to destroy a soul, he does not attempt it openly, and at once, but by various, and secret, and cunning artifices ; to praise, in the beginning, what they see laudable in the conduct of the people, passing by, for a time, their vices, until their good will and friendship be secured : to preach the Catholic truths and virtues not only in public discourses, but likewise in private conferences, and not to forget that whatever they say, even ' in the dark,' will spread abroad, and be proclaimed 'from the very house-top :' in transacting business, rather to anticipate, than defer time ; so that if any thing be promised for the morrow, let it be performed on the present day : to refuse all pecuniary compensation, even for dispensations ; but whatever moneys might be received should be given to the poor : to write to Rome frequently on their journey ; from Scotland ; as soon as they should reach Ireland ; and after-

---

* St. Basil, in reg. brev. interrog., 245.

wards, every month to give an account of their mission."*

Armed with these instructions, Salmeron bent his way, not without imminent danger, through France, as the war then raging through that country rendered suspicious every stranger who ventured to enter it. He, however, escaped, and embarked for Scotland, whence, encountering great difficulties and obstacles, he passed over to Ireland, where, under the Divine protection, he arrived about the beginning of Lent.† Here he found every thing in disorder; fear and terror occupied every heart, and the condition of the Catholics was discovered to be far worse in reality than had been described to them at a distance. The people were poor and neglected, and entirely deprived of the care and vigilance of pastors. The nobles, with one solitary exception, had succumbed to the will of the tyrant, and bound themselves by oath to burn all letters that might come from the Sovereign Pontiff, and to apprehend and imprison all who should continue faithful to the ancient

---

* Id. n. 48, 49. The principal heads of these wise admonitions of St. Ignatius are given; leaving out some, which the reader may find in full in the numbers to which he is referred.

† Id. n. 58.

Church. Under these circumstances, the Catholics did not dare receive the Father as coming with extraordinary powers from the Holy See, or even whisper abroad the object of his mission. But Salmeron and his companions did not yield to despondency, or recoil from danger. They studied their position; marked the difficulties that surrounded their path; and labored, privately at least, to master them all. They succeeded to a considerable extent; and found means to proffer their spiritual assistance to the suffering but faithful people. They encouraged and strengthened them by salutary exhortations; instructed them in the pure spirit of religion, teaching them what to retain and what to reject. To thousands they administered the sacraments; celebrated the holy mysteries; performed, with assiduous and compassionate zeal and solicitude, all the offices of their ministry, in a manner worthy the cause in which they were enlisted, and the Institute under which they acted. The joy of the Irish people was universal, their gratitude characteristic. Whoever has studied the genius of that susceptible and devoted nation, will easily understand how intense and heartfelt was their veneration of these apostolic men, who, for the mere love of their souls, had encountered the fatigues of a long journey, and the frowns of the

English government. And, were it now more universally known that Salmeron and Paschasius Broëtus, those true disciples of Ignatius, were the first missionaries sent from Rome, to comfort and strengthen the Irish Catholics immediately after the fatal Reformation in England, their names would be embalmed in the memories, and engraven on the hearts, of the children of Erin, at the present day. If the mere circumstance of my being instrumental in bringing these—their ancient benefactors—before the people of Ireland, were the only good result produced by this biography, I should, even so, consider my pains and my research more than abundantly compensated.

During thirty days, Salmeron and his companions traversed the island, giving an example of unrelenting perseverance, shining sanctity, and unparalleled disinterestedness. The fame of his spiritual exploits spread abroad, and aroused the vindictive passions of the English Protestants, who offered a large reward for his head. Dazzled by the fascinations of gold, many individuals were ready to betray and sell the missionaries. They stood in imminent peril. Their usefulness—watched and hemmed round by the venal enemies of the Church—was at an end ; and it became their duty to save their lives by withdrawing from the island. They, accordingly, fled to Scotland, obedient to the positive commands of Ignatius, that, should they deem their remaining in Ireland to be unsafe, they should, straightway, retrace their steps to Italy.* In complying with this injunction, they left behind them a blessed memory among the people, and a signal monument of apostolic virtues, for having exposed themselves to danger and to death, with a total renunciation of their own will, actuated by supernatural charity, spurning all personal consideration, and devoting their being to the salvation of their oppressed and persecuted brethren.†

On his return to Scotland, Salmeron, whose soul was still undaunted, and whose zeal was on fire, used every effort to obtain an audience of the king, with the hope of persuading that monarch to relax his rigor against his Catholic subjects. But every

---

* Id. n. 60. Ribadeneira, *Vit. Salm.* Tanner, p. 196.

† Abeunt, igitur, ex Hyberniâ, relicto apud eos populos cum desiderio non parvo tum singulari monumento virtutis, qui morte periculisque contemptis, nullâ suâ utilitate quoscunque, sed unâ dumtaxat animorum salute, ac caritate ducti, tantum itineris suscepissent. Id. n. 60. Were not such men under the guidance of the Spirit of God, that same Spirit which animated the first most glorious apostle of Ireland and the holy monk who converted England?

avenue to the throne was blocked up by the industry of the courtiers, who had abjured the ancient faith together with nearly the whole of the Scottish people. In despair of effecting his purpose, or bringing about any good result by delaying in that apostate realm, he, with his companions, crossed the Channel, and reaching again the more genial and grateful soil of France, landed at Dieppe, and pursued his journey, on foot, to Paris. There, having tarried a considerable length of time, he received letters from the Pope instructing him to return, with the same privileges and powers, to Scotland. But, on informing the Holy See of the condition—as he had witnessed it—of that country, he was ordered to bend his way directly, with his faithful associate, Paschasius, to the Eternal City. Poor and humble, like the fishermen of Galilee of old, they travelled on in safety as far as Lyons : there, in consequence of the war that was raging between the French and the Spaniards, every stranger was viewed with suspicion, and especially these two priests—the one a Spaniard, the other a Frenchman—so unusually sordid in their appearance, so singularly negligent in their dress. Wherefore, they were seized as spies, and cast into prison. Fortunately, however, they were known to the Cardinal of Tours, who happened, then, to be at

Lyons, and by him not only honorably dismissed, but provided with means and horses to continue their journey. Such was the result of the Irish mission; which, although it did not realize the, perhaps, too fervent anticipations of the Pontiff, nevertheless exhibited a shining monument of the zeal of Salmeron, of his devotion and obedience to the Holy See, and his readiness to brave any dangers, submit to any privations, nay, even expose his precious life, for the defence and propagation of the Catholic faith.

And here I must not pass over, without due commemoration, the name of Robert, Primate of Armagh. This venerable prelate was by birth a Scotchman, and had been blind from his boyhood,[*] but was distinguished for learning, and renowned for piety. When informed of the little success of this mission, "Now," he said, "I clearly perceive, that unless the sheep hear the voice of the shepherd, no good can be done." Despite his blindness, he labored vehemently for the spiritual welfare of his people, and assisted at the Council of Trent: from which, returning to Ireland, he was taken ill at Lyons, and, with these words on his lips, "Lord, if I can still be useful to thy Church, I do

---

[*] A puero cæcus, Id. n. 61.

not refuse to labor; but thy will be done,"—he expired in the arms of the Jesuits, whom he intensely loved and venerated.

After enduring great fatigue and anxiety, among a distant people, Salmeron's next destiny was to suffer a most cruel persecution in Italy. He surmounted the former with apostolic fortitude, he will subdue the latter with noble magnanimity. Invited to Modena by the Cardinal Moroni, he repaired to that city, where, during two years, he labored in the spiritual vineyard. On those fields of the Church, with the good grain planted and fostered by his hands, there grew up much cockle which the devil had sowed. The poison of Lutheranism had sunk so deeply into the hearts of many, that not only did it defy the healing power of Salmeron, but it caused them to fester with hate and malevolence against him. They had the hardihood to accuse him of teaching false doctrines, and even attacked the sanctity of his morals. Numberless calumnies against him were scattered abroad, which, as they spread, accumulated in gravity, and in apparent authenticity. The holy and injured man held his place with constancy, and, both in public and private, hazarded every thing most dear, with the hope of recalling the erring from their devious labyrinths, and the abandoned to a sense of duty and religion. With a sacred freedom he reproved vice, inveighed against abuses, and argued against heresy. But his zeal was repaid with ingratitude and injury. His enemies went so far as to depute informers to the Roman court, charging him with iniquitous conduct. On hearing this, Ignatius, who knew full well the innocence of his disciple, summoned him, nevertheless, to Rome, that he might, in person, be able to vindicate himself. In effect, he so completely confounded his enemies, and so immaculately emerged from the trying ordeal, that it is manifest Heaven subjected him to it only for the purpose of signalizing, in the clearest and brightest manner, the sanctity of its servant.*

From the arena of his triumph over the assaults of calumny, the Sovereign Pontiff, as if to decree him a solemn ovation, associated him with Laynez as an apostolic theologian to the holy Council of Trent :† as one best calculated, by his extraordinary erudition, singular prudence, and integrity of life, to combat and defeat the enemies of the Church. The honor conferred on Salmeron was

---

* Lib. iv. n. 13, 14.

† See the particulars as above related in the biography of Laynez, chap. iv.

the more signally marked, as he was, at this epoch, only in his thirty-first year.* Notwithstanding his extreme youth, so exalted was the opinion which the prelates entertained of his wisdom and abilities, that they often consulted with him in private, before they delivered their sentiments in the public sessions.† He delivered a Latin oration, of which the style and composition were so elegant, that it was published by the desire of the Council, as a masterpiece of sacred rhetoric, and was preserved as such for the benefit and admiration of posterity.‡ On the subject of Justification—an abstruse

---

* "Or quanto a Padri Laynez, et Salmerone, l'uno e l'altro eran giovani; queste ne' trent' un anni, quegli ne' trenta quattro: di che ingenio, e sapere, il vidrem poscia: che non se ne vuol ricordare altro che il zelo della fede Cattolica, e della reformazione della Chiesa, ch'era ardentissimo in amendue adunque in tante, e cosi gravissime occasioni che loro tuttodi si offerrebbono d'adoperarlo, esser pericolosi di trasandare con qualque seorso di lingua, difficillissimo a scansare, perochè altretanto difficile a conoscere."—*Bartoli*, lib. ii. p. 6.

And yet, notwithstanding their extreme youth, the reader will learn in the text, how great was the authority, how powerful the influence, which they exercised over the whole Council.

† Lib. vi. n. 23.

‡ Orlandinus, than whom no better judge could exist, de

and much vexed question—his prudence shone out in brilliant rays, especially as he was the first to deliver his sentiments concerning it. For, many and powerful objections were to be refuted, many obscure points to be made evident, and vast research to be exhibited.

The reputation, so justly acquired by Salmeron in the Council, was enhanced by his indefatigable zeal in preaching, hearing confessions, and visiting the hospitals. The prelates, assembled from all parts of the world, beheld, with amazement, the spirit of the Society exemplified in her first disciples at Trent. Its fame spread rapidly and widely among all true Catholics, while the wavering and the perverted earnestly endeavored to tarnish its glory. The Bishop of Clairmont, who, ere he witnessed, with his own eyes, the shining example of Salmeron and his companions, had been tainted with some undefined prejudice against their order, afterwards not only became conciliated and satisfied, but proved his sincerity, and signalized his friendship, by becoming the founder of no less than three Jesuit colleges in his diocese.*

---

clares: Salmeron latinam orationem habuit elegantis illius conventûs auribus dignam. Ibid. n. 24.

* Lib. vi. n. 30.

At Bologna—whither the Council was transferred—Salmeron continued his unremitting duties, as apostolic theologian, and an arduous missionary. He preached the Lent (1548), in the church of St. Lucia, introduced among the highest classes a taste and habit of prayer, and drew many of the noblemen to the sacred tribunal. Thence, at the invitation of the Bishop of Verona, Louis Lipomani, he went to that city, where, by his discourses and instructions, he produced much fruit: he confirmed in the faith the minds of many who began to doubt, recalled to the bosom of the Church several who had strayed away, and silenced the noisy declamations of Heresy against the holiness of Truth, by a public exposition of the sacred Scriptures.* Although, in general, listened to with marked respect and admiration by his auditors, he was, by some individuals—men of depraved habits or tainted minds—interrupted and opposed. He was styled the adulator of the Roman Pontiff, afraid to reveal what he well knew concerning the Church of Rome. In other words, he was accused of vile hypocrisy—the last subterfuge of the enemies of Truth; who, when argument fails them—as our daily experience teaches—always have recourse to the infamous

---

* Lib. viii. n. 28, et Lib. ix. n. 48.

logic of calumny and misrepresentation. This, it appears from the circumstance before us, was an early artifice of the Reformation ; and on this much of its declining influence reposes, after an interval of three hundred years. In our own republic, is not Catholicism identified by her opponents with Jesuitism, and is not Jesuitism confounded with mental reservation, suppression of truth, and the justification of the means necessary for the accomplishment of any object? When the ingenuous and upright mind sees through this baneful scheme of the leaders of Protestantism, what wonder is it, that it abandons them in disgust, and seeks for truth and virtue in the blessed tabernacles of Rome !

From Verona, Salmeron extended his missionary solicitude to Belluno, an ancient and elegant city in the Venetian dominions. Aware of the bitter animosity that existed there against his person and the institute of the Society, he affectionately recommended himself and his object to the prayers of Ignatius. Confident in the holiness of his cause, he commenced a public course of lectures, which were numerously frequented ; gave private instructions ; introduced the practice of prayer and meditation ; extirpated vices ; and revived a spirit of piety and devotion. His novel style of preaching excited universal admiration : all united in conceding that the true and genuine character of pulpit oratory was displayed to perfection in his f rvid and solid, his moving and convincing eloquence. Since the days of St. Bernard of Sienna—it was unanimously admitted—no preacher ever produced more general and lasting good.* To this declaration the state of society bore evidence. Violent and deadly animosities were extinguished ; errors and unsound opinions were abandoned ; the works of Luther and his fellow-gospellers were destroyed ; the sacraments were frequented ; the fasts of Lent and other penitential ordinances were revived ; and, in fine, Religion reassumed her pristine discipline and salutary sway.† The acknowledged success of Salmeron in counteracting the advancement and pernicious consequences of error at Belluno, induced Ignatius to station him in the very seat of its empire—Germany. With Jaius and Canisius he was ordered to undertake that mission at the earnest solicitation of William, Duke of Bavaria, an uncompromising defender of the Cath-

---

* Id. n. 49.

† "Denique," writes our historian, "alia id genus com plura gesta." No wonder the sons of Ignatius should be hated by the votaries of the world, and the enemies of the Catholic faith.

olic faith. To add greater weight to their project, the degree of Doctors in Theology was awarded to them all by the famous University of Bologna. This honor they received through the Cardinal John Maria de Monte, who afterwards was raised to the papal throne. At Trent, the former theatre of Salmeron's learning and eloquence, they were received, with merited distinction, by the cardinal, who commended them by special letters to the Duke of Bavaria. This noble prince, who yielded to none in his veneration for these saintly Jesuits, received them with every token of cordial affection. With public demonstrations of welcome they entered the city of Ingoldstadt, and were especially greeted by the whole academy, in a masterly Latin oration.* On the following day, in the "ancient" college, Salmeron began an explication of the epistles of St. Paul, which he continued in a series of discourses not less learned than beautiful: which were so greatly admired by the illustrious members of the academy, that they were published for the

---

* In a no less elegant style Canisius responded extemporaneously, in the name of his companions; "Cui subito et eleganter omnium nomine a Canisio responsum est," writes Orlandinus, *ubi supr.* n. 54.

perusal and instruction of all men of taste and investigation.*

A sudden order of the Sovereign Pontiff requiring his presence at Verona, suspended the great and good work he had commenced. Obedient to his supreme will, although the duke remonstrated loudly and strongly against the measure, Salmeron quitted Ingolstadt amid the tears and regrets of the Academicians. At Verona he was created Dean of Theology in the university, where he remained an entire year.

At Naples, a college was about being founded under the auspices of Hector Pignatelli, Duke of Monte Leone, and Caraffa, Count of Montorio. These distinguished benefactors of the Society wrote to Ignatius requesting him to send to that city some eminent Jesuit to preach the Lenten sermons, and negotiate concerning their meditated establishment. Salmeron was selected, and was received at Naples with solemn congratulations. Without delay, he entered upon the offices of his mission, and, at the suggestion of most noble and influential citizens, commenced, in the church of the Blessed Virgin, a course of lectures explanatory of the epistle of St. Paul to the Galatians,

---

* Id. ibid.

which he conducted with such fervid eloquence and solid erudition, that he crushed the secret spirit of heresy which was lurking in the bosom of society.*

Useful as were his labors at Naples, a more conspicuous and unlimited stage was again prepared for him by the Sovereign Pontiff. Again must he assume his post as Theologian of the Holy See in the sacred Council of Trent. He reached that city, in company with Laynez, towards the end of July, A. D. 1551 ; where, as we have related in the last chapter, he won golden opinions, both for himself personally, and for the Society which he represented.†

Three years later he visited again the city of Naples, where he resumed, with his former energy and fervor, the work of instruction and piety which had been interrupted for so long a time. To his sermons crowds flocked without number. With his irresistible eloquence and learning, he swept away, as so many flimsy cobwebs, the heresies which certain reformists had woven among the people, and revived the primitive spirit of devotion and fervor. Among other pious institutions, he es

---

* Lib. xi. n. 16.

† Id. n. 36. See the particulars in the biography of Laynez, chap. iv.

tablished two sodalities, one for men, the other for women. Of the former the object was—strengthening their resolution by receiving the holy communion every fortnight—to catechise children, instruct the ignorant, diffuse peace and concord among their fellow-citizens, entice others, by their virtuous example, to the frequentation of the sacraments, and to visit and nurse the poor and infirm.* That of the women required its members to approach weekly the holy table ; to imbue the minds of their children and domestics with the influence of religion, by reflecting it in their own conduct ; to provide for the unfortunate of their own sex who should desire to reform their lives ; and to beware of decorating their own persons meretriciously or too extravagantly, either by the use of factitious coloring or unseemly dress.† The usefulness of such sodalities to the members themselves, and to society at large, may be easily imagined : and it was in promoting such holy ob-

---

* Lib. xiv. n. 36. Of course, only the most exemplary and disinterested could obtain membership in this admirable association.

† Against the custom of painting, St. Cyprian inveighed in unsparing terms, as unbecoming Christian ladies. See Orlandinus, *ubi supr*.

jects that the disciples of Ignatius—and in this particular especially Salmeron—dedicated and devoted their talents and their lives. Europe beheld them with wonder, and looked to them as the props and ornaments of the Faith in these disastrous times. Everywhere colleges were asked for; insomuch that it was impossible for Ignatius to supply the demand for his disciples. The request of Sienna was, however, granted ; and in the erection of her college, Salmeron justly claims no vulgar merit.

That beautiful and lately powerful city had just recovered from the horrors of an exhausting war, and fallen under the dominion of Philip (1556) ; and was placed under the government of Cardinal Francis Mendoza. This noble prelate, seeing on all sides the melancholy vestiges of that fatal war, and commiserating the calamities of a people renowned for humanity and refinement, resolved to remedy the evil by blending together the Divine and human aid. To this effect, he entreated Ignatius to allow him the assistance of three members of his order, under whose auspicious and soothing influence he anticipated the happiest and holiest results. The appeal to his charity, under these woeful circumstances, awoke the deep sympathies of Ignatius; and forthwith he chose the number desired, of which the most conspicuous was Salmeron. From Poland, whither he had been sent with the Apostolic Nuncio, Louis Lipomani, (he was the first Jesuit that was ever seen in that kingdom,) by the order of Ignatius he was summoned back to Italy, and stationed at Sienna, at the disposal of the cardinal and the city.*

He was not, however, left long in that position;—scarcely long enough to accomplish all the good anticipated. His services were deemed so invaluable by the Sovereign Pontiff, that they were made to extend from kingdom to kingdom a brief but indelible influence, rather than to concentrate in any particular part. He was soon called back to Rome by the Pope, who associated him with the Cardinal de Montala in a mission to Belgium, where he laid the foundations of that firm and reverential hold which the Society secured among a truly Catholic people, who have, to the present day, cherished their faith with a primitive integrity and love, and stand in the midst of the nations of the earth a living, speaking, splendid monument of the genius, character, and influence of the Catholic faith.† The Belgians, who are now, perhaps,

---

* Lib. xvi. n. 3, 4, 5.

† See the particulars of the introduction of the Society

the most Catholic people in Europe, have not forgotten the labors of the primitive Society among them. During all succeeding times, it has been cherished and venerated : some of the most magnificent volumes which the press ever sent out into the world were the productions of her sons, and the perfection of the typographic art of their publishers. While their grateful posterity—whose ever ardent faith has been kept alive, and whose ever Catholic spirit has been perpetuated in a great degree by the Society—recurs to the annals of their history, and admires the glorious names that sparkle on every page, they will perceive none irradiated with a brighter and purer halo than that of Alphonsus Salmeron.*

---

into Belgium, as narrated in Orlandinus, lib. xvi. n. 28, 29, 30, 31, 32, et seq.

* On quitting Belgium for Rome, whilst passing through the town of Basle, he was challenged by some of the Reformists to a controversy. From this he came forth triumphantly, having crushed his adversaries under the weight of his arguments. He reached Rome in 1558, after the death of Ignatius. By Laynez, he was then sent into Naples, where he continued laboring with unceasing zeal, and wonderful success, for the salvation of souls. It was his fortune to live under five different Generals—Ignatius, Laynez, Borgia, Everardus Mercurianus. and Aquaviva, whom

Mr. Stephen, in his famous essay on "Loyola and his Associates," nominates the Numa Pompilius of the Order. Repeating these words, *Lætatur anima mea*, "my soul rejoices," with his eyes fixed upon a crucifix, he calmly expired on the 13th of February, A. D. 1585, in the sixty-ninth year of his age. See Tanner, p. 201 and 202.

Father Ribadeneira, who wrote the lives of Laynez and Salmeron, and who was their contemporary, enumerates the works composed by Salmeron, which are as follow:

I. *Liber Prolegomenon:* a commentary on the entire Scriptures.

II. *De Incarnatione:* on the incarnation of Christ.

III. *De infantiâ et pueritiâ Christi Domini:* on the infancy and childhood of Christ

IV. An evangelical history.

V. An explanation of Christ's sermon on the Mount.

VI. On the miracles of Christ.

VII. A treatise on the parables and sermons of the gospel.

VIII. *De disputationibus Domini:* on Christ's disputations.

IX. On the discourse of Christ touching the Last Supper, and the Holy Eucharist.

X. On the passion and death of Christ.

XI. On the resurrection and ascension of Christ.

XII. On the Acts of the Apostles.

Besides which, he composed nine books on the canonical Epistles of St. Paul, and the Apocalypse.

These works of Salmeron are regarded as masterpieces in point of lucid composition, learned research, and theological argument. His name ranks among the most eminent writers of the Church in the sixteenth century.

NICHOLAS BOBADILLA.

CHAPTER VI.

NICHOLAS BOBADILLA.

NICHOLAS BOBADILLA.—Becomes one of the nine. Is sent to the island of Ischia. Is destined for the East Indies, but detained by illness. Is deputed to Germany. Labors at Vienna; traverses the different cities of Germany. Refuses the Episcopal dignity. His zeal at Naples. Is made Rector of the Neapolitan College. His lenient government. His trials. His submission. His obedience and other virtues. An example to posterity.

IN the year 1525, whilst Ignatius was just commencing the magnificent work of his Society in Paris, a strange youth presented himself, desirous of obtaining an interview with that immortal man. His object was to confide to his paternal breast the story of his wants and friendless circumstances in that vast metropolis, to which he had come with the hope of being able to prosecute his theological studies. His parents had struggled to provide him with the necessary means; but in vain. And he must either relinquish the career on which he had entered with such buoyant emotions, such successful anticipations, or he must meet with some true and sympathizing benefactor, whose hand will be stretched out to support and sustain him in his hopeless condition. The name of this ingenuous and aspiring youth was Nicholas Bobadilla, a native of a village in Spain, of the same name, near Palenza. He had rendered himself conspicuous as a professor of philosophy in the University of Valladolid. At the recital of his necessitous circumstances, the paternal heart of Ignatius was moved, and he immediately obtained for him the sum necessary for the continuance of his course in the University of Paris. For these disinterested favors, Bobadilla not only returned the most cordial expressions of gratitude, but was so charmed by the manner in which they were conferred, and conceived so lofty an estimation of his saintly benefactor, that he determined to rank himself among the number of his disciples, with Faber, Xavier, and the others.* Having gone through all the requisite preliminaries, he pronounced his solemn vows with his companions—as has been stated before—on the festival of the Assumption of the Blessed Virgin, A. D. 1534.

---

* Orland. lib. i. n. 88.

From the frank and unaffected disposition evinced in the incipient career of Bobadilla, the reader may anticipate the character of his future greatness. On the former was based the latter; and he is no less admirable in the one, than illustrious and ever-memorable in the other. The breast that does not foster the elements of candor and ingenuousness can never be the seat of magnanimous aspirations. Had Bobadilla nursed in his the morbid sentiments of false pride, or *mauvaise honte*, he would have sunk into a miserable state of apathy, and neither the history of the Church nor of the Society would have treasured his name, and enshrined his memory, among the great and saintly apostles of the sixteenth century.*

---

* "Era giovane, di quanto è ingegno e scienze naturale e divine, fornito piu che a sufficienza. Poi quive stesso e in Italia, venuto formandosi nella vita spirituale, sotto la disciplina del Santo, deviene in verità uomo di riuscire a cose grandi in servigio della Chiesa: perocchè attemperandosi in lui la grazia alla natura, come per questa era di compessione focoso, cosi per quella, di spirito a maraviglia zelante; e i tempi che allora correvano disordinatissimi per la tanta libertà o del vivere, o ancora del credere . . . . abbisognavano, per ammenda, di troppa piu gagliarda, che non sarebbe mestieri in altra meno disordinata stagione." *Bartoli*, libr. iii. p. 224.

Ignatius, who with almost a prophet's intuition read the distinctive qualities of his disciples, descried in Bobadilla the spirit of conciliation and peace: and in their dispersion over the world, to him was allotted a mission of this twofold character, to the island of Ischia, in the kingdom of Naples. Among certain noble and powerful personages of that place, a fatal animosity had broken out, which was as pernicious as it was scandalous.* The happy result amply realized the sanguine presentiments of Ignatius: and, although the nature of these quarrels so auspiciously adjusted by Bobadilla is not specified by our historian, nevertheless, as that eloquent writer remarks, "it afforded an earnest of his future tact and prudence, and constituted a bright preliminary to his splendid achievements in Germany." †

It was the manifest disposition of events by Divine Providence that pointed out the destination of Bobadilla. When the distant portals of the East were opened to the missionary labors of

---

* Id. lib. ii. n. 79. Bobadilla in Ænariam ab urbe mittitur regni Neopolitani insulam ad conciliandam pacem inter graves illustresque viros.

† Specimen suæ dabat industriæ quæ postea latissimum Germania nacta campum, tanto liberius excurreret, quanto jam cohibita vidibatur angustiis. Ibid. n. 81.

the Jesuits, it was the intention of Ignatius to charge him—as one best fitted—with that momentous trust. With this view, he was recalled from Ænaria to Rome, in the beginning of the year 1540. Laboring, though he was, under a severe illness, and wasted with the fatigues of his long journey, still he showed himself ready and desirous, at the command of Heaven, to depart at once, upon the almost returnless voyage for which he was selected. But the opportunity of sailing being urgent, and the fleet in readiness, ere he had time to recover from his indisposition, the lot, which by human ordination had been intended for him, was, by Divine interposition, transferred upon another. No matter what glorious hopes the departure to the Indies of such a man might have kindled up in the Church, the splendid and almost miraculous achievements of the apostle who was substituted in his place not only remove all regret at the change, but afford the subject of immortal gratitude to God, and glory unsurpassed to Francis Xavier.*

Bobadilla arrived in Germany, hardly convalescent from his recent sickness, and proceeded to Inspruck, where King Ferdinand was residing

---

* Id. n. 88.

with his children. There, forgetful of his weakness, with intrepid zeal, he began his laborious career, and by his private conferences with the nobles, as well as the other public functions of the ministry, he devoted himself to the salvation of the people. The court being, afterwards, transferred to Vienna, he obtained access to the sovereign himself, by whom he was received with a gracious welcome, and encouraged to continue his exertions for the cause of religion. Wherefore, he resumed, with renewed fervor, his public instructions, and the other functions of the mission. He preached, gave lectures explanatory of the ancient faith, catechised the young and ignorant, devoted hours, stolen from his almost incessant occupations, to the confessional, and thus effected many conversions, even among Jews and Turks. What added the crown to all his other actions, was the fortunate effect of his conference with the king, who, animated by his vigorous and ardent expostulations, supported the cause of religion, and prevented the evil which menaced it at Ratisbonne.* So intimately did he possess the favor and friendship of the monarch, that at

---

* Lib. iii. n. 64.

Vienna, whither he was ordered to follow the court, he was not permitted to leave it; but became the cherished and venerated inmate of the palace.*

Whilst engaged in the rigid and multifarious offices of his ministry, in that great capital; whilst, with potent and eloquent energy, he maintained and vindicated the tenets of the holy Catholic Church, he was suddenly challenged by a famous Lutheran doctor to a controversial encounter. The source from which it emanated—the standing of the individual who stood forth as his antagonist—the circumstances of his own position—the public expectation—the offended majesty of Truth—the honor of the Priesthood—the character of the Society—rendered it necessary for him to set aside the strong repugnance, in ordinary cases, of publicly meeting on the arena of dogmatic disputation a presumptuous opponent. There are times, when, for a Divine, thoroughly competent to the task, to refuse the contest, would be as deserving of reproach, as for a person not perfectly armed with the weapons of learning and moderation to accept, under *any* cir-

---

* Lib. iv. n. 27. In Regis curiâ commorabatur æquè carus, utilisque proceribus.

cumstances. The former produces striking and solemn good: the latter generates mischief, and leaves no other impression on the public conviction, but that of temerity and defeat.

Bobadilla was driven upon the arena; but not without feeling himself equal to the conspicuous and, generally, dangerous attempt. He was actuated by no ostentatious desire of exhibiting his powers of elocution, or his abilities for argument, or his research and erudition. There was mixed in his pure motives no alloy of vain-glory, no secret self-complacency. His were the motives of an apostle—a germane disciple of Ignatius—an humble follower of JESUS: and impelled by these, and these alone, how could he come off from the field of controversy otherwise than victorious, and by common consent, covered and graced with the laurels of triumph?

The personage by whom the gauntlet was thrown at Bobadilla's feet was a fautor of Lutheranism, more distinguished by the nobility of his birth than by the sincerity of his faith. He held the rank of the King's Counsellor, but since his defection from the ancient faith was looked upon with unfavorable eyes by the monarch. Envious of the favor and friendship displayed by the court towards Bobadilla, this disaffected nobleman did not hesitate to declare that he was willing to argue the subject of religion with that celebrated Jesuit in presence of arbiters and judges ; avowing, that should they decide against him, he would be willing to submit : if in his favor, that he should be allowed to hold his station in court, and to persist in his doctrines.*

The king assented to the proposition, nominated seven judges, and summoned Bobadilla to the contest. The occasion precluded the possibility of his refusing to obey the summons. No alternative was left to his discretion, no choice permitted to his judgment. The sacred cause of religion demanded his defence. The enthusiasm of the nobles was excited on the subject. The king called upon him as the champion of the Church, and the city was in suspense to witness the important spectacle. In God did Bobadilla place his trust ; his heart yearned for the salvation of the sheep that had wandered from the fold of Christ, and, with the hope of bringing back at least some of the number, he presented himself, at the call of the monarch, upon the arena, before his stern antagonist. The king and most of the nobles were spectators to

---

* Id. n. 27. The description of this controversy is admirably detailed in the above reference. See it *passim*.

the novel scene, hanging on the disputation with intense anxiety for the event. The controversy soon waxed ardent and vehement. Argument was met by argument, authority by authority. But as the power of truth—vindicated as it was by the *athleta* of orthodoxy—could not be cloven down by any violence of error; nor its majesty be tarnished by the conceits and inventions of human opinion; nor its identification with the Holy, Apostolic, and Roman Church be severed apart by the logic of calumny or aspersion; the disputation was necessarily of very brief duration. Vanity was crushed by verity; the impiety of the disciple of Luther, by the orthodoxy of the disciple of Ignatius, who detected and confuted not less than fifty heresies in the doctrines of his adversary. The vain apologist of Lutheranism was silenced and confounded, and, by unanimous acclamation, Bobadilla was hailed as his unquestionable victor.*

But still, with his stake, it cannot be supposed that the Lutheran admitted his defeat. He had more to say—therefore he imagined his argumentative ammunition had not given out: his store of

---

* Bellus igitur Lutheri sectator, et tali dignus magistro, omnium calculis, suffragiisque damnatur. Id. ibid.

misrepresentation had not been exhausted—consequently he did not feel himself bound by the obligation he had made, but forgotten—or, rather, disregarded. On the contrary, to defeat he added pervicacity; and to error, perfidy. The equitable sentence of the umpires touching his erroneous doctrines he obstinately rejected, charged them with perjury, pertinaciously affirmed that he would never change his opinions, nor be any other than he had always been,—the uncompromising enemy of the Ancient Religion.*

The king, astonished not so much at the pertinacity as at the impudence of the man, who had drawn up his own conditions for the controversy, and now refused to abide honorably by them, banished him from court, and condemned him to be shut up within the inclosure of a monastery. There, stung with remorse, and impatient of the disgrace he had brought upon himself, with his own hands he attempted to put an end to his existence. The wound, however—and most providentially and mer-

---

* Ibid. Was not this disputant an accomplished exemplar of thousands of more recent date? Professing to be open to conviction, and sincere in the inquiry after truth; and yet obstinate when convinced, and, with a spiteful embrace, hugging error to their bosoms.

cifully was the escape ordained—did not incontinently prove fatal. Mercifully, indeed, was this designed by Providence: for, from the stroke which was intended to produce death, life and safety sprang. Weltering in his blood, he beheld the light of heaven shining upon his dark and desperate spirit. Instantly all was changed. His obstinacy relented; his conscience was wrung with sorrow for his crime; he repented, retracted his errors, and submitted, with humble acquiescence, to the venerable Church from whose pale he had wandered, and to whose bosom he now came back, to die—a sincere penitent, and a signal object of the Divine clemency.*

Meantime, the Diet was now in session at Nuremberg, at which, in order to protect the rights of religion, the Bishop of Caserta was present as Apostolic Nuncio. Bobadilla, whose fame the recent disputation had spread to the extreme limits of the empire, accompanied that prelate, and, through deep snows and the dangers of pestilence, proceeded in safety to the destined place. By his counsel and prudence the Nuncio was governed and directed in the Diet: and although his stay there was brief, the unremitting zeal of Bobadilla

---

* Id. ibid.

prompted him to scour the whole city, and visit all the churches. In his missionary functions he was consoled to perceive, that the clergy were more regular and less dissolute than in some other places, and bound by a stronger chain to the religion of their ancestors. To the city of Nuremberg, and that whole district of Germany, his exertions proved of infinite advantage. With the Lutheran minister—there was but one in the city—he became familiar, and won over his confidence and friendship to such a degree, that there was every reason to hope, could he have remained longer in the city, that he would have brought over to the true faith that individual, in character and sentiment totally different from the cunning and refractory Bucer.* But after the rising of the Diet—the session was short—he was obliged to return to Vienna with the Nuncio, where he was greeted by the king and court, and received with no ordinary de-

---

* Id. n. 28. Of this minister Orlandinus asserts, that he possessed "facile, et ad bonum omne flexibile ingenium." The same author styles Bucer, " vafrum atque præfractum.' Wherever good and noble qualities exist, the Catholic, carefully separating them from the errors of the individual, will be the first to acknowledge and praise them. Charity forbids him to believe that every teacher of erroneous doctrine is perversely insincere.

monstrations of honor. To narrate all that he did in that grand metropolis for the advancement of God's glory, would be an exhaustless task: one thing, however, must be mentioned,—that a noble German of very high distinction, who had, during many years past, been not only neglectful of the sacraments, but also notorious for his depraved habits of conduct, and who had withstood the remonstrances of the king, as well as the frequent solicitations of his friends, was brought to yield to one single conference with Bobadilla, and to embrace a Christian mode of life.*

His sojourn at Vienna was not long. Another Diet was convened at Spires, and thither he was sent, to accompany the Bishop of Passau, the representative of the monarch, as one so generally known to Catholics and Protestants, and whose prudence and counsel would greatly benefit the public weal. The prelate, aided by the wisdom of the Father, having succeeded to the entire satisfaction of the king, petitioned that Bobadilla might be permitted to visit Passau. The request was granted; and the magnanimous Jesuit plunged at once, as it were, into the centre of that diocese, and, with his wonted ardor, performed inestima-

---

* Id. n. 29.

ble good. The prelate, aware of the influence and authority that he exercised over the people, made abundant use of them both ; and would have taken him again to another Diet at Spires, to assist, by his erudition and experience, the assembled bishops who were to consult for the sacred cause of religion. This distinction he did not accept, on the ground that it could not be conferred except by the authority of the Sovereign Pontiff. Accordingly, he remained at Passau, engaged in the functions of the holy ministry ; when the honor, which he dared not admit when proffered by the Bishops, was suddenly forced upon him by the Cardinal Alexander Farnesius, then Legate of the Holy See at Spires. With the genuine spirit of his order, he obeyed, and took his place in that august Convention among the great and wise. To the king and court this circumstance afforded special satisfaction, whilst, at the same time, it was peculiarly beneficial to the cause of truth, which he vindicated by his sacred eloquence, and illustrated by his saint-like example.*

---

* Inspruck, Spires, Cologne, Worms, Nuremberg, and other cities, which were exposed to be infected with the Lutheran heresies, were saved by his preaching, conferences, and all-embracing zeal ; looking for no earthly reward,

The Diet having broken up, there ensued a contention among the prelates, which of them should take to his diocese this extraordinary man. But as he came with the Bishop of Passau, with him he proposed to return—and thence again to Vienna, whither the king had also repaired.* There, besides his accustomed sermons, he studied, with the co-operation of the monarch, to regulate the manners of the pastors and doctors according to the norma of ancient discipline; but nothing would he undertake without the approbation, likewise, of the bishops, whose authority he strenuously asserted, and whose character he invariably held up to the highest veneration of the faithful.† On this account, when the king addressed him a letter from Passau, requesting him to visit the monasteries of Austria, he freely replied, that he could not, without

---

spurning honors, and using the glory of the court of Ferdinand and Charles V. "as if he used them not:" living always under the simple and holy influence of his vocation. "Spregiator," writes Bartoli, "degli onori, e quel che solo gli rimaneva, ancor della propria vita in pro della vita eterna de prossimi." (P. 225.) What more perfect character could be portrayed for the admiration of the world, and the honor of the Society, which he loved as his mother?

* Id. n. 114, 115, 116.
† Id. n. 116.

the consent of the prelates. And again, when nominated by the same power to attend at the famous Synod of Worms, he declined to comply, until the nomination was sanctioned by the Holy See ; at whose bidding he departed without delay, and acted a part in that Convention which added fresh laurels to his fame, and reflected new lustre upon the Society of JESUS.

To Worms he was duly deputed with the Apostolic Nuncio, Jerome Verallo : Jaius, his companion, having accompanied the Bishop of Augsburg. Baffled in his efforts, disappointed in his hopes, of consolidating the elements of religion at Ratisbonne, Nuremberg, and Spires, Ferdinand persuaded himself that the object might ultimately be attained at Worms. But, unfortunately, up to this date (it had been convened a year before), no salutary purpose was achieved : no efficacious barrier was raised against the inroads, no sanatory antidote prescribed against the errors, of Lutheranism. In the effectuation of this twofold object, all the vigilance, all the energies of Bobadilla were called up. With unbending determination he stood forth in vindication of the Church, laboriously careful to prevent any thing—in a Council at which were present the emperor and his brother Ferdinand, together with a large number of noblemen—

from escaping, that might be, in the least, injurious to the orthodoxy of the ancient faith, or the majesty of the Holy See. But despite his powerful co-operation and that of his associate Jaius, the Council, though prolonged, had not the happy termination that had been anticipated. Nothing, however, was decreed against the Catholic Church nor was the proposal of the Lutherans admitted, to have a National Convention, although they were more numerous and more powerful than the orthodox.*

---

* Lib. v. n. 28, 29, 30, 31. All these Diets of Germany ended unfortunately. That of Spires had passed a decree, banishing from the dominions all the Sacramentarians and Anabaptists; restoring the celebration of Mass, and requiring that the gospels should be explained according to the interpretation of the Fathers of the Church. Against this decree the Lutherans protested, as contrary to Evangelical liberty; and hence they derived the name of *Protestants*.

This protestation was confirmed, in the Diet of Augsburg, by the aid—powerful indeed—of Melancthon, in the Articles presented to Charles V., commonly called the "Confession of Augsburg." This was subscribed by all the Lutheran Princes in Germany, who afterwards formed a league at *Smalkald*, to defend their sect by *force of arms*. Alarmed by this confederacy on one hand, and the formidable power of the Turks now menacing him on the other, the emperor convened the Diet of Ratisbonne; where he entered into a

It pleased God, however, whose providence often draws good from evil, to turn this Synod to a favorable account, in a twofold manner: first, by inducing the emperor, who had a fair opportunity of testing the obstinacy and impracticability of the Dissenters, to restrain and repress them more effectually than before. Secondly, by stimulating the zeal and solicitude of the pastors themselves, who having witnessed the arts and resources of so many "wolves in sheep's clothing," rendered them more vigilant over the flock committed to their sacred care.

In the year 1546, Bobadilla—then laboring at

---

kind of armistice with the Lutherans, by issuing a proclamation forbidding any one to be molested in religious matters, until the General Council should be convoked. It was held at Trent; but its authority and decrees were set aside and opposed by those very men who, at first, affected to be willing to submit to both.

It should be carefully remarked and remembered, that the recourse to arms was the act of the Protestant princes; determined to propagate their opinions by violence. At the head of this league were John Frederick, Duke of Saxony, and Philip, Landgrave of Hesse. The particulars of this religious war—in which the emperor was victorious—are related by Sleiden, libr. xvii., xviii., and xix. See Natalis Alexander, Select. Hist. Eccles. cap. &c. &c., tom. 24. Dissert. Sæc. xvi. p. 245.

Cologne for the salvation of souls—was again required to accompany the king, to whom he was very dear, to the city of Ratisbonne, where another Synod had convened. The object of this Synod was to conciliate, if possible, the Protestants, and prepare them to recognize the Œcumenical Council of Trent, already convoked, but not by them admitted as such. Of this Synod, all the acts were to be referred to the General Council.* Besides the other occupations of Bobadilla, he found time to compose a work entitled "On the Conscience of a Christian," which, on appointed days, he explained in a series of discourses, in the Latin tongue, to a numerous concourse of learned and noble men,—Germans, Italians, French, and Spaniards.†

The licentious doctrine on which Luther had erected the superstructure of the miscalled Reformation was the assumed and arrogant right of Private Judgment. Had this pretension confined itself within the boundaries of dogmatic theories, the evil might have required no other check but that of the spiritual sword: but the state began to suffer from it; the peace of the nation, the established order and system of government, the insti

---

* Lib. vi. n. 53, 54.   † Id. ibid.

tutions, which had, from immemorial ages, been regarded and respected by the people, were seriously menaced. If a set of theological demagogues, acting under the unrestrained influence of Private Judgment, would throw into confusion, and even subvert, the elements and foundations of religion; driven on by the same wild impulse, and shielding their lawless passions under the same vaunted ægis of human liberty, they will not fail to disorganize and destroy the social and political institutions of government. The emperor, unable to preserve the ancient order and secure the peace of Germany by legislative decrees, or tolerant offers of conciliation, was compelled to unsheath the temporal sword, and declare war against the domestic enemies of their country.[*]

Bobadilla, who had so often contended for the Faith on the arena of controversy and theological dispute, was now, contrary to his pacific dispositions, but in obedience to the will of his superiors, destined to mingle in the tumult and horrors of the camp. Not, indeed, himself to wield the sword, but to dispense the consolations of religion, to encourage the despondent, to absolve the penitent, to

---

[*] The reader must not forget the league of *Smalkald*; and the tolerant enactments of the Diet of Ratisbonne.

attend the sick and wounded, and to watch over the dying, and bury the dead. By the Cardinal Farnesius he was placed at the head of the hospital, within whose walls the bodies of the wounded and dying were brought. With such wasting and intense solicitude he devoted himself to these offices of mercy, that he sank under their pressure, and was prostrated with illness. And yet, when unable to stand erect upon his feet, from debility, he might be seen creeping from bed to bed, administering consolation and the sacraments to the wretched victims, and unhappy himself only from not being able to afford all the aid and attention which his generous heart desired to bestow. To him, whose soul was burning with charity, nothing was difficult, nothing arduous. My pen cannot describe his fervor in exhorting, his gentleness in reproving, his assiduity in hearing confessions, his patience, resignation, humility, and cheerfulness in all things.*

On his route back to Ratisbonne, Heaven gave him an opportunity of adding to the store of his long suffering and mortification which he had accumulated in the camp. He was captured by robbers, despoiled of all his effects, severely beaten,

---

Id. n. 55, 56.

and perhaps would have been murdered had he not been rescued by three Italians who accidentally happened to pass that way.* But the faithful servant of God was not without the highest reward—for the estimation of his sovereign, and the favor of the Holy See, might, in truth, be thus denominated. Indeed, as far as the inmost acknowledgment of the value of both could extend, he felt that they were no common remuneration, and he was grateful. But when, as a testification of the one and the other, the emperor held out the mitre to his acceptance, he shrank from the dignity with characteristic greatness of soul, and replied, "that he had been called by God to the Society of Jesus, not to receive honors and distinctions, but to practise poverty, and lead a life of humility." †

It was the desire of Ferdinand to appoint Bobadilla as a theologian in the Council of Trent, but finding his services so indispensable in the camp, he did not deem it prudent to remove him. Mean-

---

* Id. n. 57.

† Testatus se a Deo non ad honorem et amplitudinem, sed ad paupertatis humilitatem obscuramque potius vitam fuisse vocatum. Id. n. 58. Who now will presume to assert, that the followers of Ignatius were ambitious and power-loving men?

while, the justice of Heaven, as if conspiring with the efforts of the monarch and the solicitude of the Sovereign Pontiff, fell suddenly and heavily upon the author of all the calamities and errors which afflicted and agitated both Church and State. Luther, the apostate monk, after indulging freely and gayly in the luxuries of a supper, and spending the evening, as he was wont, to a very late hour in amusement, was seized with a mortal illness, during the night, and plunged into eternity.*

---

* Orlandinus, in speaking of this event, makes use of very strong, and, to the superficial admirer of Luther, very harsh language. But he speaks as a faithful historian, a contemporary, and under a perfect knowledge of all the facts and circumstances connected with his pretended Reformation. The best modern writers on this subject, even among Protestants, agree, in the main points, with Orlandinus: and concur with him in the conviction, that Martin Luther was a scourge to religion, and a man disgraced with the worst crimes. In confirmation of this, we need refer only to his own contemporaries and fellow-reformers. Hospinian declared that *he was absolutely mad:* that "he combated truth against all justice, and against the cry of his own conscience."

Œcolampadius affirmed that he was "puffed up with pride and arrogance, and seduced by Satan."

Zuinglius averred, that "the Devil had made himself master of Luther to such a degree, as to make one believe that he wished to gain entire possession of him."

But alas! the evil which he occasioned did not expire with him. The seed of error and disunion which his recreant hands scattered over the field of the Church took root, deep root, and the fruit was bitter and noxious indeed. The storm of the Reformation had raged violently in Germany, and, in its fury, overturned many of the time-honored and consecrated institutions of Catholic antiquity. "Everywhere," exclaims Orlandinus, "we behold altars laid low, monasteries desecrated and destroyed, sacred things profaned, and the dire vestiges of the most horrible crimes impressed upon the fairest portions of Europe. Wherefore," he adds, "it becomes our members to unite their strongest energies in order to extirpate, if possible, the fatal evil; for they may rest assured that a war has only commenced against the Catholic Church which will continue for ages."*

A veridical prophet has he, unfortunately, proved. Three centuries have witnessed the fatal battle

---

Calvin said that Luther had done nothing to the purpose ..... called his school a *pigsty*, addressed him with the courteous epithet of *dog, madman, huge beast*, &c., &c. See the "Amicable Discussion," tom. i. p. 69, 70.

* Id. n. 59. Here is the secret of the enmity of Protestantism to the Society of Jesus, which was established for the avowed purpose of warring against its errors.

which the spirit of the Reformation has been carrying on against the spirit of Truth and Union: a battle which has covered the world with devastation, crimsoned nations with blood, retarded the advancement of light, letters, morals, civilization, and liberty. This is no exaggerated or unjustifiable language. The entire world begins to feel its truth, while the most learned and candid Protestants themselves deplore the event, as uncalled for and unnecessary, and fraught with miserable consequences.* Would to God, that they who have begun to trace back their way to the ancient Catholic Church, may not desist from their labors until they bring about a perfect union with the Supreme Head on earth, the Vicar of Jesus Christ !

The war in Germany had now ceased. The Duke of Saxony and the landgrave had yielded to the victorious power of the emperor, and the Catholic cause began to flourish anew. Bobadilla's zeal glowed out with intense fervor. At Passau, he preached, during Lent, in the Latin language, in presence of the amiable prelate ; and exerted all his eloquence, likewise, at Ratisbonne, where many of the senators and citizens were infected

---

* See Ward's "Ideal of a Christian Church."

with the Lutheran errors. Such was the efficacy of his discourses, that he obtained a public and solemn celebration in thanksgiving for the emperor's triumph over the enemies of the Church and empire, and effected the restoration of many Catholic ceremonies which had so long been suspended.* To build up again what had been overturned and ruined by the fury of the Reformation, he went from place to place, visited church after church, remaining stationary nowhere, but, like a true Apostle, and a true Jesuit, fulfilling his vocation by traversing various parts for the promotion of God's greater glory.† Checked in his ardent course by the hand of sickness, he returned to Vienna, where Religion had resumed her pristine reign and ancient magnificence.

At Cologne, too, a fairer aspect began to appear : Hermannus, the long vacillating, but, at length, unfaithful Bishop, was driven from his see. In a former chapter, I had occasion to bring this personage before the reader's attention, and to show how lubriciously he had comported himself

---

* Lib. vii. n. 39.

† "Nostræ vocationis est diversa loca peragrare," is one of the cardinal maxims of the Society, embodied by Ignatius in his general rules.

in his relation with Peter Faber.* He now threw off the mask, and avowed himself a Lutheran. In consequence of which apostasy, he was deposed and degraded by the Sovereign Pontiff; and in his place was substituted Adolphus, of the ancient family of the Counts of Scaueburg, a man adorned with great personal qualifications, and a staunch asserter of the religion of his ancestors. With his exertions, Bobadilla, and the Society generally, co-operated firmly; and, with the blessing of Heaven, they produced, in a short time, a general change throughout the German empire.† Bobadilla, whilst he did not cease preaching to the Spanish and Italian courtiers, or relax his devotion to the duties of the confessional, found leisure to compose several works on religious subjects. By the nobility he was emulously sought after; for they felt convinced, that if ever his labors had been necessary, they were, perhaps, more necessary this year than ever; when, after the victory obtained over the Lutheran insurgents, many of the ministers and leaders, even in Saxony, evinced a desire to return to the ancient faith. The number of those who abjured their errors is, indeed, extraordinary. Two of the electors, being at Augsburg

---

* See Chap. ii.   † Lib. vii. n. 40.

with their wives, during Lent, assisted during the whole of that penitential season at the solemnities of the Church. One of them—the Elector of Brandeburg—forbade the use of flesh-meat in his dominions; in conformity with the spirit of the Church, ordered the re-establishment of confessions, the frequentation of the Eucharist, and promised to restore, in due time, all the other religious ordinances and practices which the Reformation had ruthlessly swept away from the land. The example of the orthodox—especially of the Spanish and Italian nobles—was of great advantage to the Germans. In vast numbers, and with extreme fervor, did they crowd to the Lenten exercises, and perform acts of severe mortification, to the astonishment of the Lutherans. At Ulm, more than seven thousand Germans approached the holy table, and the august sacrifice of the Mass was again offered up, after having been long suppressed and forbidden.*

Bobadilla continued at Cologne until the year 1548, when, from motives of conscience, he found it necessary to depart for Rome. A work had recently been published explanatory of the Catholic doctrines and discipline, in which certain proposi-

---

* Lib. viii. n. 34.

tions were advanced, not in rigid conformity with sound principles—in the estimation of this profound theologian. He, consequently, ever acting under the influence of sacred duty, deemed himself obliged to object to it, which he did both in word and writing. Beloved, as he was by the court, nevertheless, with the view of establishing concord, before the emperor's departure into Belgium, the imperial ministers advised him to leave the kingdom : a sentence which he received with the more composure and resignation, as he regarded it more glorious to please God, in a just cause, than to yield to the caprice of men. The stand he took was confirmed by the Holy See, which could not but disapprove of the character of that concord ; and the magnanimity he displayed in the circumstances connected with his departure to the Eternal City, caused him to be received there with every mark of admiration and respect by the Sovereign Pontiff and the venerable Ignatius.*

---

* This book had been issued with the approbation of the emperor, who, however, referred its contents to the decision of the Council of Trent. The learned Catholic doctors, and especially Bobadilla, deemed it necessary to speak out forthwith, as some essential matters were, more or less, compromised. On this account he incurred the displeasure of the oscillating ministers, and was advised to quit the kingdom

At Rome, partly within doors and partly without, he strenuously labored, until, in company with Father Michael Ochioa, he set out for Naples, where they lodged with the Benedictine monks. Immediately he opened a course of lectures in the church, in which, three times a week, he explained the epistle of St. Paul to the Romans. As yet no college had been erected at Naples; and though such an establishment was vehemently desired by the citizens, the municipal officers and the nobility had not taken any measures to commence it. In the mean while, the season of Lent coming on, Bobadilla delivered the usual sermons in an elegant and elaborate style. The fruit evinced itself in the crowds that rushed to the sacred tribune.*

After Pentecost, he visited, not without great advantage, the neighboring dioceses, inflaming with devotion the hearts of the faithful by his fervid discourses, and instructing the children in the

---

The Holy See condemned the book, and sustained Bobadilla in the answer he had published against it. Consult *Graveson, Hist. Eccl.* tom. vii. p. 83.

This book was entitled "*Ad Interim*," and created a general scandal among all thinking Catholics. See Bartoli, lib. iii. p. 226. Id. n. 35.

* Lib. ix. n. 33.

elements of the catechism, and never for a moment deviating from the high and perfect standard of duty which he had prescribed for himself from the commencement of his career.*

The proper authorities having taken in hands the establishment of a college at Naples, it soon rose from its foundation—an ample and magnificent structure—and was finished in the year 1551.† Of this college, Andrew Oviedo had been appointed the first rector, with whom, for a space of time, Bobadilla was afterwards associated. But these two eminent men—both conspicuous for their sanctity, each in his own way—did not entertain a congenial sentiment with regard to the external apparatus of discipline. The former was considered rather rigid by the latter, who conceived that discipline should not consist so much in the minutiæ and details of the rules, as in a habit of solid virtue, and strict fulfilment of essential duty. Oviedo maintained a contrary opinion, in which he was supported by Ignatius, who took occasion to express how dangerous would be the experiment of disregarding small things, and scrupulously

---

* "Ubique semper strenuus," writes Orlandinus, "semper sui similis Bobadilla." Ibid.

† See the preceding chapter.

practising greater. The wise decision of the holy founder of the Institute has ever since governed his disciples. The lenity of Bobadilla will always be considered as a mere disposition of charity to others, whilst every circumstance in his life so convincingly bears testimony of extreme rigor towards his own person. If, then, in his estimation of the proper character of general principles of discipline, he fell into an error, it was an amiable error; and his obedience in submitting his own ideas to the wisdom of their common father, Ignatius, and ever after abiding by his decision, displays again before our view the original frankness and simplicity which marked and characterized his early life. It began in humility, and ended in obedience; admirable in both, and in both a perfect model of imitation for the Society to all succeeding times.*

---

* Bartoli does not hesitate to censure the conduct of Bobadilla, and comment on it with the freedom of a candid critic and historian. He attributes it to the *infocato spirito del Bobadiglia;* regretting "that he was not, when in peace, equal to himself, as when in war." Father Oviedo he styles, *uomo santo, e maestro di grande isperienza nelle cose dell' anima.* (P. 227.)

I do not enter into the very grave and singular dispute

which Bobadilla carried on after the death of Saint Ignatius with Laynez. It will be sufficient to remark with Bartoli, that it is passing strange to see that otherwise great and excellent man contending for a trifling superiority in his order, after having so generously repudiated the mitre and crozier, offered him by Ferdinand.

His exertions for the Church did not, however, relax during the remaining portion of his life. He survived three Generals besides Ignatius, and, worn out with labors, expired in peace at Loretto, on the 23d of September, A. D 1580. He was the last survivor of the nine. After his death, it was discovered from his manuscripts that he had delivered seventy-seven sermons in Italy, Sicily, and Dalmatia, and a hundred and fifty-eight in other places. He was eminent for his virtues, especially that of evangelical poverty. He often predicted that he would survive all his companions; and when jocosely asked why, in the papal brief in which the Institute was confirmed, his name was placed last, his answer was, because he would be the last one among them to die. See Tanner, p. 231.

SIMON RODRIGUEZ.

AND

HIS FIRST COMPANIONS.

CHAPTER VII.

SIMON RODRIGUEZ.

SIMON RODRIGUEZ.—Is numbered among the Nine. Is selected for the Indies. Departs to Portugal. Is there detained. Converts the Ambassador from the Indies. His trials at Lisbon. Is made Tutor to the Son of the King. Is created Provincial. Is called to Rome. Is appointed to preside over the Province of Aragon. Is recalled to Rome. His severe trials. His extreme humility. Another shining example to his brethren for all succeeding times.

AMONG the Alumni of the Academy of Philosophy at Paris, in the year 1528, there was a Portuguese in the flower of youth, and conspicuous for his brilliant talents. He held his place in that far-famed Institution by the special favor of his sovereign. His acquaintance with Ignatius was of an earlier date than that of Xavier, Laynez, or Bobadilla. And by associating with that holy and ardent servant of God, he caught, at once, the flame of sympathy, and felt his heart glowing with a desire to abandon all terrene objects, and dedicate himself to the perfect service of the Most High. To him he communicated his inmost sentiments, revealed his secret aspirations, and entered, with a sacred enthusiasm, into all his views and designs. Thus was added a sixth companion to the number already treated of—in the person of Simon Rodriguez, born of respectable parents, at Buzella, in Portugal.*

After the nine had formed themselves into a religious and organized body—under the obligation of vows which they made, and renewed—Divine Providence decreed that they should not remain in the capital of France, but should scatter themselves —and thus propagate the Society—over the world. A fierce war broke out, after the death of Francis Sporzia, between the Spaniards and French, on account of the principality of Milan; and the emperor, Charles V., had burst into the province with a powerful army. This was the cause why the first companions of Ignatius quitted Paris earlier than they otherwise would have done. Whatever remained of their effects, they distributed among the poor.; and in the month of December, 1556, the memorable dispersion occurred.†

---

* Orlandin. lib. i. n. 88. † Id. n. 104.

Clad in coarse long gowns—the ordinary form of dress among the Parisian Academicians—each carrying his own package of books, might have been seen these wondrous men, staff in hand, and barefoot, pursuing their arduous journey.

From the fatigue and hardship, Rodriguez fell ill, after having struggled onward four-and-twenty leagues. His feet were blistered and inflamed; his shoulders laid bare by the burden he bore, and his whole body bruised, from lying at night on the hard boards, or cold ground. Pained as he was from his sores, and wasted with fatigue, his only anxiety and complaint were, lest he might not be able to continue his way with his beloved brethren.

But God, who led them out of Paris, and sent his angels to guide and support them in their journey, did not forsake his servants. Rodriguez recovered almost suddenly, and with incredible vigor and alacrity, was enabled to follow on. Every day the three who were in priestly orders—Faber, Jaius, and Broëtus—offered the sacrifice of the Mass, and the others received the holy communion. Morning and evening, they allotted a space of time for meditation and prayer; and on the road, either chanted psalms, or entertained one another with spiritual and salutary conversation;

and by this pleasing variety relieved the tedium of their journey.*

Having subdued one threatening difficulty, Rodriguez was assaulted, with greater violence, by another. He was followed by three young men on horseback, who having heard of his intention at Paris, hurried thither, with great speed, in order to dissuade him from it; and learning that he had left the capital, pursued him in hot haste. Of them, one was his brother, and the other a fellow-townsman and friend. With all the arts of persuasion they besought him to change his mind; reminded him of the bright hopes that were before him, and entreated him not to rashly waste away his youth in danger, poverty, and ignominy. They called to his remembrance the favor of the king, which he had already liberally experienced in his education, and menaced him with disgrace, and the just punishment of what they termed ingratitude.

The noble heart of Rodriguez was not to be moved by such expostulations. What recked he

---

* Id. n. 110, 111. In ipso itinere vel ex psalmis decantabant aliquid, vel de Deo agitabant inter sese dulcia et salutaria colloquia: hâc perenni vicissitudine tædia levabant itineris.

of the world's opinion, who had trodden it under his feet? or of the pageantry of life, or of the vain promises of ambition? All these he had sacrificed, and forsworn, when, at the shrine of the Virgin Mary, he told his vows of religious perfection He loved not father or mother more than Christ · and, therefore, was not unworthy of him. He looked not back, after putting his hand to the plough: he let the dead bury the dead. From his holy purpose, no persuasion could deter him. His brother, baffled in his design, retraced his way, sorrowful and disappointed, to Paris—he joyously and eagerly resumed his journey, with his companions.*

On entering Lorraine, they were exposed to new trials and dangers. That country was overrun with French troops, which had made a descent through it into Belgium, and spread such devastation around, that even the inhabitants themselves were afraid to intrust themselves on the high roads. How these pilgrim-Jesuits escaped was a subject of wonder to all: little reflecting " that they walked under the protection of Heaven."† For the soldiery, unrestrained by the

---

* Id. n. 112. Nondum edocti quantum sit in Dei tutelâ præsidii. † Id. n. 113.

principles of religion, unchecked by the fear of God, gave loose reins to their rapacity and passions. At Metz, which was surrounded with a military force, they were permitted, with much difficulty, to pass, under the name of French Academicians. They then proceeded through the frozen regions of Germany, in the depth of winter, in the midst of snow, until they reached Bâsle, a celebrated but unfortunate city, where hardly a vestige of the ancient religion could be perceived, among the fatal errors of the Reformation. There Carlostadius ruled with dogmatic tyranny—the opponent of Luther and of Rome. Cursed by the former, anathematized by the latter—and yet maintaining a kind of anomalous ascendency, in the vulgar estimation, over the one and the other. A reformist, on Protestant principles, and yet, on the same inconsistent and incoherent principles, disowned and persecuted by the Patriarch of all reformists.*

Headed by that recreant monk—the first to break his monastic vows—a number of Lutheran ministers met the strangers, and instantly proposed a controversy on the disputed points of doctrine. Their object was, evidently, not the desire of seek-

---

* See Audin's Life of Luther.

ing after truth, but of provoking a discussion; and consequently the Jesuits, anticipating no good from a contest of that description, contented themselves with an indirect refutation of the calumnies attributed to the Church, by their holy example, their salutary admonitions, their earnest instructions. So generally were they esteemed, wherever they tarried, that the hospitality not of Catholics only, but of Lutherans also, was generously extended to them.*

At Constance, wearied as they were from their journey, the curate, who had taken a wife to his arms, and thrown off the Divine yoke of the Church, came at the head of seven principal citizens, and challenged the strangers to a disputation. From this they found it impossible to escape, and, therefore, entered upon the controversy with so great ardor and erudition, that the apostate priest was driven to such an extreme, and pursued with such relentless vigor—especially by Laynez—that he was forced to exclaim: "I am hemmed in at all points! I know not which way to turn!" † "Why, then, do you follow that sect," retorted one of the Fathers, "which you are not able to defend?"

---

* Lib. i. n. 113.

† Includor undique, et ubi verser ignoro. Id. ibid.

"To-morrow," he savagely replied, "I will have you bound with irons, and will teach you how to abuse my sect."

He then abruptly left them, muttering, I know not what threats, in the German language. The Jesuits, rejoicing in their triumph over error, disregarded his threats; for, they were ready to lay down their lives, if necessary, for the faith. The rude menaces evaporated, however, in angry words and oaths.* On the following morning, they were merely required to depart from the city, under the guidance of an individual who treated them with kindness, and accompanied them, to the distance of eight miles, on their way.

In the year 1537 they arrived at Venice, and proceeded thence, through Ravenna and Ancona, to the Eternal City, where they were graciously received by the Sovereign Pontiff, Clement VII., as related above.†

The merit of Rodriguez could not be better understood, than from the fact, that on him Ignatius had originally fixed his eyes as a fit apostle to the

---

* Orlandinus expresses in graphic terms the fury of the minister: "Nescio quid germanicè cum jurgio effutiens," he writes. Ibid. n. 114.

† Chap. iv.

far-off and perilous mission of the East Indies : and his nomination was, not without mature reflection and deliberation, confirmed by the concurrence of all the other Fathers.*

He, accordingly, quitted Rome, and proceeded to Portugal by sea. After a short voyage, he reached Lisbon, where he found an individual waiting for him, sent by the king for the purpose of escorting him to the palace. But, requesting the messenger to return his heartfelt thanks to the monarch, he retired to Alcarer, laboring under a quartan fever. He had hardly been there eight days, before he was again sent for by the king, whose desire to see and converse with so extraordinary a man was not to be controlled. Rodriguez consented to gratify it, but on condition that he should be permitted to live according to the spirit of his order, and beg his bread from door to door. The public hospital was, therefore, assigned him for his residence : in which, besides attending the sick, he devoted himself to hearing confessions, and the care of souls.†

Three days later, he was joined by Xavier, who had made the journey by land. Both were invited

---

* Lib. ii. n. 87. † Id. n. 101.

to the palace, where the king and queen listened, with extreme attention and interest, to the history they gave of the rise, progress, institute, and scope of the Society, and the odium and persecution which it had already excited. Among the people, so sedulous was their zeal, so unremitting their exertions, for the salvation of men, that they went by the name of "the apostles." The king, seeing the unprecedented success of their ministry, by the advice and desire of the nobles, resolved to lay aside the project of the oriental mission, and to retain the Fathers in Portugal. Ignatius having been consulted, referred the matter to the Sovereign Pontiff, who left it entirely to the pleasure and determination of the monarch. This Ignatius expressed in a letter to the Fathers; proposing, at the same time, that all difficulty might by obviated by keeping Rodriguez in Portugal, and sending Xavier to the Indies. To this suggestion, the king made no objection, and Xavier was ordered to prepare for his embarkation. Rodriguez, however, after having sounded the intentions of the king, and finding that all hope of establishing a college in Portugal had, at least for the present, vanished, began to think of secretly flying from Lisbon, and sailing, with his companion, for the East. But this design he could not accomplish: and **submit-**

ting to the disposition of Providence, he remained in that city, devoting himself to the salvation of the people.* By his exertions, a House of Refuge was erected for the reception of unfortunate women, where they might not only reform their lewd and criminal habits, but, likewise, have the opportunity of practising piety and devotion. This institution was highly approved by the public, and extremely salutary, not only to the penitents themselves, but to the young men also, of the city, and especially of the university. He received into the Society several distinguished members, among whom were Melchior Nunnius, a celebrated canonist and jurist: Consalvez Silveria, son of the Count of Sortella, a youth of mature judgment, acute discernment, and naturally prone to piety—only in his twentieth year; and Melchior Carnerio, afterwards Bishop, and a devoted laborer in the island of Macao.*

With indefatigable zeal he advanced the cause of religion in the court, where his reputation for sanctity awakened a peculiar veneration for his person; and in the whole region, throughout which he spread the odor of his own example, gained over many souls to God, and dissipated every remnant

* Lib. iii. n. 44.   † Lib. iv. n. 55 56, 57, 58.

of prejudice against the Society from the minds of those who were once under its influence, especially in the university of Coimbra. Wherefore, animated by the general feeling, the king resolved to commence at once the erection of the college, over the building of which—not to cumber the Father's time with such an occupation—he placed, as superintendent, a skilful and accomplished architect. In order to allow them ample leisure and facilities of attending to their many and arduous duties, Rodriguez associated with the priests a certain number of lay-brothers, who, after the example of those selected by the apostles, should minister at the table, and take care of the domestic concerns.[*]

He excited, moreover, universal attention, by the conversion of the ambassador from the Indies to the court of Lisbon. He visited that remarkable stranger, and endeared himself to him in so intimate a manner, that the ambassador listened with interest and pleasure to the doctrines which he taught and explained, yielded to the power of truth, abandoned his idolatrous rites, and received baptism with great fervor and gratitude to God, who deigned, through the agency of Rodriguez, to bring

---

[*] Lib. iv. n. 59.

him out of darkness into "the admirable light" of the gospel.*

Saintly men must have their alternations of prosperity and persecution ; and from this rule Rodriguez could not be exempted. Calumnies of a serious nature were industriously propagated against him and the Society by a certain licentiate of the university of Coimbra, by the name of Ferdinand. With the most tranquil composure, and in the deepest silence, he bore them all ; although, by his influence with the king, he might have avenged his innocence with extreme severity. But instead of calling for a just retribution, he implored the monarch to pardon the culprit. The king's justice would not be propitiated even by the prayers of the innocent man. He condemned the base calumniator to be exiled from the kingdom. The nature of the calumnies was as follows : he accused the Society of having forged all the immunities and privileges which its members claimed, and Rodriguez personally with having asserted that they were subject to the Apostolic See only, and not to bishops or ordinaries, to whose tribunal

---

* Id. ibid. "Ergo," writes our author, "brevi, Deo collustrante, se dedit, et nefaria detestatus idola, veterem, per baptismum, abjecit Adam."

they were not amenable, by whose authority they were not obligated. Of being independent of all canonical discipline, and bound by no laws, but governed by the will of Rodriguez alone : who, were it not for the favor and protection of a few, and the flattery and applause of the ignorant, would long since have been deserted by his own, and opposed by the public. These and similar charges were alleged, which now fell, of themselves, to the ground. For, two letters of the Holy See, confirming the Institute of the Society, were exhibited, as well as the diploma by which the Sovereign Pontiff had adorned it with numerous and extraordinary privileges. Thus the cloud, which the spirit of jealousy had gathered around this holy order, was dispersed by the light of evidence and truth, and the Society and Rodriguez emerged from it more brilliantly than ever.*

The king reposed unbounded confidence in Rodriguez, and even condescended, when about selecting ambassadors and prelates to assist at the great Council of Trent, to consult him by letter on that important matter. Nor was this the only singular token of his veneration for him : there was

---

* Lib. iv. n. 133.

another, if not of a higher, at least of a more personal character, namely, the intrusting to his care the young prince, whose education hitherto had been watched over by John Suarez, afterwards Bishop of Coimbra. The permission of Ignatius was asked: who, though unwilling that his disciples should become too familiar with the courts of monarchs, could not, in this particular case—considering the extraordinary piety and numberless acts of benevolence of the king towards the Society—withhold his approbation.*

The number of candidates for the new order was very great; and so widely had it already spread itself over Portugal, that, in the year 1546, that kingdom was erected into a province, of which Rodriguez was created the first Provincial. He was yet—having in his charge the prince—residing at court: but his spirit and influence were diffused in every part, in aid, both of the temporal and spiritual wants of the faithful. Amid the splendor of the court he looked, with undazzled eye, upon the vanity it revealed; and his heart, long since detached from the world, grew, if possible, more insensible to its fascinations. It was still fixed upon his first destination

---

* Lib. v. n. 57.

It yearned to be emancipated from the gorgeous trammels with which, by circumstances, it had been enveloped, and to pant—in the liberty of an apostle's mission in uncivilized lands—for the distant shores of India.* Or, at least, if he could not advance thus far, to go as far, at least, as the regions of Brazil, which had recently been discovered by the Portuguese. But the ways of Heaven are not always conformable with the inclinations of the human mind; and provided to them it submit with the acquiescence becoming a Christian, the more abundant will its merit prove. The soul of Rodriguez burned for perils and privations in far-off missions—and could it have put on the "wings of the morning," would have flown away to the remotest East: and, nevertheless, obedient and resigned to the supreme will of God, who takes care of the destinies of all mankind, he remained in his office and at his post, and by his wise administration contributed to the happiness and welfare of all under his charge.†

Towards the end of the year 1550, Ignatius summoned in the city of Rome a Council, at which all the principal Fathers from the various

---

* Id. n. 58. † Lib viii. n. 74, 75.

parts of Europe were required to be present. At the bidding of their saintly Founder and Superior —putting aside every inconvenience, except what might accrue to religion—as many as could possibly absent themselves from their different avocations instantly obeyed the call. Among these were Araozius, Strada, Oviedo, and Borgia, from Spain; Laynez from Sicily; Salmeron, Miona, Frusius, and Polancus, and Rodriguez; all, except Strada, bound by the solemn vows of profession. The last-mentioned Father had been sent for expressly, by Ignatius, who desired particularly to have him among the number to be convened, aware of the light which his long experience in a difficult position in Portugal would shed over their deliberations, and, at the same time, that he might take back to his province the uniform standard of discipline which was observed in that—the fountain-source—of Rome.*

The object which Ignatius had in view in the convocation of this Council, was to submit to its inspection and consideration the Constitutions which, at the urgent solicitation of the first Fathers and of all the Society, he had drawn up. These were subjected to the scrutiny of each, with

---

* Lib x. n. 47.

the privilege of suggesting any change or addition Their saintly author possessed too deep a knowledge of the human heart, and was governed by too much prudence, not to perceive the advantage that would accrue to his work, by having it approved by those who were to be regulated by it.

His Constitutions were designed for all nations, and to be rendered compatible with every variety of habits and customs, and every form of government, and every future generation ; and, therefore, he desired to have them stamped with the sanction of individuals of various provinces and countries : not only of those present, but likewise of all scattered through the world, whose occupations prevented them from attending at the Council. By all, these admirable Constitutions—which had cost Ignatius so much time, study, and prayer—were read and approved ; yet, their holy author, in order to mature them thoroughly, and leave them still open for amendment, did not publish them until the year 1553.* He then sent them to Spain, Portugal, and some other provinces, not, indeed, as perfect, but to be tried, in their application to circumstances and their adaptation to places : **and not to be considered binding or indispensable,**

---

* Id. n. 50.

until they should have merited the approbation of the entire Society. This approbation was solemnly given, in the year 1558, in a Council of Fathers, held for the purpose of electing a General, after the demise of Ignatius.* Laynez was chosen: when they were again subjected to the revision and re-examination of all assembled, and unanimously approved and confirmed. Four Cardinals were, afterwards, designated by Paul IV., to pass their judgment on them, by whom they were returned, without any change or the alteration of a single word.

In the year 1552, so great was the increase in the members of the Society in Spain, that it became necessary to divide that province into two: of one part Anthony Araozius, who before had presided over the whole, was left Provincial; of the other—the kingdom of Aragon—Simon Rodriguez was appointed, having been removed from Portugal.† Of this change the occasion was, because in Portugal the Society had been planted and matured under circumstances different from those in any other country. For, as everywhere else it had been founded in poverty, in troubles, and in all manner of suffering, here, on account of the

---

* Id. n. 51.　　　　　† Lib. xii. n. 53.

friendship of the monarch, it was quite the contrary. And as the immense harvest, now whitening through the boundless regions of the East, invited to an increase of missionary labor, fostered under the munificent influence of the sovereign's favor, numbers of candidates were received into the ranks of the Society, and the Alumni of the College of Coimbra amounted to a hundred and forty. As yet no uniform discipline had been framed for the noviceship, and the domestic rules were few. Rodriguez labored to govern after the model of Ignatius, on which he himself had been formed: but yielding to his too indulgent and lenient disposition, his government assumed a character which, though not remiss, was easily abused by a numerous community, made up of individuals of every variety of temperament, and most of them in the ardor of youth. He was beloved by all as their kind and common father: to the more careless he was endeared by his meekness, while the more rigid and wiser members did not criticise the conduct of their companions, much less find fault with the mildness of their Superior.*

It was under circumstances of this delicate na-

---

* Id. n. 53, 54, 55.

ture that the wisdom of Ignatius most perfectly displayed itself. Aware of the exalted merit and qualities of Rodriguez, and yet watchful over the stern requirements which must be maintained by his order, he deemed it proper to remove that saintly man to a sphere more appropriate to the bent of his disposition, and better adapted to the temper of his discipline. He left him to choose the mission of Brazil, which he had long sighed for, or the office of Provincial to the new-formed province, and addressed letters of this his intention to the king of Spain, his queen, Catherine, and the Cardinal Henry. At the same time, he stationed Michael Turrianus and Francis Borgia in Portugal. The king could not oppose the change, coming, as it did, with so much wisdom, and desired with so much earnestness by Rodriguez, as well as by Ignatius. For, to Rodriguez, the tidings were most acceptable. In token of his joy, he was seen to press to his lips and breast the letter that liberated him from so heavy a burden, so awful a responsibility. To his successor, Muroni, he instantly forwarded the diploma of his appointment, and to the Alumni of the College of Coimbra wrote an affectionate epistle, conjuring them to pardon the faults and errors he might have committed during his administration. Muroni received his papers with tears, dreading the mighty yoke which was laid upon his shoulders as successor to Rodriguez. This venerable Father —having taken all circumstances into consideration—did not deem himself justifiable, ardently as he panted for the Indies, in quitting Europe; and he was, therefore, created, according to the original view of Ignatius, Provincial of Aragon.*

In this capacity, he continued for the space of about one year; after which, he retired to Lisbon on account of ill-health, and was ordered thence, by Ignatius, to Rome. There were, in that capital of the Christian world, in the year 1554, when Rodriguez repaired thither, about a hundred and forty members of the Society; although many had, during the course of the year, been sent to other cities to establish colleges and communities. The Roman College enjoyed—and deserved—the highest renown for learning. In the Church of the Professed House, *theses* were publicly disputed, touching all the branches taught by the Society, leaving to all the spectators the privilege of entering the lists. So great was the crowd which these disputations attracted, that for eight days not a single member of the college

---

* Id. p. 56.

could have an opportunity of proposing an objection.*

The Professed House, though already enlarged, was much too small for its inmates. Ignatius determined to add amply to its dimensions, or rather almost to rebuild it entirely. For this purpose, he invited Cardinal Bartholomew Cucuanus to place the foundation-stone, in presence of Alphonsus Alencastrio, the orator of the king of Portugal, and many illustrious noblemen. The Cardinal, who had a profound reverence for Ignatius, refused to perform the ceremony, observing that it would better become him, who had laid the foundation of so celebrated an order, to place the corner-stone of the Professed House. Ignatius, however, modestly persisting in his first determination, the good cardinal insisted upon his acting, at least, in conjunction with himself; and both at the same time handed over the stone to the skill of the architect.†

I must not omit in this, its proper place, a fact of a very remarkable nature, which occurred at this epoch in the Society. At the suggestion of the king of Portugal, Pope Julius required Ignatius to send some Fathers into Ethiopia, out of

---

* Lib. xiv. n. 1. † Id. n. 2.

which number one should be created bishop and patriarch. Ever obedient to the will of the Supreme Head of the Church on earth, Ignatius immediately complied with his command, and nominated, as worthy of the exalted honor, a learned and holy man, John Nunnius, and designated two others as his companions—viz., Andrew Oviedus, and Melchior Carnerius; of whom the former—after struggling against the dignity with all his might—was, by the command of the Sovereign Pontiff, compelled to be consecrated bishop.*

In the mean time, Heaven had in store a severe trial—still more to purify his affections and enrich his merits—for Simon Rodriguez. A few pages above, the reader saw that the too lenient disposition of that excellent disciple of Ignatius had suffered the reins of government to become rather loose in the province of Portugal. A visitor of the name of Consalvi had been sent thither to take cognizance of affairs, and he now returned to Rome, confirming the complaints that had been made. Ignatius,

---

* Lib. xiv. n. 4. "Eum item per litteras hortatus est Ignatius, ut teneret in recusando constantiam." But when the voice of God spoke definitely through the Pontiff, both were obliged to yield. " Verum Pontifex imperavit."

with his wonted prudence, referred the whole matter to a tribunal composed of several Professed Fathers, empowering them to investigate, but reserving to himself the right of animadversion. After calm deliberation, accompanied by fervent prayer, they decided that their beloved brother, Father Rodriguez, was not without blame. The sentence was pronounced in presence of Rodriguez, who received it with a humility worthy his calling and his heroic virtues. Before it was published, he had seen it in writing, and approved it: after hearing it read, he fell at the feet of his brethren, and testified his readiness to submit to any penance. Ignatius, delighted with his simplicity and humility, enjoined no severer penalty upon him than not to return to Portugal. In this manner, Ignatius, without respect to individuals, sustained the vigor of discipline, and yet, breathing nothing but love for his children, was perfectly satisfied with the submission of Rodriguez; transmitting thus to posterity a twofold lesson : one, the necessity of keeping the sinews of government well strung, under all circumstances ; the second, of the necessity of superiors acting always under the holy influence of charity in their relations with those whom they are appointed to govern. As for Rodriguez himself, nowhere does he appear more admirable or great, than at the feet of his judges, acknowledging his error, and craving forgiveness for the disedification which his example, perhaps, might have given to his brethren.*

In order to atone for his imperfection—which, in truth, was the mere result of his amiable qualities too injudiciously infused into the spirit of his administration—Rodriguez obtained permission to go to Jerusalem, with the view of establishing a college in that holy city. He departed from Rome, accompanied by another Father. But at Venice he was taken ill, and was compelled to give up the great and interesting project. He recovered, however, and survived, persevering in the practice of all the virtues proper to his vocation, until the year 1579. On the fifteenth of July, having received the viaticum and extreme unction, with the most fervent sentiments of piety and devotion, he breathed out his soul into the hands of his Creator. His venerable remains were followed to the grave by an immense concourse of people of all orders, by whom his demise was deplored as a common and public calamity.†

---

* Id. n. 5, 6. † Tanner, p. 160.

CLAUDIUS JAIUS.

CHAPTER VIII.

CLAUDIUS JAIUS.

CLAUDIUS JAIUS.—He joins Ignatius. Is sent to Brescia and Favenza. Goes to Germany. Is persecuted. Labors at Ratisbonne and Ingoldstadt. Succeeds Eckius in the Chair of Theology. Attends the Diet of Worms. Founds Seminaries. Is sought after by various Princes. Is sent to the Council of Trent. Refuses the See of Trieste. Goes to Ferrara, at the invitation of the Duke. Goes to Augsburg. Thence to Vienna. Dies. His eulogy. His monument. His immortality.

THE precise time in which the seventh Companion—a native of the Diocese of Geneva—associated himself with Ignatius cannot be ascertained. Orlandinus himself is at a loss to designate it, merely remarking, that it must have been previously to the year 1536.* With the others, he was present at the renovation of their vows made on Mont-Matre: and devoted himself to the spiritual exercises un-

---

* Claudius Jaius Gebennensis theologus item ac Sacerdos —quanquam certum tempus non planè constat—ad alios septem .... accesserat. Lib. i. n. 101.

der the guidance of his Holy Father, in which he passed three days in severe and continual austerities, eating nothing, except what was necessary to sustain life. Jaius caught the spirit of his Institute, and to exalted piety added extraordinary prudence. His first mission afforded him a signal opportunity of exercising both. In the town of Balnerregia, in Tuscany, a serious and fearful discord had arisen between the clergy and the people—to allay which he was chosen as an umpire, and deputed thither on this difficult and delicate errand. On his arrival, which, at first, seemed not to be too acceptable to either party, he convened them together, and, after giving the reasons why he was sent among them, conciliated, at once, the good-will, and secured the confidence, of all who were present. Thousands flocked to hear his sermons; and so great was the number of those who had recourse to the sacred tribunal of Confession, that he was obliged to spend day and night in receiving them. As to the disputes, to arrange which was the object of his mission, they were completely removed, to the universal gratification of all concerned. Nor was the reconciliation merely of a cold and formal nature: but the parties, on the contrary, might have been seen pressing one another to their bosoms; and in ratification of their restored friendship they received the Holy Eucharist—the source and pledge of supernatural peace.*

This great end being triumphantly accomplished, Jaius repaired to Brescia, where the "enemy" had scattered the noxious seed of heresy, for the extirpation of which he determined to exert all his energies. In this enterprise he consumed the entire year (1539) with consoling effect. Thence he proceeded on a similar undertaking to Favenza, where, by his indefatigable efforts and exemplary deportment, he restored the ancient discipline of the Church, and instituted a sodality, of which the members bound themselves to approach the holy table at least once a week, and to perform, with peculiar devotion, offices and acts of mercy and charity in the city. He appointed a Physician out of that body, and also an Advocate, who contributed their services gratuitously, the former to the destitute sick, the latter to the poor in cases of lawsuits. Some collected alms for the needy; some acted as tutors for orphan-boys; some provided for helpless females; and all exhibited so striking an example, and spread abroad so benign an influence, that, ere long, the city—recently disgraced by the dissolute and irreligious tendencies of its inhabitants, now

---

* Lib. ii. n. 93.

assumed a splendid position in the eyes of the Church, and in the gaze of the world.*

From this field of his labors, the Sovereign Pontiff destined him to depart to a more extensive and important arena. He was commanded to accompany Bobadilla to Ratisbonne, to succeed in the place of Faber, who was sent into Spain.†

Without delay, he entered, with extreme alacrity and intense fervor, upon his arduous duties. Often did he visit the Bishop, and remind him of his duty. The Canons he incited to every good action: and in his own dwelling, stimulated all who advised with him to virtue and piety, either by salutary admonitions or by the spiritual exercises. He addressed the senate in a strain of noble eloquence, and everywhere planted, with the sweat of his brow, the good grain in these vast and neglected fields of the Church.‡ His efforts, however, to remove from the office of preaching a Lutheran minister who had ingratiated himself into general

---

* Quin ea, quam dixi, sodalitas illas sibi partes quoque imposuit, ut peculiari quodam studio misericordiæ tuerentur officia...... ut viderentur omnia Faventiæ priscâ quâdam religione fervere. Lib. iii. n. 25. Was not this, in its largest acceptation, the spirit of the Gospel?

† Lib. iii. n. 25.

‡ Id. n. 62.

favor, excited the odium of the reformed clergy against him. The apostles of truth are never exempt from trials and persecutions. Jaius had now to bear his cross, with which—keeping before his eyes the example of his Divine model, JESUS—he continued on his way rejoicing. So inveterate did the hatred of the Lutherans become, that they threatened to precipitate him into the Danube : to which menace his only reply was, that "he could reach Heaven as well by water as by land."* Nor was he the less undaunted when informed that he was in danger of being poisoned, or certainly driven into exile. His courageous example was regarded with admiration by all good men, especially by the Catholics and the Bishop, who rejoiced to see him defy the malicious schemes of the wicked, and remain, supported by the consciousness of innocence and truth, in the midst of the snares that were spread around his path. With unshrinking intrepidity, he began a public explanation of the Epistle of Saint Paul to the Galatians, which was attended by a vast concourse of all ranks and orders, and even by many Lutherans also. And though in that city there were already established two Lutheran

---

* Respondebat intrepidus in cœlum se tam facile aquâ quam terrâ ire posse. Id. ibid.

churches, in which discourses fraught with errors were assiduously delivered, nevertheless, with such perseverance, and in such numbers, did the citizens crowd to his lectures, that he could not interrupt them, even during the usual autumnal vacation.*

The effects of the so-called Reformation had been severely felt over all Europe: its bitter fruits had been tasted, presented to the unwary and unstable under the most specious and inviting appearances. The cry of liberty was raised: but it meant licentiousness for those only who raised that cry, while their victims were ground down under despotic bigotry and cruel fanaticism. Evangelical doctrines were the boast of recreant and faithless monks and priests, who certainly were determined not to be restrained by the evangelical counsels: and these vaunted doctrines—all negative, all Protestant—multiplied and increased with terrible and pernicious fecundity: giving birth to Socinianism, Arianism, and latitudinarianism of every hue and shape, and at the same time generating disorder, schism, anarchy, and desolation.† In Germany, the

---

* Id. n. 63. Ut ne per autumni quidem vindemias, ut mos erat, intermitti sacram illam paterentur explanationem.

† The picture of these times, as drawn by the caustic and

evil had seated itself so deeply in the nation's heart, that Jaius, Faber, and Bobadilla, in their letters to Ignatius, declared that nothing short of the Divine

---

graphic pen of Erasmus, in a letter, written in 1525, is most melancholy. "One sect," he writes, "will not hear of baptism; another rejects the sacrament of the Eucharist; a third teaches that a new world will be created by God before the day of judgment; another that Christ is not God: in short, one this, another that. There are almost as many creeds as individuals. There is no fool, who, when he dreams, does not believe that he is visited by God, and that he is endowed with the gift of prophecy."

And again: "When the Apostles tamed serpents, healed the sick, raised the dead, men were forced to believe in them, although they announced incomprehensible mysteries. Among these Doctors, who tell us so many wonderful things, is there one who has been able to cure a sick horse? Give me miracles..... What must I believe, when I see, in the midst of contradictory doctrines, all laying claim to dogmatical infallibility, and rising up with oracular authority against the doctrines of those who have preceded us? Is it probable, that, during thirteen centuries, God should not have raised up, among the numerous holy personages he has given to his Church, a single one to whom he revealed his true doctrine?" *De Libero arbit.*

The curious discussion, as related by Audin, pp. 322, &c., between Luther and Carlostadius, bears testimony of the spirit by which both—as well as all their associates—were actuated.

mercy could rescue and save that fated land. The reformists traversed the empire, with untiring and fatal strides, strewing their errors whithersoever they went, and leading the people captive to their pretended authority: whereas, many of those who were appointed watchmen on the towers of the Church, either deserted their posts, or stood idly and negligently looking on the spreading calamity. The clergy had, for the most part, lost their energy, and given up all vigilance. The blind lust of gain, the mad determination of living without restraint, threw every thing into dire confusion.* A sad picture, but not the less faithful, of the state of Germany, when Jaius and the other Fathers of the Society first dared to encounter the evil in that afflicted land. They could be deterred by no obstacle or opposition: neither by the magnitude of the enterprise, nor the impending dangers, nor the number and hostility of their powerful adversaries. To the newly-broached heresies, they boldly opposed the clearest truths of antiquity; and to the poison of error, applied with skilful and fearless assiduity the antidote of pure and undefiled religion. With the ministers and chiefs of the sect, they did not, when duty required it, flinch from controversy; nor

---

* Lib. iv. n. 19, 20.

did they cease to warn and animate the Catholic pastors and prelates of their solemn duties, and of the necessity they were now under—more than at any other time—of watching over their flocks, and preserving them intact from the pervading contagion.*

Jaius, as before stated, was now at Ratisbonne, in which, being a free city and immediately subject to the emperor alone, the Catholic cause suffered the more severely, as the magistrate had not conspired with the Bishop in the extirpation of heresies. On the contrary, the senate seemed to favor the novelties, by not using the influence it possessed to prevent their growth. I do not mean to insinuate that violence and persecution should have been recurred to. Far from it. Such weapons but ill become a Christian State, and should never be wielded by any power. Nor do I find fault with the toleration of Lutheranism by the senate, and its protecting those citizens who should choose to worship in Lutheran temples. But there was another kind of power, which it should have exerted against the inroads of the Reformation. Namely, a wakeful solicitude, and ardent zeal, in behalf of the ancient doctrines which they had received, as a sacred heirloom,

---

* Id. n. 21.

from the orthodoxy and piety of their forefathers; and which were a guaranty not only for the peace of their consciences, but, likewise, the safety of the commonwealth.*

---

* Protestantism has been intolerant, from the period of the Reformation. It was born with the germ of persecution in its breast, and wherever it gained the ascendency, and possessed the power, proscription and disaster were the fatal consequences. I make no rash assertion. The annals of history are my vouchers. The lives of the Reformers themselves—as well as their own acts and writings—are the indisputable testimonies to which I appeal.

Hear how Roscoe, in his *Leo X.*, censures "the severity with which Luther treated those who unfortunately happened to believe too much on the one hand, or too little on the other, and could not walk steadily on the hairbreadth line which he had presented." Dr. Sturges, a violent Protestant, admits that "Luther was, in his manners and writings, coarse, presuming, and impetuous."—*Reflections on Popery.*

Robelot, in his great work, "*Influence de la Reformation,*" p. 71, relates that the Reformers met at Cadan, and declared that they would not *tolerate*, or suffer to *remain in the country*, any sect not Lutheran.

The Convention of Smalkald, held in 1536, proclaimed that "to believe that any one who opposed the Reformation *should be tolerated*, was an error!"—Robelot, *ut supr.*

A Synod at Hamburg, in the same year, decreed, that "whoever rejects baptism, or transgresses the orders of the

The difficulty position in which Jaius found himself under these circumstances, and the onerous task he had undertaken to achieve, can easily be

---

magistrates, or preaches against taxes, or teaches community of goods, or usurps the priesthood, ... or sins against faith, *shall be punished with death.*"—Idem, ibid.

From these few authorities, the reader may now form his own judgment, whether it was bigotry, or prejudice, or rashness in me to assert, that intolerance and proscription were the characteristics of Protestantism, in the days of the mis named Reformation. In England, the unrestrained use of the Bible was forbidden under Henry VIII. "He had," says Dr. Lingard, "formerly sanctioned the publication of an English Bible, and granted permission to all his subjects to read it; but it had been represented to him that even the authorized version was disfigured by unfaithful renderings; and that the indiscriminate lecture of the Scriptures had not only generated a race of teachers who promulgated doctrines the most strange and contradictory, but had taught ignorant men to discuss the meaning of the inspired writings in alehouses and taverns. To remedy the first of these evils, it was enacted that the version of Tyndall should be disowned altogether, as *crafty, false,* and *untrue;* and that the authorized translation should be published with note or comment. To obviate the second, the *permission of reading the Bible in public to others was revoked;* that of reading it to private families was *confined to persons of rank,* .... any other woman or artificer, apprentice, journeyman, servant, or laborer, who should presume to open the sacred volume, was

imagined. His opponents were many and active, and to his tireless exertions on the side of truth, they opposed an indomitable reaction on the side of error. Still, by his admirable discourses—which were frequented and appreciated as well by Lutherans as Catholics—and by his other missionary functions, he preserved thousands from contamination, and brought back many to the "one fold." He implored the Bishop to take every means to reform and purify the morals of the people, but to execute this duty in so conciliatory and prudent a manner, as not to give them any offence. The senate, likewise, he exhorted and entreated not to connive at the increasing errors of the reformists. His zeal and influence stirred up the angry passions of these men; and the persecution commenced against him, the preceding year, was now renewed with deadlier acrimony. But the ægis of Providence not only covered him from the arrows of their revenge; they were blunted in their force, and fell innocuously at his feet. Hatred he overcame by charity; insolence by mansuetude;

---

made liable for each offence to one month's imprisonment." Such was the boasted liberty, such the supposed enlightening and emancipating spirit of the Reformation! See Stat. 34 Henry VIII., I.

and he persevered in his station, preaching, counselling, suffering, and displaying heroic virtues, which commanded the reluctant admiration and respect even of his most inveterate opponents.*

Some, however, continued to harass and persecute him. Especially when, at his suggestion, the Bishop promulgated in Germany the jubilee extended by the Sovereign Pontiff to the whole Christian world. The infinite good which this measure produced was hailed with rapture by the Catholics, but viewed with jealousy by the Lutherans. Yet, in return, Jaius evinced towards them the greatest meekness and the purest charity: and the better to adapt himself to their feelings, to open an easier avenue to their minds, and to make himself all to all, he applied himself—though now advanced in years—to the study of the German language.†

Among his deadliest adversaries, two are particularly designated by Orlandinus: one a physician, the other an apostate and married friar of the

---

* Perseveravitque monitis et consiliis optimè quoque de malevolis et ingratis in sua statione mereri. Orlandin., *ut supr.* n. 22.

† Id. n. 23. Our author styles the study of that language 'linguæ asperæ disciplinam."

order of St. Francis. The former was the first who ventured to persuade the senate to introduce communion under both kinds. The latter, having thrown off the habit and the cowl, assumed the character of a Lutheran preacher, and the appendage of a handsome wife. These Jaius had long and earnestly endeavored to reclaim from their evil ways. But they repaid his zeal and charity with animosity and hate, until the hand of Divine vengeance fell dreadfully upon them both: for both were carried off by a sudden and frightful death.*

The senate was not, however, terrified by this manifest visitation of God's justice on these unfortunate victims. On the contrary, it seemed to rush more recklessly into the precipice, until nearly the whole city, as Jaius bitterly lamented, wondered to see itself infected with the spirit of Lutheranism. The efforts of one distinguished personage to stay the evil cannot be sufficiently praised. William, Duke of Bavaria, comes down to Catholic posterity with a name hallowed and renowned by his unshaken constancy in defending the ancient faith. And although to some who may not take into consideration all the circumstances

---

* Ibid. n. 24.

of the case, he may appear to have enacted too severe a law against the innovators, yet, when the peace and order, the happiness and perpetuity of his government were at stake, he felt himself justified in protecting and securing these for the many, by menacing, even by capital punishment, the lives of a few. Such was the nature of the heresies of the sixteenth century, that they threw open, at one and the same time, the gates of the sanctuary and the state to disorder and licentiousness. They were not then, as they now are, mere human theories conflicting with Divine convictions. The warfare between them was not a spiritual conflict: but it became a conflict between two temporal powers: the new one struggling to inoculate the old with a blighting virus of innovation: and the old resisting the destructive violence of the new, by opposing, in self-defence, a counteracting violence. The character of the warfare between error and truth has, in the lapse of years, undergone an essential change, which, we may fervently trust, will preclude, forever, the necessity of capital enactments, or of personal proscriptions.

The decree of the Duke against the intrusion of Lutheranism into his dominions was attended by such fortunate results, that, "to this day," writes

Orlandinus, "Bavaria has escaped the tumults and horrors of a civil war."*

Jaius mourned the ruins in which the Church of Ratisbonne was laid; and to restore which he had spared no pains, and had given himself no repose, during the space of two years. He was now commanded to extend his labors to another direction. For the Apostolic Nuncio, departing from Ratisbonne to Nuremberg, required Jaius to accompany him thither. Hardly had he commenced his mission at Nuremberg, before he was sent to Ingolstadt, where, notwithstanding the precaution of the Duke of Bavaria, the errors of Lutheranism began to insinuate their poisonous influence. Here he spent the summer; and whilst he reclaimed many from the paths of destruction, shed abroad a bright halo of sanctity, and exhibited a profound fund of erudition. By the advice of Robert, Primate of Armagh, of whom I made mention before, and at the solicitation of the Doctors of the city, he consented to fill the chair of Theology, which had been left vacant by the death of the renowned and learned Eckius.†

---

* Itaque ad hodiernum usque diem, cernimus Bavariæ provinciam nil bellicis periclitatam tumultibus. *Ubi supr.* n. 25.

† Ibid. n. 26.

So great was his celebrity throughout the German Empire, that many Prelates, anxious for the salvation of those over whom he presided, sought for his co-operation and aid. His virtues and erudition were dreaded by the Lutherans, and they formed, wherever he displayed them, a powerful rampart against the reputation of the reformers. The Prelate whose fortune it was to secure his services, at this juncture, was Otho Truchses, who was afterwards created Cardinal : a personage of great influence at the Roman Court, and in high favor with the Sovereign Pontiff. Every exertion was made to retain Jaius at Ingolstadt. But neither munificent remunerations, nor the honors of the chair in the University, nor the expostulations of the citizens, could make any impression on him, whose breast was animated by no other spirit than that of the welfare of the Church. The city offered him, on his departure, liberal donations, which, however, he refused to accept.*

At Este, he was retained, with the consent of Otho, then at the Council of Spires, by the Bishop of that city : where, during two months, he labored, with immense advantage and success, among the faithful. At Dilinghen, he conceived the liveli-

---

* Ibid. n. 110.

est hopes for the cause of Religion, under the patronage of Otho, who was adorned with all the virtues, and actuated by the zeal, worthy the Prelates of the primitive ages,—virtues which had been happily cultivated, zeal which had been duly directed, by the spiritual exercises which that Bishop had performed under the guidance of Faber. This great and saintly man passed through Dilinghen, at this conjuncture, on his way to Rome. Jaius deplored the departure from Germany of so useful, so apostolic a missionary, and wrote, by him, to Ignatius, expressing his grief at that occurrence. For his very name was a tower of strength to the Catholic cause: his eloquence and wisdom had attracted back to her fold numbers of the most distinguished persons; and his sanctity had given a singular *éclat* to the name of the Society. In this well-merited strain of eulogy did Jaius write of Faber to his Holy General, Ignatius.*

At Dilinghen he did not long remain, but repaired to Salzburg, at the request of the Archbishop, the brother of the Duke of Bavaria. A provincial Council had been convoked in that city, at which the Bishops of Augsburg and Este were both to be

---

* Ibid. n. iii. For the justness of this eulogy, let the reader revert to Chap. II.

present. Jaius was their attendant and consulter; and by them his opinions were always asked, before they would come to a decision on any grave point.*

The object of the late Council of Spires having been to discuss the articles which were disputed between Catholics and Sectarians, and it now being resolved to transfer the assembly to Worms, the question to be determined was, what would the Emperor think of that measure. This question appeared to Jaius delicate and difficult; and he affirmed that it was not reasonable to expect that, as the Sovereign Pontiff had deputed him to Germany, he would assist at that Council without the approbation of the Holy See. He, accordingly, begged the Archbishop to excuse his non-attendance. The Prelate yielded, on condition that he should remain at Salzburg during the entire session of the Synod; and that when consulted by the Prelates, he should at least privately give his opinion. To this he could not object; and to him all the gravest questions were submitted ere they were discussed in Council. Two things were unanimously agreed upon. First, that, in a religious convocation, nothing should be decided by lay

---

* Ibid. n. 112.

and popular votes. And secondly, that the Protestants, though they should admit all Catholic doctrines, were, nevertheless, to be considered Schismatics, if they refused to acknowledge the supremacy of the Pope.*

The result of the Council was pleasing and satisfactory to Jaius. He rejoiced to see the firmness with which the Archbishop exerted his influence and power against the encroachments of the Reformation; and, with fresh courage and renewed confidence, returned to Dilinghen,† whence, after an interval of a few days, he was ordered by the Bishop to accompany him to the Synod of Worms. The affairs of the Church in Germany were in so critical a condition, that Jaius felt convinced that nothing short of a General Council would be able to meet the impending danger. He exhorted the Bishop not to listen to the proposition, made by the Lutherans, of a national convocation, and he made Ignatius acquainted, by letter, with all the particulars of his own position, and of the circumstances of the Church in these lamentable times.‡

The Diet of Worms was occupied rather in useless altercations, than in salutary and grave debate. Jaius, however, was not inactive, or

---

* Ibid. n. 112.   † Ibid. n. 113.   ‡ Ibid. n. 114.

wanting in his duty. He aided and animated the Bishops in sustaining the interests of religion; and vindicated truth and confuted error in his frequent sermons to the people. During the season of Lent, 1545, he preached before an immense concourse of noblemen and the king with such ardor, learning, and eloquence, that he moved, convinced, and enraptured all. Of the incalculable good produced by his instrumentality in Germany, not only the Bishop, whom he followed to Worms, but likewise the Papal legate, Cardinal Alexander Farnesius, bore splendid testimony. By the latter, he was cherished and admired: and not only admitted to his familiarity as a friend, but consulted, in difficult questions, as an oracle.*

Among the meritorious objects to which he turned the attention of the German Prelates, that of the institution of Theological Seminaries—a measure which Ignatius had recommended to him when departing on this mission—was, perhaps, the most important for the permanent wants of the empire. The study of theology had, of late years, been much neglected, while the inutility of it, and the change in its whole system, were the themes of

---

* Lib. v. n. 30. His associate, in this Synod, was not less esteemed, as the reader saw in Chap. VI.

the reformers. This change was gratifying to the natural propensities of the mind and heart; it proclaimed a liberation from the yoke of ancient discipline, as well as ancient doctrine, and left the one and the other discretionary with the caprice of the individual who abjured the supremacy of the Roman Pontiff. The fancy of youth was delighted with these privileges and conceptions, and, not being thoroughly grounded in the study of theology, many were lured from the old path by the pleasures and charms of the new. Jaius now suggested the plan of selecting a number of children, who should be regularly trained up to the liberal sciences, and then formed in seminaries, for the ministry, by a solid and well-directed course of theology, especially of a dogmatic character, which would render them able disputants, and learned controvertists. By this means, the reformed ministers, who came fresh and educated before the people, declaiming against the ignorance and newly discovered errors of the Church, might be met, breast to breast, on the arena, by champions equal in acquirements, and superior in argument; and, thereby, vindicate the majesty and sanctity of the Church.*

---

* Inviando il Santo alla Germania il Padre Claudio Jaio, l'anno 1541, strettamente gl' inguinse, di mettere ogni possi

The project was eagerly approved by the Bishop of Salzburg and Este : and, in order to spread it more generally through the German empire, Jaius was invited by the other Prelates to visit their various dioceses. But, as he had been placed, by the command of the Pope, at the disposal of the Bishop of Augsburg, he was obliged to decline the honor, and return to Ingolstadt, where he resumed his former functions, preached in the open streets to countless auditors, and brought back numbers to the pale of the Church.*
Several Catholic Princes desired, at the same time, the services of Jaius ; so universal was the fame of his piety and erudition. But his destination to the Council of Trent, which had now been

---

bile opera nel condurre quanti i più potesse de Vescovi di colà ad abbracciare un così profittevol consiglio : e la Dio mercè gli venne felicemente fornito, e con alquanti altri, e singolarmente col Truchses, Cardinale d'Augusta ... E fin da quel medesimo primo anno, i Legati proposero al Pontifice Paolo III., fra partiti più necessari, e più utili alla Riformazion della Chiesa, l'istituir Seminari .... Consciosiecosa che, non l'avere altro, onde sperar sicuro il rimettere in piè la disciplina abbatuta, che ben' allevare in servigio della Chiesa la gioventù : essondo vero, che tali si hanno gli nomini in tutta l'eta, quali si formano nella prima. Bartoli, libr. ii. cap. ix. p. 91.

* Ibid. n. 31, 32.

convoked, disappointed all their expectations The Bishop of Augsburg, having been decorated with the Cardinal's hat by Paul IV., deputed Jaius, in his name, together with a learned Canon of the Cathedral, to that august convention. By the Cardinal of Trent—where he arrived in the month of December—he was very graciously received. But the humble Jesuit, declining the splendid hospitalities of the palace, took up his lodgings in the hospital. By the Apostolic Legates, he was, likewise, welcomed with distinguished kindness and respect, not so much, perhaps, in consequence of the high position he held as the representative of an illustrious Prelate, as of the celebrity of his own name and the renown of his past labors in Germany.*

In the Council, he exercised a powerful influence ; in private, he was consulted by the Bishops ; and in public, his decisions were heard with singular respect and veneration. Nor did he neglect the ordinary duties of the Society. But, with the approbation of the Cardinal of Trent, preached the word of God, administered the Sacraments, and uniting his great efforts with those of his brethren, Laynez and Salmeron, he gave a

---

* Ibid. n. 33.

lustre to the Society which time will never be able to extinguish.*

On the demise of the Bishop of Trieste, Ferdinand resolved to offer the vacant See to Jaius, the sanctity of whose life, and the solidity of whose erudition, would, he felt convinced, prove a mighty bulwark in favor of the Church, during these calamitous times. He, accordingly, urged the Father, by letter, not to refuse the burden, so worthy of his solicitude and vigilance, should it be imposed upon him by the Sovereign Pontiff. Nothing, he assured him, would be more agreeable to the people, nothing more gratifying to his own desires.†

Jaius, who from his youth had imbued his heart with sentiments of unaffected humility, and whose maturer reflection, and, above all, whose vow of poverty, had confirmed his natural aversion to honors and preferment, no sooner received the intimation of the king's intention, than he began to take effectual measures against its consummation. To this end, he wrote, immediately, to Ignatius, conjuring him to avert the impending danger, by interposing his influence both with the king and Pontiff: affirming that, unless compelled by obedi-

---

* Lib. vi. n 19. † Ibid. n. 31.

ence to remain at Trent, he would rescue himself by timely flight and concealment.*

Justly did this wise and holy man dread those honors at which the greatest and most venerable Fathers trembled: and which, according to St. Gregory Nazianzen, who fled from the Episcopal dignity, should be most feared, because they are the most pregnant with responsibility and danger. Wherefore, when the king's Confessor repaired to Venice, where Jaius then was stationed, for the purpose of comunicating to him the royal pleasure, "Give me one hour," was his reply, "to deliberate on the subject." After which time, he declared that, having recommended the affair to God in fervent prayer, he was fully convinced that he was not competent to the onerous charge with which the king wished to intrust him.† Ferdinand addressed to the Sovereign Pontiff, also, a most feeling letter, entreating him to appoint to the vacant See of Trieste an ecclesiastic of exemplary piety and singular learning, and in every way qualified for the high office of Bishop. These letters

---

* Ibid. n. 32.

† Ibid. Et jure vir sapiens sibi metuebat.... nec ignorabat quod scriptum Nazianzenus cum Episcopatum fugeret, reliquisset: *metum hunc omnium maximun metuum esse, et hoc periculum omnium periculorum extremum.*

were delivered to the Father of the faithful by his ambassador, who had brought the affair nearly to its termination, before Ignatius discovered the design. All hope of averting the sentence seemed to have fled. The ambassador was instructed to persist in his postulation: the Cardinals would not interfere. The Pope—despite the representations and entreaties of the Society—seemed determined to confirm the nomination made by the king. Ignatius, amid these threatening difficulties, fled to prayer, and fixed his confidence in God, who inspired him with the resolution to expostulate with the king, by a letter addressed immediately to his majesty himself, the substance of which was as follows: "The desire you have expressed, most illustrious monarch, to honor the Society, and your zeal in the cause of the spiritual welfare of your people, are not unknown to us. For both we return you our warmest thanks, beseeching the Divine goodness to inspire your majesty with the most effectual means wherewith to accomplish such noble views. But the greatest favor, and the truest kindness that you could exhibit in our regard, would be to allow us quietly and sincerely to pursue the path of our profession; to which all honors, we are persuaded, are so opposed, that we openly and conscientiously declare, that we regard the Episcopacy as the worst evil that can befall us. For of all, who have embraced the institute of the Society, the single intention and object has been to go to any part of the world to which the Sovereign Pontiff might send them, for the advancement of religion : so that the first and germane spirit of the Society is, that its members should travel from province to province, and from city to city, in all simplicity, for the glory of God and salvation of souls : and not confine their labors to any particular place. This mode of life was not only approved by the Apostolic See, but God has shown, by many evidences, how pleasing in his sight and beneficial to the Church it has been. Wherefore, as in the conservation of the first spirit is seated, as it were, the very soul of religious orders, there can be no doubt that, by retaining it, we will preserve—by abandoning it, we will destroy—our Society. From this it will clearly be perceived how dread a calamity we regard the impending honors of the Episcopacy. At this time, we are only nine professed Fathers, and to four or five the Episcopal dignity has already been offered, and by all resolutely declined. Had each of them yielded, others would have fancied themselves privileged, also, to accept it ; and thus not only would the Society degenerate from its original spirit, but, its members gradually being taken away, would be soon entirely dissolved. In fine, as by examples of humanity and holy poverty this little Society has prospered, if men were to see us honored and wealthy, their good opinion of us would be changed, and the door of future usefulness, not without scandal, would be closed. But it is not necessary to accumulate reasons. We throw ourselves upon the wisdom and clemency of your majesty : to your faith, to your protection, we confide ourselves, praying and conjuring you, through the blood of Jesus Christ, that since these honors would be, we are confident, the destruction of the Society, to avert, in your goodness and love of religion, this awful calamity, and to preserve this least and infant order, to the glory of the Eternal Majesty. May He enrich your majesty with an abundance of celestial gifts !"*

This respectful but cogent epistle of Ignatius produced the desired effect. The king relented, and ordered his ambassador to desist from the action which had well-nigh been accomplished. The reasons so forcibly urged not only satisfied the monarch, but convinced the Pope, likewise, of the wisdom of the Society in not permitting

---

* Ibid. n. 34.

her children to aspire to ecclesiastical preferment.*

Towards the end of July, 1547, Jaius repaired to Ferrara, at the solicitation of the duke, Hercules, who desired to have as the director of his conscience, and as a faithful adviser, a holy and prudent priest. The selection of such an individual being left to his Confessor, Guido Guidonio, he cast his eyes upon Jaius, whose fame was now universal, and whose place of nativity would render him peculiarly acceptable to the duchess, who was a native of France. The duke immediately wrote to the Sovereign Pontiff and Ignatius, requesting that they would approve of his choice. Ignatius replied, that he felt happy in serving a prince who had proved himself so favorable to the Society, and would ever entertain towards him the liveliest sentiments of gratitude. He, likewise, instructed Jaius in what manner he should act and comport himself towards his illustrious benefactor, and amid the blandishments of the court.†

On arriving at Ferrara, Jaius first presented

---

* To the reasons expressed in his letter to the king, Ignatius added several others in that to the Sovereign Pontiff, which I gave at length in the first chapter of this work.

† Lib. vii. n. 34.

himself to the duke, and then proceeded, straightway, to the hospital, where he devoted himself to the spiritual and corporal comfort of the inmates. The munificent accommodations offered by the duke he declined ; affirming that he enjoyed more pleasure in the company of the poor than amid the gorgeous luxuries of the court. In the asylum for widows, which was founded by the duke under the appellation of *Sancta Maria de Rosa*, he instructed, and administered the Sacraments ; and devoted a large share of his time to the hospital of Saint Anne, in which, the more effectually to reap the abundant fruits of his untiring zeal, the Cardinal Bishop of the city conferred on him all power and authority.* By the duke he was consulted concerning the affairs of his soul and the government of his people ; was intrusted with the care of the duke's children, whose spiritual guide he was appointed ; and besides these duties, applied himself, moreover, to the functions of preaching and lecturing, and hearing confessions. "In a word," adds Orlandinus, "he discharged numberless other offices, which the fear of satiating the attention of the reader, alone, induces me not to mention more in detail."†

---

* Ibid. n. 25. † Lib. ix. n. 47.

Meanwhile, William, Duke of Bavaria, the noble defender of the ancient Church, mindful of the infinite good achieved by Jaius at Ingolstadt, and of the influence and benevolence which rendered him distinguished in that part of Germany, requested the Pope to appoint three theologians—naming as one whom he most esteemed, Jaius—who should teach the sacred sciences in the University of Ingolstadt. The Pope signified the duke's pleasure to Ignatius, who could not hesitate to acquiesce in it. Quitting Ferrara, with the permission of Hercules, he proceeded with his companions, Salmeron and Canisius, to Bologna, where the degree of Doctor was awarded to each one by the famous University of that city. Decorated with this new title—which they earned by a previous disputation held with two of the most learned theologians—they continued their journey to Trent, where they were received with distinguished attention by the Cardinal, and reached their destination amid the gratulations and cordial greetings of the Duke of Bavaria. It was here that the immortal Eckius formed towards the Fathers of the Society that intimate friendship which he cherished to the end of his life. By the University of Ingolstadt, they were welcomed with unanimous applause, and addressed in a Latin

occasion, to which Canisius returned an extemporaneous, but eloquent reply.*

The following day they were escorted to the "Ancient College."† They soon entered upon their respective duties. Salmeron commenced an explanation of the Epistle of St. Paul; Jaius, of the Psalms; and Canisius, of the Master of Sentences: and so highly were they admired, that the members of the University expressed their gratification, in a printed document, to the following effect: "We are at a loss how to give utterance to the pleasure we have derived from the arrival amongst us of the three theologians, Claudius Jaius, Alphonsus Salmeron, and Peter Canisius: whose presence, far from diminishing the greatness of their reputation, has increased it. Their wonderful knowledge of the sacred sciences, their general erudition, and their sanctity of manners, not only equal, but far surpass, our sanguine anticipations.‡

This was the declaration made in favor of these

---

* Ibid. n. 54.

† Postero die in Collegium, quod apellant "vetus," cum aonore deducuntur. Id. n. 54.

‡ Nuper quantam lætitiam ceperimus omnes ex adventu trium Theologorum, vix dici potest. Quorum præsenta non-solum famam de ipsis excitatam non minuit, verum etiam

first Jesuit Fathers—these disciples of Ignatius—by the far-famed University of Ingolstadt; a declaration which afforded great joy to the neighboring Bishops, who had hitherto endeavored, in vain, to revive the sacred sciences, so long dormant, amid the increasing innovations of the times. In order to perpetuate the good work, the duke determined to take measures for the foundation of a College of the Society at Ingolstadt; a project which met with the cordial approbation and concurrence of the illustrious Chancellor Eckius.*

---

auget. Quorum singularis in Sacris studiis Scientia, tum in omnibus disciplinis exercitatio, postremo sanctimonia vitæ expectationem omnium eamque maximam non solum æquat-verum etiam superat.—Ibid.

* This was the renowned champion of the Church, who had earned immortal laurels from the disputations he held at Vienna and Bologna; laurels which Luther and Carlostadius afterwards sought to wrest from his brows. To the ninety-five propositions put forth by the former, he boldly replied and triumphantly opposed the theological arguments, which excited the jealousy of the Archdeacon of Wittemberg, who, at that time, was Lecturer of Divinity. Eckius was accordingly challenged to enter the lists with him. The city of Leipsic was chosen as the arena of the controversy—being famous for its trade and university. The conflict was short. Carlostadius found to his shame, as well as confutation, that his shallow theology could not withstand the deep and

After the death of William, Duke of Bavaria, his successor, Albert, who cherished an equal affection for Jaius and his companions, earnestly conjured the Pope, by letters, and by his ambassador, not to remove them from his dominions. But the Cardinal of Augsburg had already obtained permission for Jaius to aid him, in his diocese, in promoting the Catholic cause, and to be present at the Council which was soon to be held in the metropolis. Ignatius, convinced that the labors of Jaius would be more required there than at Ingolstadt, ordered him to take his departure thence; which he did, followed by the regrets of Albert, and the lamentations of the whole city.*

In the year 1550, the Council of Augsburg

---

sweeping force of his adversary's, a man of acute mind, splendid genius, boundless erudition, and unfailing memory.

Carlostadius yielded the field—routed and confounded—to Luther, who, in his turn, was reduced to the necessity of admitting much of what he had previously uttered against penance, indulgences, and priestly absolution. Luther being silenced, his once-defeated vindicator attempted to breast anew the torrent of Eckius's controversy. But again he was oppressed by its irresistible tide. And the arena and all the laurels of the day were awarded, by acclamation, to the Catholic disputant. For further interesting details, consult Graveson, Hist. Ecc. vol. vii. p. 79 et seq.

* Lib. x. n. 102.

was convened. In the midst of the august personages and learned men who were present, Jaius stood conspicuous, and devoted himself, with assiduous attention and care, to the duties assigned him: now displaying his wisdom by his counsel; now contributing his invaluable aid to the labors of the Prelates; shedding, meanwhile, upon all around, the influence of his example, and seeking light and prudence from above, in the habitual exercise of prayer and meditation. He converted from the errors of Lutheranism not a few; among whom were several young men of excellent disposition and talents, who had been swept away in the torrent of the Reformation: and, by means of the spiritual exercises infused into the clergy—many of whom were noble and opulent—the spirit of their vocation. From the public places he caused all indecent statues, and from private houses unseemly pictures, to be removed; and induced the wealthy to apply a portion of their riches to the wants of the poor.

At Vienna, Ferdinand, king of the Romans, of whose piety and zeal for the Catholic cause I have already related many examples, desirous of restoring the University, in which the taint of error had contaminated most of the professors, and of restraining the progress of Lutheranism, as well as reforming the morals of the faithful, obtained thirteen members of the Society, solid men, and well versed in the art of administering the business connected with a University. Among these, the most prominent was Jaius.*

Such was the lamentable condition of Austria, at this epoch (1551), that of the provinces subject to the sway of Ferdinand hardly the tenth—or as others have surmised, even the thirtieth—part could be said to be free from the contagion of heresy. The Reformation had swept its direful way into the heart of the empire. Its teachers had scattered, in thousands, volumes teeming with abuse, calumny, and error, from which the credulous minds of youth drank in the agreeable poison, which, mingling itself, as it were, with the blood in their tender veins, incorporated with their beings. Well did the reformists understand the pernicious art of instilling indelible prejudices into the unwary breast, through the medium of pleasing and elegantly-published books.† The monasteries

---

* Lib. xi. n. 39.

† The leading and wealthiest publishers at this fatal period had gone over to the cause of the Reformation: and the recreant members of the monastic order, who had acquired, in their communities, the art of copying, in elegant style, the ancient manuscripts, gave themselves up to the business of

were deserted. Monks and priests were held up to public scorn and ridicule, insomuch that few had the courage to devote themselves to the ministry. Orlandinus states, that during the long course of twenty years not one individual received sacred orders in the celebrated University of Vienna.* Many weak Catholics, ashamed of the opprobrious title of papists, by which the Lutherans designated them, dissembled their faith; and to this evil, which was daily spreading wider and wider, no remedy seemed to be at hand. The king, who possessed extraordinary discrimination, did not see any men perfectly fitted to undertake

---

type-composition and proof-reading in Lutheran establishments. The press, by this means, assumed a Protestant ascendency. The works of the reformists were beautifully and sumptuously edited, while those of the Catholics—even of Eckius and Erasmus—were so clumsily executed, that they excited the ridicule of the Frankfort merchants. Cochlœus, p. 58, 59. Erasmus, in an epistle to Henry VIII., regrets that "he could find no printer who would dare publish any thing against Luther."—Epist. p. 752.

Cochlœus relates, that an infinite number of apostate priests procured their living by strolling through Germany, selling Lutheran books.—P. 58.

For innumerable details with regard to these facts, the reader is referred to Audin's Life of Luther.

* Lib. xi. n. 40.

the government of the Churches, or to be raised to the Episcopal dignity. In all Vienna, not a single person could be found willing to devote himself to holy orders. The parishes were either destitute of pastors, or else occupied by men unworthy their ecclesiastical profession. The sacraments were entirely neglected. The Eucharist was administered under both kinds; the confessional was dispensed with. Preachers treated, in their discourses, of faith alone, and the merits of Christ: but not a word was uttered concerning fasting, prayer, alms-deeds, and other good works. It was amid all these abuses, while this dense cloud of error was brooding over the Church, that Jaius and his companions appeared at Vienna.* The scene was soon changed. A School of Theology was immediately opened, to which, in a few days, upwards of fifty young men repaired, who, in due time, were promoted to holy orders, and began to combat the prevailing heresies, with a courage and success to which the empire of Austria is greatly indebted for the preservation of the faith.†

Under the pressure of his continued and wast-

---

* Ibid. n. 41. In has errorum tenebras, atque in hos mores incidit societatis adventus. Quos ut corrigeret sanaretque divino auxilio nixa suos omnes nervos et curas intendit.

† Ibid. n. 42.

ing labors, Jaius now began to sink. In the month of August, 1552, he was attacked by a mortal illness; not, indeed, of a painful or lingerin nature, but the consequence of incessant and devouring solicitude and fatigue. Being duly fortified with the last sacraments of the Church, and calmly commending his spirit into the hands of his Creator, in the sweet odor of sanctity, he departed to a better world. His death excited universal mourning. The venerable remains were exposed in the church of St. Nicholas, which appertained to the Franciscan Convent, where they were bedewed with the tears of the illustrious Doctors, as well as of the ingenuous youth, of the University. To the grave they were followed by all who appreciated learning, admired eloquence, esteemed virtue; and his memory will be held in benediction by the Society of Jesus and the Catholic Church. He was, indeed, a great man, an indefatigable apostle. Never shall his exertions in favor of religion be forgotten, in Italy, Bavaria, and Germany. In the Council of Augsburg, and other Synods, he vindicated, nobly and powerfully, the Holy Roman Catholic Church. His influence over the people was unbounded, and his wisdom was the guide of Princes and of Prelates. In character, he was naturally most amiable; of pleasing manners, and cheerful disposition : at the same time, his deportment was always marked with dignity and gravity. He loved poverty, and often appeared in the company of the great with a coarse and tattered habit. He was devoted to prayer and meditation ; scrupulously careful of time ; reserved in conversation ; and modest in every action. In him there was nothing arrogant, nothing haughty. Though mighty and uncompromising in disputation with the Lutherans, still charitable and considerate ; and thus not only confirming the faith of the orthodox, but, likewise, conciliating the attention of heretics. His mode of teaching in the schools was plain, distinct, and firm. With wonderful clearness and precision, he explained the doctrines of Justification, Predestination, Faith, and Good Works. In a word, so precious was the memory of his virtues and erudition, that, after his death, he was styled by the people " an angel of God, and the Father and Patron of Catholics." Even the great Canisius did not hesitate to denominate him the " Apostle of Germany."*

A monument was erected to his name, in the University of Ingolstadt, with the following in-

---

* Lib. xii. n. 36, 37.

scription : "Claudius Jaius, a Doctor in Theology, a Professor of the Society : a man of gentlest manners, who always united learning with piety. Here, in this School, he won the reputation of sanctity among the highest, the middle, and the lowest ; to all equally dear and useful : he was one of the ten by whom the holy Society of Jesus was originated and founded. Called hence—at Vienna in Austria—he took his flight to those heavenly realms which had always been in his heart and before his eyes, in the year of our Lord 1552."[†]

[†] Claudius Jaius, Theologus Doctor, Professor Societatis, vir placidissimorum morum, et qui doctrinam cum pietate perpetuo conjunxit. Hic, si quispiam alius, in hâc scholâ, sanctitatis opinionem apud summos, medios, infimos sibi comparavit ; cunctis æquè carus et salutaris ; qui etiam ex primâ decade fuit eorum qui Sanctæ Societatis Jesu auctores et fundatores extiterunt. Hinc evocatus, Viennam in Austriâ, et ea quæ semper in pectore tenuit et ob oculos habuit æterna migravit gaudia, anno MDLII.

JOHN CORDURIUS.

CHAPTER IX.

JOHN CORDURIUS.

> JOHN CORDURIUS.—One of the Companions. His career brief, but bright. Was destined for Ireland. Was appointed Confessor to Margaret daughter of Charles V. His death revealed to Ignatius on the Bridge of Sixtus.

BRIEF and bright is the history of this holy man: who seems to have been ordained by Providence merely to inscribe his name on the rolls of the infant Society, and then to disappear. All of him, however, died not.* His virtues, his example, and his memory, lived after him, and *they* are immortal. Had he been spared to exercise his ardent zeal, and devote his shining talents, to the cause of the Church, during these troublous and melancholy times, what tongue can tell the incalculable good, which, in concert with his associ-

---

* *Non omnis moriar.*—Hor. lib. iii. *od.* xxx.

ates in the Company of Jesus, he would have achieved. Had Xavier been taken from the field of promise, ere he had reaped the vast and glorious harvest which renders his fame unequalled in modern ages, no mind would have been able to conjecture, much less foresee, the stupendous result of his missionary labors. So are we utterly incapable of forming any idea of the usefulness of Cordurius in the Church, had he been permitted to measure the ordinary number of years allotted to man. But of him may it emphatically be said: *Consummatus in brevi explevit tempora multa.**

In the year 1536, Ignatius, having quitted Paris, and departed, on important affairs, into Spain, confided to Faber the care of his companions: exhorting them to look up to him, on account of the dignity of his priesthood, and the priority of his vocation; and to reverence him as their Father.†

Faber, who had already completed the course of his studies, and acquired great renown for his learning and sanctity, was not unfaithful to his

---

* Being made perfect in a short space, he fulfilled a long time. For his soul pleased God: therefore he hastened to bring him out of the midst of iniquities. Wisdom, chap. iv v. 13, 14.

† Orlandin. lib. i. n. 99.

important trust; but watched over those committed to his charge with prudence and gentleness, and, under all circumstances, comported himself as a worthy disciple, and representative of Ignatius.

It was during the absence of the venerable founder of the Society that, through the salutary admonitions, and by the saintly example, of Faber, John Cordurius, a native of France, was induced to add his name to the number of the first companions.

The business which required his presence in Spain being accomplished, Ignatius returned to his beloved companions, who were now at Venice, in the beginning of January, 1537. He was received with filial rejoicing and tender embraces by them all, who united in their most fervent thanks to Heaven, for having restored their Father to their bosoms. Cordurius, with the other companions, departed for Rome, leaving Ignatius behind to make arrangements for their intended pilgrimage to the Holy Land. In the city, they scattered themselves in every quarter, devoting themselves to acts of charity and mercy: and after obtaining, as was before related, the benediction of the Sovereign Pontiff, Paul III., they retraced their steps to Venice, where the sacred order of Priesthood was conferred upon all, on the feast of St. John the Baptist (1537), by Vincent Negosantio, Bishop of Arbe, a man not less renowned for the nobility of his birth, than the splendor of his virtues.* In the various occupations in which these extraordinary men were employed, none evinced a more devoted spirit than Cordurius. When he made his solemn vows, so vivid was the expression of his piety, so great was the force and exuberance of his divine consolation, that, in spite of every effort to conceal them, they burst from the depths of his soul in frequent sighs, and in involuntary sobs.†

When making the pilgrimage, with Laynez, to the Seven Churches, he would wander over the fields in order to give vent, if possible, unperceived, to his lamentations. Such sensibility seemed not fitted for the cold meridian of earth; and Heaven decreed that he should not be suffered to sojourn long amid its sorrows and cares. He foresaw the speedy coming of the angel of death, and prepared for his exit from this mortal existence, with the resignation and piety of one predestinated to immortal bliss. On the festival of St. John the Baptist, whose name he bore—the anniversary of

---

* Lib. ii. n. 3, 10, 12. † Lib. iii. n. 19.

his promotion to priestly orders—he calmly breathed his soul into the hands of his Creator.

Orlandinus relates, that Ignatius, on going to offer the holy sacrifice of the Mass for his recovery, in the church of St. Peter in Janiculo, suddenly stopped on the bridge of Sixtus, as if wrapt in amazement; and then turning to his companion, Baptist Viola, "Let us return home," he said; "our dear Cordurius is no more.*

In this short space is contained the whole history of John Cordurius. Of his sanctity, Ignatius entertained the highest opinion: and of the prudence which distinguished his earliest career, there can be no better evidence than of his having been appointed Confessor to Margaret, daughter of Charles V., and afterwards selected to undertake the mission to Ireland.† In a letter to Faber, Ignatius mentions the death of Cordurius, as of his beloved child, taken prematurely, indeed, from his brethren on earth, but transported to the bright and glorious company of the angels and saints in heaven.

---

* Referamus, inquit, no domum: Cordurius noster dicessit Ibid. n. 20.

† Ibid. n. 46.

PASCHASIUS BROËTUS

CHAPTER X.

PASCHASIUS BROËTUS.

PASCHASIUS BROETUS.—The last of the Nine. Is sent to Ireland. Is captured at Lyons as a spy. Is sent to Monte Pulciano, and to Favenza. Is deemed worthy to be made Patriarch of Ethiopia by Ignatius. Goes to Bologna. To Ferrara. Is made the first Provincial of Italy. Is sent to France. Labors to establish the Society at Paris. Opposition of the Sorbonne. Triumph of justice. His patience and other virtues. Styled by Ignatius the "Angel of the Society."

BERLINCOURT, a town near Amiens, in Picardy, claims the honor of having given birth to this ninth and last of the companions of the Founder of the Society; who, with Cordurius, added his name to their number, under the influence of Faber, during the absence of Ignatius from Paris, in the year 1536. At this period, he was already adorned with the priestly character, and, with the others, was present at the renovation of vows on Mont-Matre, having gone through the ordinary ordeal of the spiritual exercises under the direction of Ignatius; giving, during many days, an example of rigid abstinence and fasting, "which," in the language of Orlandinus, "is more to be admired than to be imitated by posterity."*

---

* Quorum admiranda magis quam imitanda viderentur exempla.—Lib. i. n. 102.

The first stage of the public functions of Broëtius was Ireland, that oppressed and afflicted land, whose children, despite the newly enacted penal laws, and the utter want of spiritual aid, continued firm and faithful to the religion which their ancestors had received from their glorious apostle, St. Patrick. Of the details of this his great mission, I have already treated in the history of his fellow-Jesuit and co-laborer, Alphonsus Salmeron.* It will be unnecessary to repeat their sufferings, dangers, exploits, and privations in Ireland, their escape at Lyons, where they were arrested as spies, and their difficult return to Italy. In every variety of circumstances, Broëtus proved his zeal, disinterestedness, and perseverance, ready to lay down his life, if necessary, for the magnificent end which the Society proposed to his view in all things: viz., the advancement of God's glory, and the salvation of the human race.†

On his return from Ireland, Broëtus was sent, by Ignatius, to Foligno, at the solicitation of Blosius, bishop of that city, who had recently been decorated with the Cardinal's hat. There a wide field expanded to his labors, among all classes and orders of society. To the convents he restored the fervor of their ancient discipline: and among

---

* Chap. v.   † Lib. iii. n. 62.

the clergy—who had degenerated into ignorance as well as negligence of their duties—diffused the spirit of knowledge and letters, as well as of regularity and zeal. The vices of the people he, in a great degree, abolished, and produced a general reform, which seemed the work more of divine power than of human agency. The Cardinal, who witnessed, with admiration, this wondrous change, requested him to exert his influence also at Monte Pulciano, the birthplace of that eminent Prelate. With alacrity he entered upon a similar career in that place; and not without equal success, preaching, and catechising, and reviving religion and piety, to the universal satisfaction and joy of the inhabitants.*

He remained among them three months ; when, by another Cardinal, his presence was solicited in France. This was Rudolphus Pius, to whose protection and encouragement the Sovereign Pontiff had commended the Society in its cradle, bestowing on him, to this effect, the title of "Protector."† The main object held out to the wisdom and zeal of Broëtus in this mission, was the restoration of

---

* Lib. iv. n. 11, 12. Pari incolarum tum utilitate, tum gaudio. Utrobique præter cætera, in tradendis Christianæ Fidei elementis.

† Orlandinus calls him *præstanti prudentiâ virum.*—Ibid. n. 77.

discipline in the monastic institutions. In the discharge of this delicate office—especially in the female establishments—he conducted himself with extreme lenity and indulgence, by which he gained the confidence and affection of the inmates. He introduced the primitive spirit of prayer and meditation among them, mildly exhorting them to look to heaven for the grace necessary for the attainment of that perfection to which they had devoted their lives. On all occasions he acted under the influence of that memorable maxim of St. Augustine, that the eternal noise of reproach would be idle if there were not an interior voice whispering to the consenting heart.* Such gentle admonitions steal insensibly into the soul, and excite those sympathies and affections which severity and stern rebuke are often only calculated to stifle One bland and tender word is frequently more effectual, in changing the sinner's heart, than long and bitter denunciations. This proved to be the case in the present remarkable instance. The monastic communities yielded, at once, to the sweet violence of persuasion: they sought enlightenment and grace in fervent and common prayer, and, re-

---

* Inanem esse strepitum monentis vocis, nisi sit intus qui doceat.—Agust. Ep. i. Joann. Tract iii.

penting of their errors, submitted to the authority of their Prelate—from whom they had, ere this, been alienated—and, with renovated fervor, practised the virtues and exercises of their holy state.*

Providence, as if desirous of crowning these rare merits of Broëtus, visited him, at this juncture, with a severe and dangerous illness; but, nevertheless, spared his bodily life for the spiritual welfare of others. Hardly had he arisen from his bed of sickness, before he was sent—still infirm but obedient—at the request of the same Cardinal, to Favenza.†

The aspect of that city, as represented by Orlandinus, was of the most melancholy character. It had long been deprived of all spiritual aid, in consequence of which universal depravity of morals prevailed, and the sacred exercises of religion had, in a great measure, disappeared. Intemperance, discord, enmities, and other deadly vices, reigned abroad. The use of the sacraments had ceased, and the infamous habit of swearing had extended to all classes, even to the very children themselves. Crimes the most flagrant in their nature had lost their turpitude and guilt; and, as is usually the case, this dissoluteness of morals was followed by perverse and temerarious opinions in religious faith. Into

---

* Lib. iv. n. 77. † Ibid. n. 78.

the bosom of this city the errors of Luther had found an easy avenue; especially as they were introduced by a man who, adorned by nature with the gifts of noble eloquence, converted to the destruction of souls his fatal talent, which had been bestowed upon him for their salvation. This individual was the famous Bernardinus Ochinus, who, having laid aside the cowl and sandals of the Capuchin friar, assumed the gown and habits of a reformer, and disseminated his errors throughout this fatal city.* So that the laborer in his shop would interrupt his work to catch the grateful novelties so plausibly diffused; and the lounger in the tavern, as he emptied his wine-cup, would drink in with keen delight a doctrine that freed the mind from all control, and the passions from all restraint.†

It required no ordinary man to meet Ochinus, on

---

* Ochinus had been the Superior of the Capuchin Friars in Italy. But leaving his order, in which he had acquired great reputation, both for austerity of life and his extraordinary talent for preaching, he joined Peter Martyr in Switzerland; and afterwards lapsed into Arianism. Beza, in his letter to Diducius, charges him with the basest crimes and the utmost impiety: "he has become a fautor of the Arians, a mocker of Christ and his Church."—Fiorim. p. 296.

† Passim, ut in tabernis officinisque pestilentis venena magistri impunissimè tractarentur.—Lib. v. n. 18

nis natal soil, and to counteract his mighty and popular influence. To effect this, it was necessary that national prejudices should be overcome, notions of religion agreeable to human reason should be sacrificed, and a system of morality gratifying to the natural appetites should be destroyed. Ochinus was an Italian. Broëtus was a Frenchman. But the former was an apostate; the latter a Jesuit. The one a fautor and promoter of schism and heresy; the other a vindicator and apostle of unity and truth : with him was the Spirit of God, and the issue of his ministry at Favenza proves that that Spirit must prevail against any antagonist.

Broëtus calmly surveyed the prospect, and studied the dispositions of the people, which discovering to be lofty and generous, he deemed it necessary to undertake the mission allotted him with caution and circumspection. Individuals of superior qualities, and disposed to piety, he gained over by bland and conciliatory conversations; and then facilitated the work of reform in morals and of conviction in truth. With all classes, he began his task with an affectionate and kind spirit, under the deep impression that the divine clemency is most easily excited by benevolent and charitable actions. At this period the city was filled with a multitude of poor and desolate beings. To the relief of their wants, and the solace of their miseries, he labored to devise some efficient remedy. With this view, he established a Sodality, over which he himself presided, of which the object was, that its devoted members should afford assistance, not merely of a corporal, but what was infinitely more important, of a spiritual, nature. At their head, he scoured the whole city, seeking after and aiding the wretched and forsaken; supplying the indigent sick with medicines and the attendance of physicians, as also with necessary and proper nourishment, and performing other works of charity among them.*

The result of these efforts surpassed all anticipation. The Sodalists, by their own virtuous example, shed throughout the city a salutary influence, while the good deeds they performed increased the fame of Broëtus, and excited general admiration. Encouraged by this auspicious experiment, he now ventured to stand as a public instructor before the people, and explained, in a simple and unostentatious style and manner, the elements of Christian doctrine. This was a novel scene, which attracted a large concourse of all ages and classes. Nor did he confine this exercise to the churches, but carried it into the schools, with the approbation

---

* Lib. v. n. 19.

of the teachers and parents of the children, and thereby implanted in the pliant and ingenuous hearts of youth the germ of truth and piety. The effect produced was so general and excellent, that in schools containing sometimes more than four hundred pupils not an oath, or an obscene word, was heard to drop from their lips. To these exercises, he added, moreover, public exhortations to the people in general, and private conferences with individuals in particular. By which means religion, which, on his arrival, seemed to be tottering hopelessly to ruin, was once more restored to its primitive vigor, and placed upon a solid foundation. Peace was effected among many of the principal families which had been torn by dissension; hundreds of individuals at a time were seen meeting in an appointed place for the purpose of being reconciled, and of pardoning one another, in the presence of the blessed peace-maker, Broëtus.*

The manners of the people being happily reformed, the task of removing from their minds the errors which had been instilled into them, became comparatively easy. The consequences of those errors were now dispassionately viewed, and bit-

---

* "*Blessed* are the peace-makers." The first Jesuits were eminently the friends of peace.

terly deplored. The license which they granted to private judgment and human passions not only tended to the subversion of all ecclesiastical authority, and the destruction of unity, but likewise to the rejection and violation of all law and order. The citizens of Favenza, brought back to a sense of sober reflection by the convincing and touching remonstrances of Broëtus, recognized in his ministry the interposing mercy of God: and, as it were with one accord, repudiating the novelties of Luther and Ochinus, threw themselves again into the arms of their Holy Mother, the ancient Catholic Church.*

---

* "Far above all the rest," writes Hallam, "the Jesuits were the instruments for regaining France and Germany to the Church they served.... They knew how to clear their reasoning from scholastic pedantry and tedious quotation, for the simple and sincere understandings which they addressed. The weak points of Protestantism they attacked with embarrassing ingenuity: and the reformed churches did not cease to give them abundant advantages by *inconsistency, extravagance, and passion.*"—History of Literature, vol. i. ch. x.

This learned author might have given other equally powerful reasons for their success in reclaiming such numbers of persons back to the Church: he might have referred to their untiring zeal, their incontaminate lives, their magnanimous motives, their vast learning, and their extraordinary eloquence: all of which were under the heavenly influence of that Society, to whose institute and rules they had vowed obedience. Lib. v. n. 20.

Broëtus continued at Favenza during the entire year, when, in 1550, he was called to Bologna But his assiduous mental and bodily fatigue brought on him a violent disease in the head, for which, by the advice of his physician and Confessor, he retired to Monte Pulciano, for the benefit of the baths. Nor was he inactive even there. For the benefit of the Catholics of that place, he celebrated the Divine Mysteries, heard confessions, and gave public meditations, at which the Cardinal and other distinguished personages assisted.*

His health being restored, he returned to Bologna, where, during the space of an entire year, he continued in the unceasing exercise of his zeal, aided by the powerful co-operation of Salmeron, while that great man was attending the Council sitting in that capital. With what efficacy he labored for the salvation of souls, the change wrought among all classes—especially among the clergy—bore unequivocal testimony. Numbers who had been infected with the Lutheran errors were induced to abjure them, and reconcile themselves to the Church : and a permanent establishment of the Society was commenced, two buildings adjoining the church of St. Lucia having been given for this purpose.†

---

* Lib. vii. n. 25. † Lib. viii. n. 26.

Many Colleges, besides those of Sicily and Naples, had now been erected in Italy, so that it was necessary for Ignatius, who was oppressed with duties and labors, to divide the burden he had hitherto borne. Accordingly, uniting all those Colleges as it were into one province, he confided the charge of it to Broëtus, under the title of Provincial. He was, therefore, the first Father who ever filled that important office in Italy. The colleges of Palermo and Naples, Ignatius still continued to administer in person.* In this responsible and honorable station, Broëtus remained until the year 1552, when he was called to France, leaving the province in the hands of the venerable Laynez.†

At Paris he found a boundless theatre for his zeal and perseverance. In the Church of St. Germain he devoted himself to the confessional, to which numberless penitents flocked for consolation and the remission of their sins. The crowning achievement, however, of his devoted life remained still to be accomplished. This was the introduction of the Society, with the due approbation of parliament, into his native country. He had already secured the interest of the Cardinal of Lorraine, and

---

* Lib. xi. n. 35.

† The reader is referred to Chapter IV., where he will be edified by the humility of that great man.

the concurrence of Henry, king of France. The parliament, with a wavering and timid policy, had delayed taking any definitive action on the matter, and, at length, resolved to remove the responsibility of it from their own body to the Bishop, and University of Sorbonne. Among the Senators as well as Doctors, there were many who disproved of all new religious orders, without exception; whilst the Bishop professed an open hostility to the Society in particular, affirming that its privileges and inmunities conflicted whith the prerogatives and authority of the Hierarchy.*

The position in which Broëtus found himself, under these circumstances, was precarious and discouraging. He saw a thousand difficulties to be overcome, numberless contentions to be silenced, and sundry conflicting prejudices to be harmonized Nevertheless, he threw himself into the midst of the business : with his usual blandness persuading some, reasoning with others, and triumphantly vindicating the " Book of Exercises," against which, both here and elsewhere, a very strong opposition had grown up. This extraordinary book, as the reader saw above, had been approved by the Apostolic See, in the year 1548, and earnestly recom-

---

* Lib. xiii n. 38.

mended to the faithful, as containing exercises which, if devoutly practised, will conduce to piety and perfection.* Among the most learned and distinguished apologists whom it numbered, at this early period, Bartholomew Torres, Bishop of the Canary Islands, stands pre-eminent. The testimony which he rendered of its value and excellence is recorded in the pages of Orlandinus ; and I cannot omit in these, at least the substance of that memorable document : "God is my witness," he writes, "how cheerfully and willingly I pronounce my opinion concerning the Exercises of the Society of Jesus. I desire what I write to be known of the whole world. And lest it should be supposed that I am influenced by any private partiality, I declare that I am not a member of that Society : but, likewise, affirm that, although I am the least learned of Doctors, yet am I able to satisfy any one on this point ; since I have known the Society from its foundation, and have been a familiar associate of Ignatius at Salamanca : with his followers, also, I have had much intercourse, and have carefully and vigilantly observed their conduct. I, moreover, declare, that from the time when I first became acquainted with this holy Society, not a crime, not an

---

* See Chapter L.

error, have I been able to detect among its members. With regard to the 'Exercises,' no one, who has not gone through them, can be a proper judge of their spirit and virtue. I have seen learned men, who cannot understand their character and value; while others, of less erudition, who have tried them, perceive nothing in them but what is perfectly conformable to the Scripture and the Holy Fathers. It is one thing to comprehend the literal meaning, and another to appreciate the spirit of this book. Prayer, study, and the practice of virtue are necessary, in order to derive the proper benefit from it. For my own part, I acknowledge that I performed these 'Exercises' at Compostella; and God is my witness, that during that time I learned more than in the space of thirty years spent in the study of philosophy, and in the teaching of theology. If this declaration appear extraordinary to any Doctor, who is satisfied with his erudition, let him make the experiment: if he will but submit to the trial, he will come forth with the same experience. I will add, that I have known not a few who have gone through them, and many at my persuasion, as well religious as secular persons; of whom there was not one who did not become benefited, and did not proclaim them above all other human institutions. Would to God we could all understand how precious a treasury they contain !—of prayer, meditation, direction, and government of the soul, and wisdom, which are condensed and comprised within so small a compass. If, then, any one desires to know what these 'Exercises' are, I reply, that they are nothing else than attentive and profound consideration of the dogmas, law, and precepts of the Gospel; of the benefits bestowed by the Almighty on the human race; of the life and death of Christ; of the state of our past lives, accompanied by salutary resolutions for the future. I, moreover, declare, that the 'Exercises,' and all they contain, have generally and particularly, been confirmed by the authority of the Holy See; and have been recommended by the Sovereign Pontiff, as of great utility to the faithful. The objections which are alleged against them are very trivial, and in some points, too, ridiculous; for it is unworthy a wise man to affirm that a book, approved by the Holy See, could contain any thing contrary to pure morals and sound doctrine."*

---

* Lib. xiii. n. 34, 35, 36, 37, 38. The "Spiritual Exercises," in the language of the judicious Mr. Stephen, "form a manual of what may be called the act of conversion. It proposes a scheme of self-discipline by which, in the course of four weeks, that mighty work is to be accomplished. In the first, the penitent is conducted through a series of dark retro-

This was the nature of that Book of "Exercises," which the Parliament of France, from the fact—as Torres justly remarks—of their being ignorant of its heavenly spirit, hesitated to admit, with the Society to which it belonged, into their dominions. Such the Book which the Doctors of the Sorbonne—for the same reason—opposed and proscribed ; and was made the theme

---

spects to abase, and gloomy prospects, to alarm him. These ends obtained, he is, during the next seven days, to enrol himself—such is the military style of the Book—in the army of the faithful, studying the sacred biography of the Divine Leader of that elect host, and choosing, with extreme caution, the plan of life, religious or secular, in which he would best be able to tread in his steps and to bear the standard emblematic at once of suffering and conquest. To sustain the Soldier of the Cross in this protracted warfare, his spiritual eye is, during the third of his solitary weeks, to be fixed in a reverential scrutiny into that unfathomable abyss of woe, into which a descent was once made to rescue the race of Adam from the grasp of their mortal enemies ; and then seven suns are to rise and set, while the secluded but now disenthralled spirit is to chant triumphant hallelujahs, elevating his desires heavenward, contemplating glories hitherto unimaginable, and mysteries never before revealed ; till the Sacred Exercises close with an absolute surrender of all the joys and interest of this sublunary state, as a holocaust, to be consumed by the undying flame of Divine love on the altar of the regenerated heart."—*Critical Miscellanies.*

of denunciation in the pulpit, in the Chair of Theology, in private circles, and in public harangues.

All these persecutions Broëtus suffered with unruffled patience, and unshaken constancy: and he would have inevitably been crushed under their violence, could his enemies have infused their prejudices and animosities into the heart of Henry II. But instead of yielding to the popular feeling, that excellent monarch assured Broëtus and the Cardinal of Lorraine, that the Society was shielded by his protection, and never should he consent to abandon it. The members, however—and particularly Broëtus—were exposed to continual insults. Strange rumors concerning them were spread among the populace, so that they could not appear in public without being covered with scorn and contempt. Broëtus bore these injuries with silent forbearance; but deemed it, at the same time, more prudent to suspend the public functions of his ministry. In private he continued, with unwearied zeal, to instruct and direct those who put themselves under his care. Meanwhile, the Sorbonne published a severe decree against the Institute, and fraught with misrepresentations of the character, rules, and customs of the members themselves: concluding with the momentous accusation of their being "dan gerous to the faith, destructive to the peace of the Church, and eve sive of the monastic institutions."*

Broëtus, having consulted Ignatius with regard to the proper measures to be taken on this grave subject, received the following answer, which is stored with the usual wisdom and magnanimity of the great and venerable man from whom it emanated: "I desire you to bear in mind the words of Jesus Christ addressed to his disciples, when on the point of departing from them: *My peace I give unto you. My peace I leave unto you.* Imagine these words to have been uttered in your presence. Let nothing be published, nothing be done, that might engender acerbity of feeling. It is often better to be silent, than to speak. Nor is there any need of a revengeful style, when truth is her own avenger. The authority of the Doctors of Paris is, doubtless, very great, and, on that account, the more to be dreaded by us. Yet, let not even that disturb us. Nothing can long prevail against truth, which may, indeed, be opposed, but never overcome. Let not the passions be stimulated by the bitterness of retort, but appeased by the humility of silence. God is our protection:

---

* Lib. xv. n. 45.

to Him we commit our cause, and it must triumph."*

The Cardinal of Lorraine saw, with exceeding grief, the storm excited against the Society, for which—knowing it better than its maligners—he cherished the tenderest regard and affection. In order to allay it, he proposed that four Doctors of the Sorbonne should accompany him to Rome, where they should converse with Ignatius in person, and also confer on the subject with four of his order, whom he should select for the purpose. This proposition was accepted; and four Doctors were deputed with him; whose names were Pansa, Sausciera, Brixante, and Benedict, the authors of all the mischief. They were met by Laynez, Olauius, Polancus, and Frusius. Benedict attempted to defend every accusation alleged in the decree: but the Fathers refuted his objections, elucidated the character of their order, and triumphantly vindicated the Institute. The substance of the conference was committed to writing; and the task of reducing it to a regular form, for the purpose of transmitting it to the Sorbonne—and to posterity —was allotted to Olauius, a man of eminent learning, splendid talents, and exalted piety. This he

---

* Ibid. n. 43.

effected in a masterly composition, in which elegance of style, courteousness of manner, terseness of argument, and eloquence of diction are combined with admirable and brilliant felicity *

On the minds of most of the Doctors of the Sorbonne, this apology produced the desired effect: so that they declared, that had they been better informed on the nature of the Institute, they would not have published their decree against it.† And what proves the thorough change that was effected on the Doctors of that famous University, was the fact, that, forty years later, another excitement having been raised against the Society, their Faculty pronounced that it ought to be retained in France.‡

Thus may the recognition in that kingdom of this wonderful order be, in no small measure, attributed to the zeal and prudence of Broëtus, who, in every capacity and station, proved himself a worthy and saintly disciple of his immortal founder The last, but not, therefore, the least, of the admirable nine: a band of noble spirits, associated under the same divine influences, shedding over the world

---

* The whole paper may be seen in Orlandinus, lib. xv. n. 46, 47, et seq. A portion of this noble vindication of the Society was spread before the reader in the first chapter of this work I refer his particular attention to it.

† Ibid. n. 62. ‡ Ibid.

—as has been shown in the preceding pages—" a burning and a shining light," in darksome and troublous days, and contributing their support, like so many grand and stately columns, to the edifice of the Church. His more than ordinary merit, his great and solid qualities, were well known to Ignatius; who, when there was question of appointing one of his disciples Patriarch of Ethiopia, nominated him to that sublime dignity. In concluding, the rarest tribute that mortal tongue could pay him was bestowed by the same discerning and impartial man, when he honored Broëtus with the title of "the Angel of the Society."*

---

* When there was question of appointing a Patriarch of Ethiopia, St. Ignatius recommended Broëtus in these terms: " Paschasius is so pure a man, that we esteem him as the angel of our Society. Besides his great learning, he has had no little experience in visiting and reforming monasteries and dioceses. Moreover, he has been Vicar Apostolic in Ireland. No one member of the Society has discharged as many offices of this kind: and he has discharged them, too, in such a manner, that to whatever work he applied his labors, in that he always admirably proved his ability. By nature he is very persevering," etc..... See Tanner, p. 78, and Drews, *Fast. Soc.* part III. p. 329.

He was carried off by the plague at Paris, in which more than eighty thousand persons perished. His death occurred on the feast of the exaltation of the cross, September the 4th, A. D. 1562, in the fifty-sixth year of his age

PUBLICATIONS OF P. J. KENEDY,

EXCELSIOR

Catholic Publishing House,

5 BARCLAY ST., Near Broadway,

Opposite the Astor House, NEW YORK.

All for the Sacred Heart of Jesus. Dedicated to associates of League of Sacred Heart. Net	50
Adelmar the Templar, a Tale of the Crusades	.40
Adventures and Daring Deeds of Michael Dwyer	1.00
All about Knock. Complete account of Cures, etc	1.00
Apparitions and Miracles at Knock, paper cover	.25
Atala. By Chateaubriand. Doré's Illustrations, 4to gilt	3.00
Battle of Ventry Harbor, paper cover	.20
Bible, Douay. Octavo, large print. Vellum cloth	2.50
The same, American Morocco, gilt edges	5.00
The same, Turkey Morocco, antique, gilt edges	10.00
Bible, Haydock's, Style G.Fr. Morocco paneled, 2 clasps	18.00
The same, Style H., Turkey Morocco beveled	25.00
Blanche, or the great evils of Pride	.40
Blind Agnese, Little Spouse of the Blessed Sacrament	.60
British Catholic Poets, red line, gilt edges	1.25
Brooks (Senator) and Hughes (Archbishop) Controversy	.75
Burke's Lectures and Sermons 1st series, cloth	2.00
The same, full gilt side and edges	3.00
Burke's Lectures and Sermons, 2d series cloth	2.00
The same, full gilt side and edges	3.00
Burke's Lectures and Sermons in Ireland, cloth	2.50
The same, full gilt side and edges	3.00
Burke's Lectures—The set complete, 3 vols, plain	6.00
The same gilt	9.00
Burke's Reply to Froude, Ireland's case stated	1.00
Cannon's Poems and Dramas. Red line, gilt edges	1.25

Catholic Prayer-Books, 25c., 50c., *up to* 12 00

☞ Any of above books sent free by mail on receipt of price. Agents wanted everywhere to sell above books, to whom liberal terms will be given. Address

P. J. KENEDY, Excelsior Catholic Publishing House, 5 Barclay Street, New York.

Publications of P. J. Kenedy, 5 Barclay St. N. Y.

Canon Schmid's Exquisite Tales, 6 vols, Illustrated...	3.00
Cannon's Practical Spelling Book	.25
Captain of the Club, a Story for Boys..............	.75
Carroll O'Donoghue. By Christine Faber............	1.25
Carpenter's Speller and Definer....................	.25
Catechism Third Plenary Council, large, No. 2, paper.. per 100 net	2.50
The same, abridged No. 1, paper per 100 net.....	1.50
The same, No. 2, cloth flexible, per 100 net.......	5.00
The same, No 1, " " " " "	3.50
Catechism, General, National Council, paper per 100 net.	2.00
The same, abridged paper cover, per 100 net........	1.50
Catechism, Butler's large, paper per 100 net......	2.50
The same, abridged, paper per 100 net......	1.50
The same, cloth, Illustrated Mass Prayers..........	.30
Catechism, The, or Short abridgment, New York, per 100 net.......	2.00
Catechism, Boston. Prayers at Mass, etc., paper per 100 net........	2.00
Catechism, Keenan's Doctrinal, cloth...................	.50
Catechism, Poor Man's, large and thick.	.40
Catechism, Spanish, Ripalda, paper cover.............	.12
Catechism, Spanish, Astete, paper cover..	.15
Catechism, Spanish, Nuevo Caton, paper cover........	.15
Catholic Christian Instructed, paper .20, cloth.........	.30
Catholic Excelsior Library, 6 vols, per set...........	4.50
Catholic Faith and Morals, By L'Homond.............	1.00
Catholic Fireside Library, 10 vols, per set...	7.50
Catholic Flowers from Protestant Gardens, gilt..	1.25
Catholic Home Library, 8 vols, per set...	4.00
Catholic Juvenile Library, 6 vols, per set...... ,....	2.40
Catholic Keepsake Library, 6 vols, per set.............	4.50
Catholic Missions and Missionaries. By Shea...	2.50
Catholic Offering or Gift Book. By Abp. Walsh	1.00
Catholic Piety, (Prayer Book). Prices range upwards from...	.60
Catholic School Book.....	.25
Chambers' English Literature, 2 vols, Octavo..........	5.00

Catholic Prayer-Books, 25c., 50c., *up to* **12 00**

☞ Any of above books sent free by mail on receipt of price. Agents wanted everywhere to sell above books, to whom liberal terms will be given. Address

P. J. KENEDY, Excelsior Catholic Publishing House, *5 Barclay Street, New York.*

Publications of P. J. Kenedy, 5 Barclay St. N. Y.

Chancellor and his Daughter. Sir Thos. More	1.25
Christian Etiquette. For Ladies and Gentlemen	1.25
Christian Maiden's Love. By Louis Veuillot.	.75
Christian's Rule of Life. By St. Liguori	.50
Christian Virtues. By St. Liguori	1.00
Christopher Columbus. Illustrated, 4to gilt	3.00
Chivalrous Deed. By Christine Faber	1.25
Clifton Tracts. Library of Controversy, 4 vols	3.00
Collins' Poems. Red line, gilt edge	1.25
Converted Jew. M. A. Ratisbonne	.50
Countess of Glosswood	.75
Crown of Jesus (Prayer Book). Prices range upwards from	1.00
Daily Companion (Prayer Book). Prices upwards from	.25
Daily Piety, (Prayer Book). Prices upwards from	.30
Dalaradia. By William Collins	.75
Davis' Poems and Essays, complete	1.50
Devout Manual, 18mo, (Prayer Book). Prices upwards from	.75
Devout Manual, 32mo, (Prayer Book). Prices upwards from	.35
Dick Massey, a Story of Irish Evictions	1.00
Diploma of Children of Mary Society, per 100 net	8.00
Doctrinal Catechism. By Rev. Stephen Keenan	.50
Dove of the Tabernacle. By Rev. T. H. Kinane	.75
Drops of Honey. By Father Zelus Animarum	.75
Drops of Honey Library—9 volumes, per set	6.75
Elevation of the soul to God	.75
Empire and Papacy. The Money God	1.25
Epistles and Gospels, 24mo. Good Type	.20
Erin go Bragh, Songster. Paper cover	.25
Evenings at School. New edition Net	1.00
Exercises of the Way of the Cross, paper cover	.05
Faber's (Christine) Works, 4 vols, large, 12mo. per set	5.00
Fair France during the Second Empire	1.00
Fair Maid of Connaught. By Mrs. Hughes	.75
Faugh a Ballagh Songster. Paper cover	.25
Feasts and Fasts. By Rev. Alban Butler	1.25

Catholic Prayer-Books, 25c., 50c., *up to* **12 00**

☞ Any of above books sent free by mail on receipt of price. Agents wanted everywhere to sell above books, to whom liberal terms will be given. Address

P. J. KENEDY, Excelsior Catholic Publishing House, *5 Barclay Street, New York.*

Publications of P. J. Kenedy, 5 Barclay St. N. Y.

Feast of Flowers and The Stoneleighs	.75
Fifty Reasons why the R. C. Religion, etc.	.25
Flowers of Piety (Prayer Book). Prices upwards from.	.35
Following of Christ. A Kempis, 1.25, 1.00 and	.40
Foster Sisters. By Agnes M. Stewart	1.25
From Error to Truth, or the Deacon's Daughters	.75
Furniss' Tracts for Spiritual Reading	1.00
Gems of Prayer, (Prayer Book). Prices upwards from.	.25
Glimpse of Glory and other Poems. E. C. Kane	.50
Glories of Mary. By St. Liguori. Large, 12mo.	1.25
Golden Book of the Confraternities	.50
Golden Hour Library, 6 vols. red edges. per set.	3.00
Good Reading For Young Girls	.75
Gordon Lodge, or Retribution	1.25
Grace O'Halloran. By Agnes M. Stewart	.75
Green Shores of Erin. Drama, net	.25
Grounds of the Catholic Doctrine	.25
Guardian's Mystery. By Christine Faber	1.25
Handy Andy. By Lover. Large edition	1.25
Hay on Miracles. Explanation, etc.	1.00
History of the Catholic Church in the U. S. J. G. Shea.	2.00
History of Ireland. By Moore. 2 volumes	3.00
History of Modern Europe. By J. G. Shea	1.25
History of the United States. By Frost	1.25
Hours with the Sacred Heart	.50
Irish Fireside Library, 6 vols. 16mo	6.00
Irish Fireside Stories, Tales and Legends	1.25
Irish National Songster. Comic and Sentimental	1.00
Irish Patriot's Library, 6 vols, 12mo.	7.50
Irish Race in the Past and Present	2.50
Irish Rebels in English Prisons	1.50
Irish Scholars of the Penal Days.	1.00
Jesus in the Tabernacle. New Meditations	.50
Keenan's Doctrinal Catechism	.50
Keeper of the Lazaretto. By Souvestre	.40
Key of Heaven, 18mo, (Prayer Book). Large. Prices up from	.75

Catholic Prayer-Books, 25c., 50c., *up to* **12 00**

☞ Any of above books sent free by mail on receipt of price. Agents wanted everywhere to sell above books, to whom liberal terms will be given. Address

P J. KENEDY, Excelsior Catholic Publishing House, *5 Barclay Street, New York.*

Publications of P. J. Kenedy, 5 Barclay St. N. Y.

Key of Heaven, 24mo, (Prayer Book). Medium. Prices up from	.60
Key of Heaven, 32mo, (Prayer Book) Small. Prices up from	.50
Kirwan Unmasked. Paper cover. By Abp. Hughes..	.12
La Fontaine's Fables. Red line, gilt edge	1.25
Last of the Catholic O'Malleys	.75
L'Ange Conducteur, (French Prayer Book)	.75
Latin Classics, Expurgated. Volume 1. Net.	.40
Latin Classics, Expurgated. Volume 2. Net	.50
Legends and Fairy Tales of Ireland	2.00
Library of American Catholic History, 3 vols. set	6.00
Library of Catholic Novels, 6 vols per set..	7.50
Library of Catholic Stories, 6 vols "	7.50
Library of Controversy. Clifton Tracts, 4 vols "	3.00
Life of Archbishop Mac Hale. Paper .25, Cloth gilt....	1.00
Life of Christ. By St. Bonaventure	1.25
The same, gilt edges	1.50
Life of Pope Pius IX. By Monsignor B. O'Reilly....	2.50
Life of Robert Emmett. By Madden	1.50
Life of St. Bridget. Paper cover	.10
Life of St. Ignatius, 2 vols. By Bartoli	3.00
Life of St. Liguori. By Mullock	.50
Life of St. Louis, King of France	.40
Life of St. Mary of Egypt	.60
Life of St. Patrick. By O'Leary, 16mo	1.00
Life of St. Winefride, 18mo. Cloth	.60
Life Stories of Dying Penitents	.75
Lily of Israel, Life of the Blessed Virgin Mary	.75
Little Flowers of Piety, (Prayer Book), 1.75–1.25 and..	.75
Little Follower of Jesus. By Rev. A. M. Grussi	.75
Little Lace Maker or Eva O'Beirne	.75
Little Lives of the Great Saints. By John O'Kane Murray	1.00
Little Man'l Bl. Trinity, (Prayer Book). Prices up from	.75
Little Office of the Immaculate Conception. Per 100 net	2.50
Lives of St. Ignatius and his Companions.	.75

Catholic Prayer-Books, 25c., 50., up to **12 00**

☞ Any of above books sent free by mail on receipt of price. Agents wanted everywhere to sell above books, to whom liberal terms will be given. Address
P. J. KENEDY. Excelsior Catholic Publishing House, *5 Barclay Street, New York.*

Publications of P. J. Kenedy, 5 Barclay St. N. Y.

Lives of the Japanese Martyrs. Spinola, etc.	.75
Louisa Kirkbride. By Rev. A. J. Thèbaud, S. J.	1.50
Love of Christ. By St. Liguori	.50
Maidens of Hallowed Names. By Rev. Chas. Piccirillo, S. J.	1.00
Maltese Cross and a Painting and its Mission	.40
Manual of the Bl. Trinity, (Prayer Book). Prices upwards from	1.00
Manual of Catholic Prayers. (Prayer Book). Prices upwards from	.37
Manual of the Children of Mary. 448 pages.	.50
The same, for Pupils of the Sacred Heart	.25
Manual of the Crucifixion, (Prayer Book). Prices upwards from	.63
May Brooke. By Anna H. Dorsey. New edition	1.25
Meditations on the Incarnation. St. Liguori	.75
Merchant of Antwerp. By Hendrik Conscience	1.25
Mirror of True Womanhood. By Rev. B. O'Reilly	2.50
The same, gilt side and edges	3.00
"Mirror" and "True Men"—2 vols. in one, gilt	3.50
Mission Book, 18mo, (Prayer Book). Prices upwards from	.75
Mission Book, 24mo, (Prayer Book). Prices upwards from	.50
Mission Cross and Convent at St. Mary's	.75
Mission and Duties of Young Women. By Rev. C. I. White. D.D.	.60
Monsieur le Curé. Drama. Net	.25
Month of Mary. By D. Roberto	.50
Moore's Poetical Works, Complete. Octavo gilt	3.00
Mother Goose Melodies. For Children	.20
Mother's Sacrifice. By Christine Faber	1.25
Mysteries of the Living Rosary. Per hundred Sheets Net	2.50
Nannette's Marriage. Translated from the French	.75
Nelligan's Speeches and Writings	1.25
New Ireland By A. M. Sullivan	1.25

Catholic Prayer-Books, 25c., 50c., *up to* **12 00**

☞ Any of above books sent free by mail on receipt of price. Agents wanted everywhere to sell above books, to whom liberal terms will be given. Address

P. J. KENEDY, Excelsior Catholic Publishing House, *5 Barclay Street, New York.*

Publications of P. J. Kenedy, 5 Barclay St. N. Y.

New Seraphic Manual, (Prayer Book). For use of members of third order St. Francis. Cloth, red edge	.75
New Testament, 18mo. Small edition, good type	.50
New Testament, Octavo. Large type, vellum cloth	1.50
New Testament in Spanish. El Nuevo Testamento	1.50
Nobleman of '89. By M. A. Quinton	1.50
Oramaika. A Catholic Indian Story	.75
Our Country, History of the U. S. By John G. Shea	.50
Pastor's Visit to the Science of Salvation	.60
Pearl in Dark Waters	.75
Pocket Key of Heaven, (Prayer Book). Prices range upwards from	.25
Poor Man's Catechism. By Rev. Mannock, O. S. B	.40
Prairie Boy. A Story for Boys	.75
Prayer, the Great Means of Salvation. By St. Liguori	.50
Priests' Blessing, or Destiny	1.25
Procter's Poems. Red line, gilt edge	1.25
Procter's Poems. Presentation edition. Octavo	4.00
Purgatory Opened. Month of November	.40
Queen's Confession. By Raoul de Navery	.75
Religion and Science. By Father Ronayne, S. J.	1.25
Rival Mail Carriers. Drama. Net	.25
Rodriguez. Christian Perfection, 3 vols	4.00
Rome, its Churches, Charities and Schools	1.00
Rosario, a Tale of the Sixteenth Century	.75
Rosary Book. Illustrated. Paper Cover	.10
Rose of St. Germains, or Florence O'Neill	1.25
Rose of Venice. A Story of Hatred and Remorse	.75
Sacred History. By Bishop Challoner	.50
Scapular Book, approved by Abp. of New York	.10
Seraphic Staff—3d Order St. Francis	.25
Seven of Us. Stories for Boys and Girls	.75
Silvia, a Drama by John Savage. Net	.90
Sixteen Names of Ancient Ireland. O'Leary	.50
Solitary Island. By Rev. John Talbot Smith	1.25
Sophie's Troubles. By Comtesse de Segur	.75
Southern Catholic Story. Minnie Mary Lee	1.25

Catholic Prayer-Books, 25c., 50c., *up to* **12 00**

☞ Any of above books sent free by mail on receipt of price. Agents wanted everywhere to sell above books, to whom liberal terms will be given. Address

P. J. KENEDY, Excelsior Catholic Publishing House, *5 Barclay Street, New York.*

Publications of P. J. Kenedy, 5 Barclay St. N. Y.

Speeches from the Dock, Emmett, Wolfe Tone, etc....	1.25
Spirit of St. Liguori. Visits to Blessed Sacrament......	.75
St. John's Manual, (Prayer Book). Prices upwards from..	1.50
Stations of the Cross. By Rev. G. J. Misdziol. Paper.	.10
Stories for Catholic Children. Rev. Grussi............	1.00
Story of Italy, or Lionello. By Bresciani.............	1.25
Strayed from the Fold. Minnie Mary Lee.............	1.25
Sunday School Teacher's Class Book. Per doz. net....	1.20
Sybil, a Drama. By John Savage. Net...............	.50
Sure Way to find out the True Religion. Rev. Baddeley.	.25
Tales of Flemish Life. By Hendrik Conscience... ...	1.25
Talks about Ireland. By James Redpath. Paper....	.30
Think Well On't. By Bishop Challoner..............	.40
Three Kings of Cologne. Rev. Titus Joslin	.20
Tracts for the Young—1st and 2d Series. Each.......	.50
True Men as we need Them. Rev. B. O'Reilly.......	2.50
Turf Fire Stories and Fairy Tales of Ireland..........	1.25
Two Cottages. By Lady Fullerton....	.50
Two Brides. By Rev. Bernard O'Reilly.............	1.50
Universal Irish Songster. Profusely Illustrated......	1.50
Ursuline Manual, (Prayer Book). Prices upwards from.	.75
Vision of Old Andrew the Weaver....................	.50
Visits to the Blessed Sacrament. Red edges..........	.50
Vultures of Erin. A Tale of the Penal Laws.	1.25
Waiting for the Train. Drama. Net	.15
Western Missions and Missionaries. De Smet.......	2.00
Wild Irish Girl. Lady Morgan....	1.00
Willy Reilly. Large edition. 12 full page illustrations.	1.25
Within and Without the Fold......................	1.25
Year with the Saints, 12mo. Red edges. Net.	1.50
Young Captives. St. Augustine, etc.................	.40
Young Poachers. Drama. Net................... ..	.25
Youth's Director. Familiar Instructions...	.50
Zozimus Papers. Blind Story Teller of Dublin........	.75

Catholic Prayer-Books, 25c., 50c., *up to* **12 00**

☞ Any of above books sent free by mail on receipt of price. Agents wanted everywhere to sell above books, to whom liberal terms will be given. Address
P. J. KENEDY, Excelsior Catholic Publishing House, *5 Barclay Street, New York.*

www.ingramcontent.com/pod-product-compliance
Lightning Source LLC
Chambersburg PA
CBHW020311240426
43673CB00039B/768